PUBLISHER'S NOTES

All European domestic league infographic data runs up until the end of the 2014–2015 season.
All team names printed in accordance with UEFA.

THIS IS A CARLTON BOOK

Published in Great Britain in 2016 by
Carlton Books Limited
20 Mortimer Street
London W1T 3JW

Infographic statistical data © Perform Media Channels Limited

All other text, graphics and design © 2016 Carlton Books Limited

A CIP catalogue for this book is available from the British Library.

Editorial Manager: Martin Corteel
Design: James Pople
Editorial: Malcolm Croft
Picture Research: Paul Langan
Production: Lisa Cook & Maria Petalidou
Text: Adrian Besley
Infographics and Visualisation: Visual Evolution (www.visualevolution.co.uk)
Opta Data: Duncan Alexander & Tom Ede

ISBN 978-1-78097-772-0

Printed in Dubai

10 9 8 7 6 5 4 3 2 1

opta

WORLD FOOTBALL INFOGRAPHICS

The Beautiful Game in Brilliant Detail

Trends, Statistics and Data Analysis

CARLTON
BOOKS

WORLD CUP

EUROPE

NORTH & CENTRAL AMERICA

CONCACAF GOLD CUP

MLS

SOUTH AMERICA

COPA AMÉRICA

COPA LIBERTADORES

AFRICA

AFRICAN CUP OF NATIONS

ASIA

AFC ASIAN CUP

VARIOUS

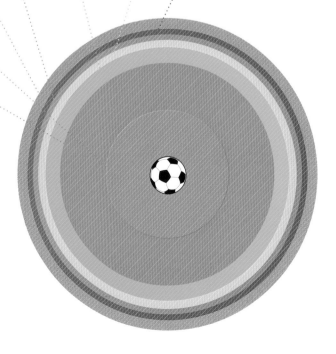

opta

Foreword

Since 1996, Opta has been at the forefront of the collection and analysis of detailed sports data. If you watch football on television, read about it online or in newspapers, place the occasional bet on a game, follow prominent players, journalists and pundits on social media, or even play at a professional level yourself, it's likely that you will have encountered Opta data. You might even be one of over 1.25 million people that follow us across our many Twitter accounts.

Originally, our statistics were collected by hand. A dedicated band of people would watch, pause and rewind video tapes of Premier League matches in order to make sure we could be as accurate as possible, before sending out statistics to journalists the day after the games had finished. Now, thanks to an army of data collectors using proprietary software in collection centres across the world, we are able to collect between 1600 and 2000 data points (including 16 different types of pass!), live from every single game, on more than 40 global leagues and tournaments. This live data is being used to power TV broadcasts, websites, apps, fantasy games and live blogs across the world.

Infographics have become one of the most quickly-developing trends in sports data analysis. As datasets become more complex, infographics are an invaluable way of displaying complex information in a clear, concise, attractive way. The unique infographics created for this book, incorporating comparisons between players, teams and leagues for almost every continent, showcases the mass of detailed data now available from right across the world of football.

Enjoy the book,

Rob Bateman (@Orbinho), Opta

Opta is part of Perform Content, a division of Perform Group (www.performgroup.com). To learn more about Opta's work, head to www.optasports.com or follow @OptaJoe on Twitter.

Introduction

It's a question that has been asked a lot recently. Can the instruments of maths and graphic design really translate the thrills and skills, triumphs and trophies of the beautiful game into a set of thought-provoking graphs, diagrams and charts? The answer is yes, absolutely. You'll be amazed at what emerges from the technicolour infographics in the pages that follow. From the statistics that make the Messi–Ronaldo rivalry even more compelling than when the players collide on the pitch right through to the different parts of the body used to score World Cup goals. It's all here... and more.

Our fascination with football takes many forms. We can admire the breathtaking skills of Mesut Özil, Zlatan Ibrahimović, Neymar and other magicians on the ball. It is their flair, their passion for the game played well, that keeps the fans coming back for more. That will never change. However, in recent years, another facet of the game has become as passionately talked about as decent ball skill – sports data analysis. Statistics, trends and data collection have become a commonplace appendix to the beautiful game to the extent that fans now have more numbers, averages and decimal points thrown at them by pundits and commentators than ever before. And this is no bad thing. Because where there is data there are infographics that unlock the power of big data and show it off in a brilliant, visually interesting way.

This invaluable book uses infographics to take a topical look at the trends and data in football at both domestic and international levels. It compares the top leagues and players across Europe, including the Premier League, La Liga, Bundesliga, Ligue 1 and Serie A. And the greatest footballing show on earth, the World Cup, is also represented in vibrant infographics, revealing many vital statistics and trends behind every competition since 1930 with further analysis on noteworthy goalkeepers, goal recreations, perfect penalty placements and the women's tournament.

Thanks to the rich and compelling information supplied by data providers such as Opta, football is no longer just a simple game of two halves. The doors have been blown open and the beautiful game is just that little bit more beautiful.

1966 WORLD CUP GOALS

Many nations fancied their chances of winning the World Cup in 1966 with West Germany, Argentina, Brazil and England all confident it would be their turn to lift the Jules Rimet trophy. Despite being blighted by the barbaric treatment of Pelé and some controversial refereeing, the tournament was enlightened by the giant-slaying North Korea, the brilliance of Eusébio and a nail-biting, but triumphant, final for the host nation. The 1966 World Cup also saw goals that would become legendary, including the lung-bursting run from West Germany's Franz Beckenbauer, an outside-of-the-foot free kick from Brazil's Garrincha and Geoff Hurst's monumental hat-trick in the final – the first ever in a World Cup final.

GEOFF HURST – England vs West Germany

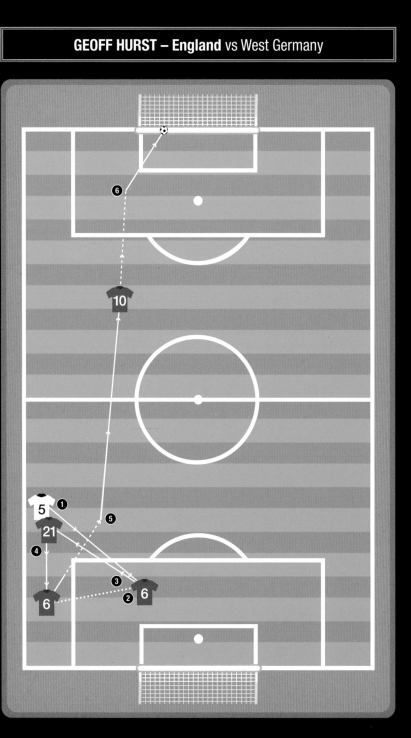

England's Geoff Hurst scores that famous 4th goal to put England 4–2 up against West Germany after extra time, 30 July 1966.

1. Pass (chipped, cross) **Schulz**
2. Ball recovery **Moore**
3. Pass **Moore**
4. Pass **Hunt**
5. Pass (chipped, long ball) **Moore**
6. Goal **Hurst**

KEY

Ball movement	Player with ball
Shot	Player without ball

LUIS ARTIME – Argentina vs Spain

1. Interception **Más**
2. Pass **Más**
3. Pass **Solari**
4. Pass **Rattín**
5. Pass **Onega**
6. Pass **Solari**
7. Goal **Artime**

FRANZ BECKENBAUER – West Germany vs Switzerland

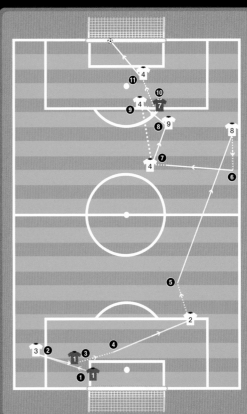

1. Goal kick **Tilkowski**
2. Pass **Schnellinger**
3. Keeper pick-up **Tilkowski**
4. Keeper throw **Tilkowski**
5. Pass (chipped, long ball) **Höttges**
6. Pass **Haller**
7. Pass **Beckenbauer**
8. Through ball **Seeler**
9. Take on **Beckenbauer**
10. Challenge **Führer**
11. Goal **Beckenbauer**

JÁNOS FARKAS – Hungary vs Brazil

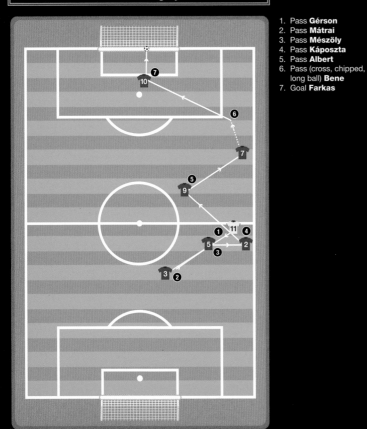

1. Pass **Gérson**
2. Pass **Mátrai**
3. Pass **Mészöly**
4. Pass **Káposzta**
5. Pass **Albert**
6. Pass (cross, chipped, long ball) **Bene**
7. Goal **Farkas**

EDUARD MALOFEYEV – USSR vs DPR Korea

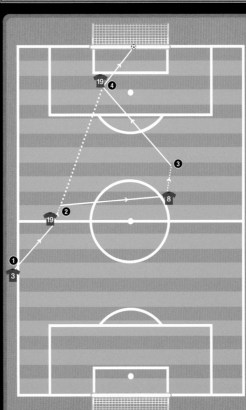

1. Throw in **Ostrowskiy**
2. Pass (chipped, long ball) **Malofeyev**
3. Pass (chipped) **Sabo**
4. Goal **Malofeyev**

PREMIER LEAGUE FOULS AND CARDS

The number of bookings and dismissals has been gradually increasing since the Premier League began in 1992. Although referee clampdowns and new rules to protect players from reckless challenges have increased the tally, statistics reveal a large number of indiscretions are due to rash decisions and second-offences. It appears that as the game gets quicker, and more skilful, tackling becomes a much riskier business. So, hats off to Ryan Giggs. He managed 632 Premier League appearances without seeing red once.

CHELSEA 1406
EVERTON 1349
ARSENAL 1309
ASTON VILLA 1287
TOTTENHAM HOTSPUR 1263

MANCHESTER UNITED 1193
WEST HAM UNITED 1185
NEWCASTLE UNITED 1160
BLACKBURN ROVERS 1111
LIVERPOOL 1105

MANCHESTER CITY 1026
SUNDERLAND 953
MIDDLESBROUGH 896
SOUTHAMPTON 880
BOLTON WANDERERS 845

LEEDS UNITED 790
FULHAM 708
DERBY COUNTY 538
WIGAN ATHLETIC 513
WEST BROMWICH ALBION 500

LEICESTER CITY 499
STOKE CITY 496
COVENTRY CITY 481
BIRMINGHAM CITY 428
CHARLTON ATHLETIC 408

WIMBLEDON 407
PORTSMOUTH 398
QUEENS PARK RANGERS 364
SHEFFIELD WEDNESDAY 341
CRYSTAL PALACE 340

NORWICH CITY 333
NOTTINGHAM FOREST 287
HULL CITY 261
WOLVERHAMPTON WANDERERS 255
SWANSEA CITY 202

IPSWICH TOWN 183
SHEFFIELD UNITED 170
READING 142
BURNLEY 121
WATFORD 115

BRADFORD CITY 113
OLDHAM ATHLETIC 70
BARNSLEY 66
CARDIFF CITY 50
BLACKPOOL 47

EVERTON 79   **ARSENAL 77**   **BLACKBURN ROVERS 76**   **NEWCASTLE UNITED 73**   **CHELSEA 69**

TOTTENHAM HOTSPUR 59   **MANCHESTER CITY 58**   **WEST HAM UNITED 58**   **MANCHESTER UNITED 57**   **SUNDERLAND 55**

ASTON VILLA 53   **LIVERPOOL 51**   **MIDDLESBROUGH 44**   **BOLTON WANDERERS 43**   **SOUTHAMPTON 41**

FULHAM 36   **LEICESTER CITY 32**   **LEEDS UNITED 28**   **WIGAN ATHLETIC 27**   **WEST BROMWICH ALBION 27**

BIRMINGHAM CITY 26   **WIMBLEDON 26**   **QUEENS PARK RANGERS 26**   **COVENTRY CITY 24**   **STOKE CITY 24**

CHARLTON ATHLETIC 24   **PORTSMOUTH 20**   **SHEFFIELD WEDNESDAY 19**   **HULL CITY 19**   **DERBY COUNTY 17**

CRYSTAL PALACE 16   **SWANSEA CITY 12**   **NORWICH CITY 12**   **WOLVERHAMPTON WANDERERS 11**   **NOTTINGHAM FOREST 10**

SHEFFIELD UNITED 9   **READING 9**   **IPSWICH TOWN 6**   **WATFORD 6**   **BARNSLEY 4**

OLDHAM ATHLETIC 4   **BURNLEY 4**   **BLACKPOOL 2**   **BRADFORD CITY 2**   **SWINDON TOWN 1**

CARDIFF CITY 1

Total Fouls since 2003

ASTON VILLA **6145**	BLACKBURN ROVERS **5044**	SOUTHAMPTON **2367**	BURNLEY **867**
EVERTON **5904**	BOLTON WANDERERS **4871**	CHARLTON ATHLETIC **2013**	WATFORD **597**
MANCHESTER CITY **5732**	WEST HAM UNITED **4502**	HULL CITY **1996**	LEEDS UNITED **583**
CHELSEA **5475**	SUNDERLAND **4265**	WOLVERHAMPTON WANDERERS **1901**	DERBY COUNTY **548**
TOTTENHAM HOTSPUR **5374**	WIGAN ATHLETIC **4042**	NORWICH CITY **1837**	SHEFFIELD UNITED **510**
NEWCASTLE UNITED **5354**	PORTSMOUTH **3728**	SWANSEA CITY **1501**	BLACKPOOL **440**
LIVERPOOL **5332**	WEST BROMWICH ALBION **3680**	CRYSTAL PALACE **1500**	CARDIFF CITY **345**
MANCHESTER UNITED **5301**	STOKE CITY **3368**	READING **1341**	
ARSENAL **5240**	MIDDLESBROUGH **3166**	QUEENS PARK RANGERS **1262**	
FULHAM **5233**	BIRMINGHAM CITY **3085**	LEICESTER CITY **1026**	

Source: Opta (August 2015)

AFRICAN CUP OF NATIONS TROPHIES AND GOALS

What began in 1957 with a three-team competition has developed, 30 tournaments later, into a month-long, 16-team extravaganza. The tournament has witnessed many great moments, including Cameroon's Samuel Eto'o converting a penalty against Sudan in 2008 to become the tournament's record scorer; South Africa's Benni McCarthy netting four goals in 13 minutes against Namibia in 1998; and the incredible 2015 final when Ivory Coast's second-choice keeper Boubacar Barry saved two penalties and struck the winner himself in the dramatic shoot-out.

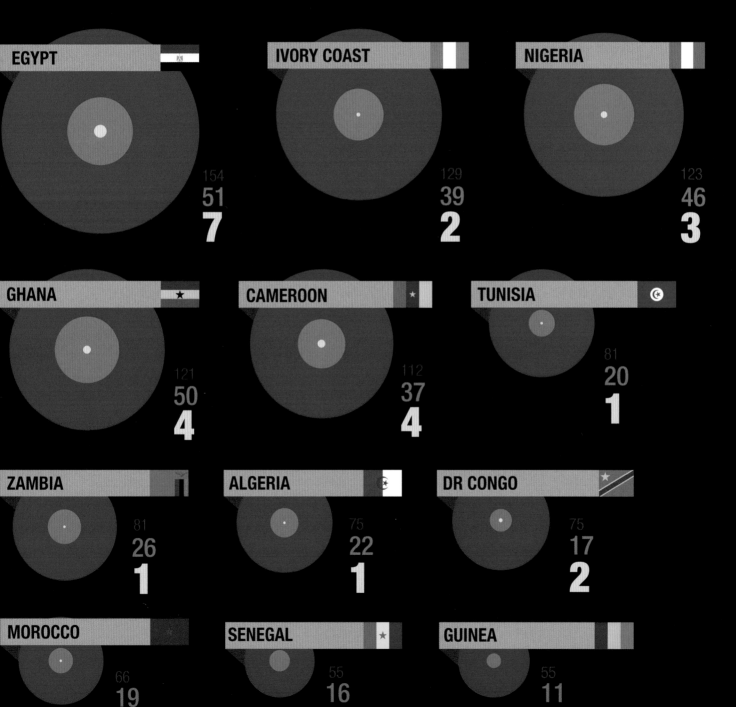

EGYPT
154
51
7

IVORY COAST
129
39
2

NIGERIA
123
46
3

GHANA
121
50
4

CAMEROON
112
37
4

TUNISIA
81
20
1

ZAMBIA
81
26
1

ALGERIA
75
22
1

DR CONGO
75
17
2

MOROCCO
66
19

SENEGAL
55
16

GUINEA
55
11

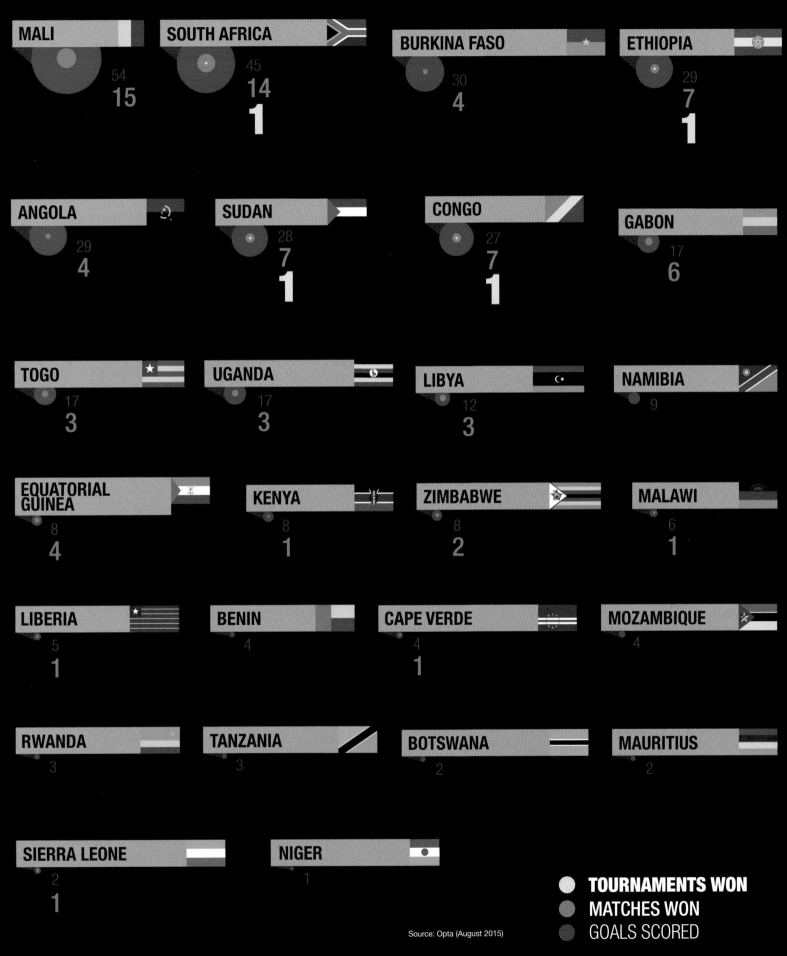

MALI 54 15

SOUTH AFRICA 45 14 1

BURKINA FASO 30 4

ETHIOPIA 29 7 1

ANGOLA 29 4

SUDAN 28 7 1

CONGO 27 7 1

GABON 17 6

TOGO 17 3

UGANDA 17 3

LIBYA 12 3

NAMIBIA 9

EQUATORIAL GUINEA 8 4

KENYA 8 1

ZIMBABWE 8 2

MALAWI 6 1

LIBERIA 5 1

BENIN 4

CAPE VERDE 4 1

MOZAMBIQUE 4

RWANDA 3

TANZANIA 3

BOTSWANA 2

MAURITIUS 2

SIERRA LEONE 2 1

NIGER 1

● **TOURNAMENTS WON**
● **MATCHES WON**
● **GOALS SCORED**

Source: Opta (August 2015)

13

WORLD CUP FINALS RESULTS 1930–2014

The FIFA World Cup has grown from a small tournament comprising 13 teams from Europe and South America (USA and Mexico participated too) to 32 nations from five continents battling it out in the most widely followed sporting event in the world. There have been 20 to date, each one as spectacular as the last. Every tournament has had its amazing stories, controversies, moments that took our breath away and heartbreak that saw us plunge into despair. Behind all these iconic events all that remains (apart from memories) are these simple facts – the statistics that mark each country's triumphs and disappointments in black and white. Make of these what you will…

Source: Google (October 2015)

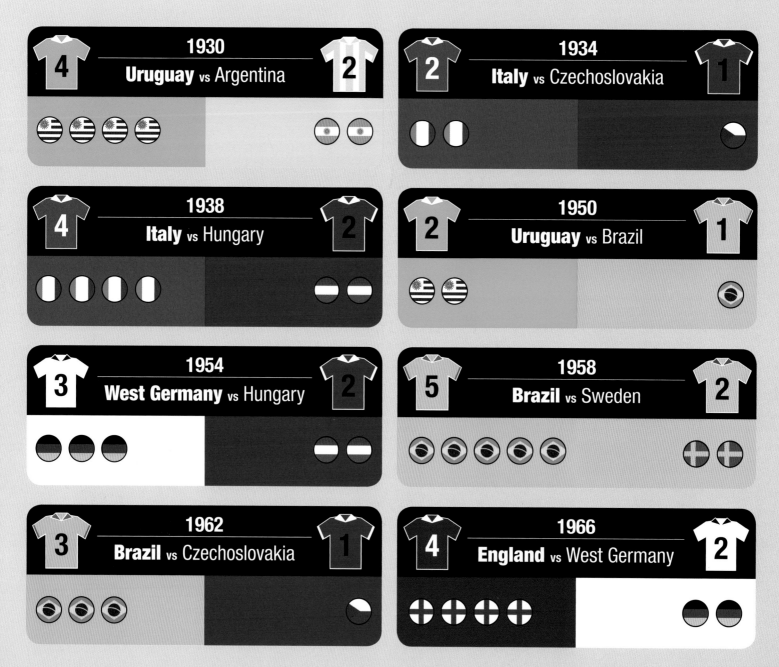

1930	1934
4 Uruguay vs Argentina **2**	**2** Italy vs Czechoslovakia **1**

1938	1950
4 Italy vs Hungary **2**	**2** Uruguay vs Brazil **1**

1954	1958
3 West Germany vs Hungary **2**	**5** Brazil vs Sweden **2**

1962	1966
3 Brazil vs Czechoslovakia **1**	**4** England vs West Germany **2**

1970 — **Brazil** vs Italy — 4–1

1974 — **West Germany** vs Netherlands — 2–1

1978 — **Argentina** vs Netherlands — 3–1

1982 — **Italy** vs West Germany — 3–1

1986 — **Argentina** vs West Germany — 3–2

1990 — **West Germany** vs Argentina — 1–0

1994 — **Brazil** vs Italy — 0–0 PENALTIES

1998 — **France** vs Brazil — 3–0

2002 — **Brazil** vs Germany — 2–0

2006 — **Italy** vs France — 1–1 PENALTIES

2010 — **Spain** vs Netherlands — 1–0

2014 — **Germany** vs Argentina — 1–0

ENGLISH PREMIER LEAGUE SHIRT COLOURS

English football has been seeing red for much of the last 50 years. The success of Liverpool, Manchester United and Arsenal has led to a red-shirted dominance among the Premier League's top clubs. Only the relatively recent emergence of the blues of Chelsea and Manchester City have threatened this dominance. Long tradition plays a major part in most teams' shirt selection, from the yellow and green of Norwich City to the black and white of Newcastle United, with clubs using second and third kits to experiment with colour.

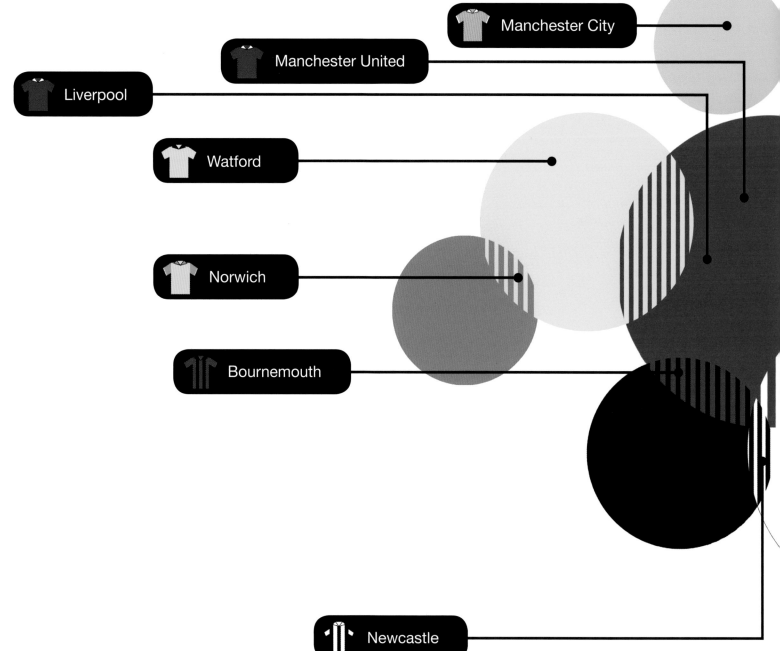

Manchester City

Manchester United

Liverpool

Watford

Norwich

Bournemouth

Newcastle

Source: Google (October 2015)

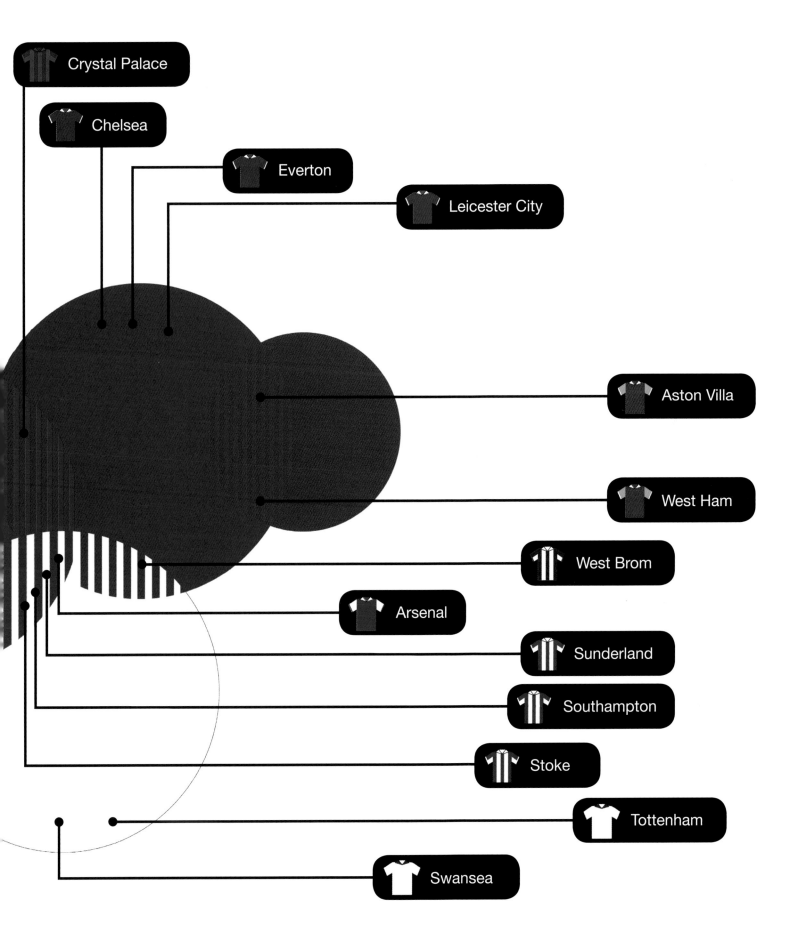

Crystal Palace

Chelsea

Everton

Leicester City

Aston Villa

West Ham

West Brom

Arsenal

Sunderland

Southampton

Stoke

Tottenham

Swansea

17

UEFA EUROPEAN CHAMPIONSHIP RECORDS BY NATION

The brainchild of Henri Delaunay, the secretary of the French Football Federation, the European Championship has been held every four years since 1960.

Qualification for the first two tournaments was conducted on a home and away knockout basis with the group qualification format beginning in 1968. Originally only four teams qualified for the finals. This was extended to eight teams in 1980 and then to 16 from 1996. In 2016 the finals will be further expanded to include 24 nations.

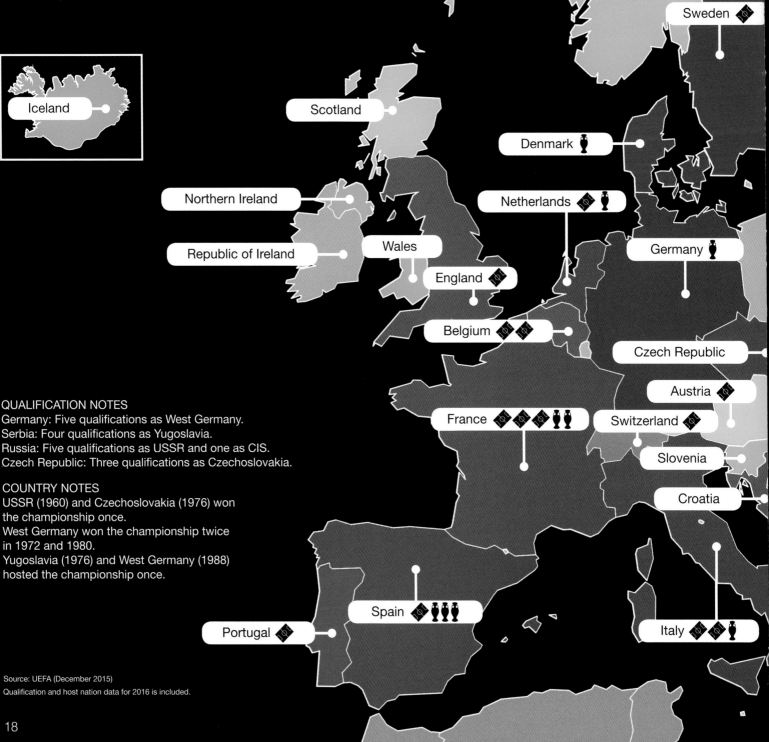

Norway

Sweden

Iceland

Scotland

Denmark

Northern Ireland

Netherlands

Wales

Germany

Republic of Ireland

England

Belgium

Czech Republic

Austria

France

Switzerland

Slovenia

Croatia

Spain

Portugal

Italy

QUALIFICATION NOTES
Germany: Five qualifications as West Germany.
Serbia: Four qualifications as Yugoslavia.
Russia: Five qualifications as USSR and one as CIS.
Czech Republic: Three qualifications as Czechoslovakia.

COUNTRY NOTES
USSR (1960) and Czechoslovakia (1976) won the championship once.
West Germany won the championship twice in 1972 and 1980.
Yugoslavia (1976) and West Germany (1988) hosted the championship once.

Source: UEFA (December 2015)
Qualification and host nation data for 2016 is included.

Qualified

0
1
2
3
4
5
6
7
8
9
10
11
12

Finland

Estonia

Latvia

Lithuania

Poland

Belarus

Russia

Kazakhstan

Slovakia

Ukraine

Hungary

Moldova

Romania

Bosnia and Herzegovina

Serbia

Bulgaria

Georgia

Albania

Armenia

Azerbaijan

Turkey

Greece

Cyprus

Winner

Host

FOOTBALL RIVALRIES, PART 1

History, tradition, passion and pride – these are the elements that come to the fore when great footballing rivals collide. Every nation has its rival teams. Some, such as Tottenham Hotspur and Arsenal, are born from geographical proximity – they're based four miles apart. France's Olympique de Marseille and Paris Saint-Germain may reside further apart, but the rivalry between the North and South, and the country's two biggest cities, makes the "Le Classique" derby just as bitterly fought.

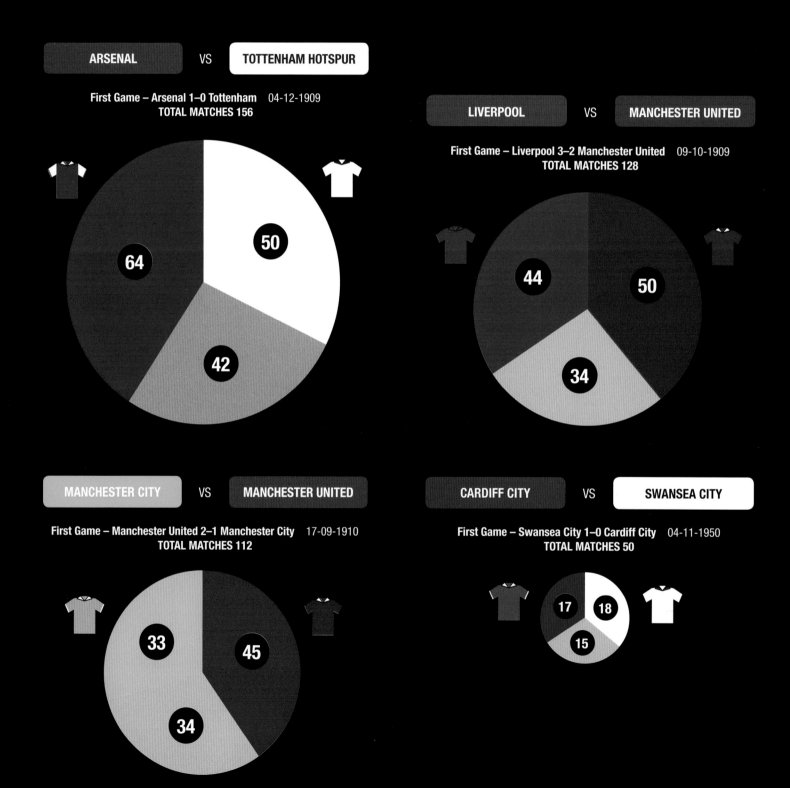

ARSENAL VS **TOTTENHAM HOTSPUR**

First Game – Arsenal 1–0 Tottenham   04-12-1909
TOTAL MATCHES 156

64   50   42

LIVERPOOL VS **MANCHESTER UNITED**

First Game – Liverpool 3–2 Manchester United   09-10-1909
TOTAL MATCHES 128

44   50   34

MANCHESTER CITY VS **MANCHESTER UNITED**

First Game – Manchester United 2–1 Manchester City   17-09-1910
TOTAL MATCHES 112

33   45   34

CARDIFF CITY VS **SWANSEA CITY**

First Game – Swansea City 1–0 Cardiff City   04-11-1950
TOTAL MATCHES 50

17   18   15

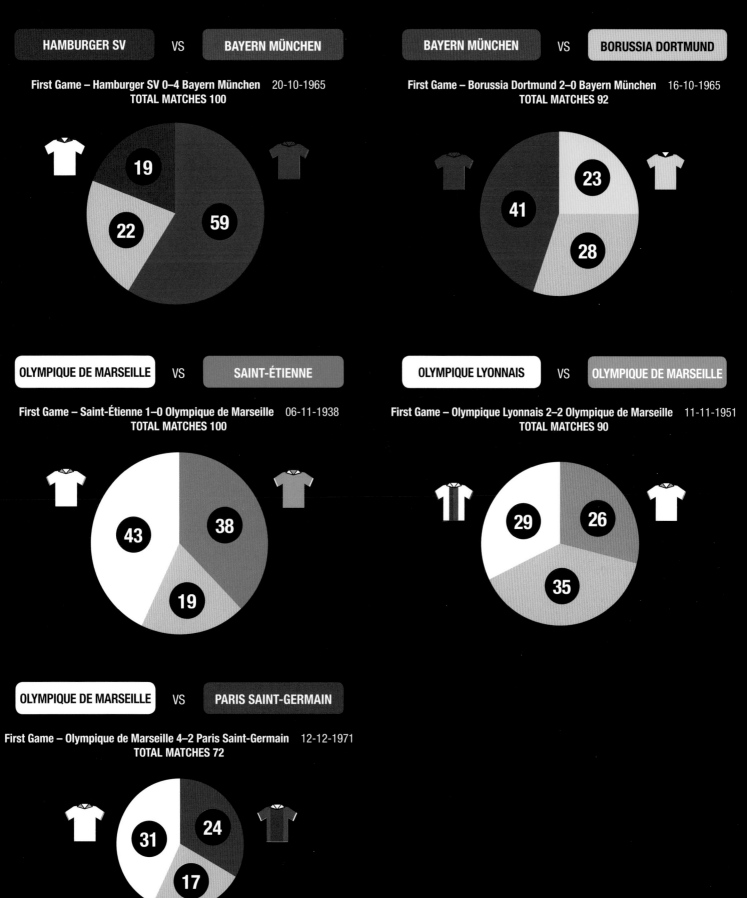

HAMBURGER SV VS **BAYERN MÜNCHEN**

First Game – Hamburger SV 0–4 Bayern München   20-10-1965
TOTAL MATCHES 100

19
22
59

BAYERN MÜNCHEN VS **BORUSSIA DORTMUND**

First Game – Borussia Dortmund 2–0 Bayern München   16-10-1965
TOTAL MATCHES 92

23
41
28

OLYMPIQUE DE MARSEILLE VS **SAINT-ÉTIENNE**

First Game – Saint-Étienne 1–0 Olympique de Marseille   06-11-1938
TOTAL MATCHES 100

43
38
19

OLYMPIQUE LYONNAIS VS **OLYMPIQUE DE MARSEILLE**

First Game – Olympique Lyonnais 2–2 Olympique de Marseille   11-11-1951
TOTAL MATCHES 90

29
26
35

OLYMPIQUE DE MARSEILLE VS **PARIS SAINT-GERMAIN**

First Game – Olympique de Marseille 4–2 Paris Saint-Germain   12-12-1971
TOTAL MATCHES 72

31
24
17

Source: Opta (October 2015)

GOOGLE GIANTS OF FOOTBALL

Google is the world's most popular search engine and football is one of the most-searched categories. If you type "Manchester United" into your search you will receive around 148 million results whereas a search for Luxembourg champions "Fola Esch" will yield only 386,000 results. It is an interesting insight into their global popularity. In this word chart, the more answers given to a particular search, the larger the name appears on the chart.

Sergio Agüero

Zlatan Ibrahimovic

Benfica

Tottenham Hotspur

David Beckham

Zenit St Petersburg

Rangers

Juventus

Real Madrid

Manchester

Chelsea

Arsenal

Thomas Müller

Celtic
Everton

Robert Lewandowski

James Rodríguez

Thiago Silva

FC Porto

Sporting Lisbon

Roma

Eden Hazard

Gareth Bale

Luis Suárez

PSG

Atlético Madrid

Sevilla

Team

Player

22

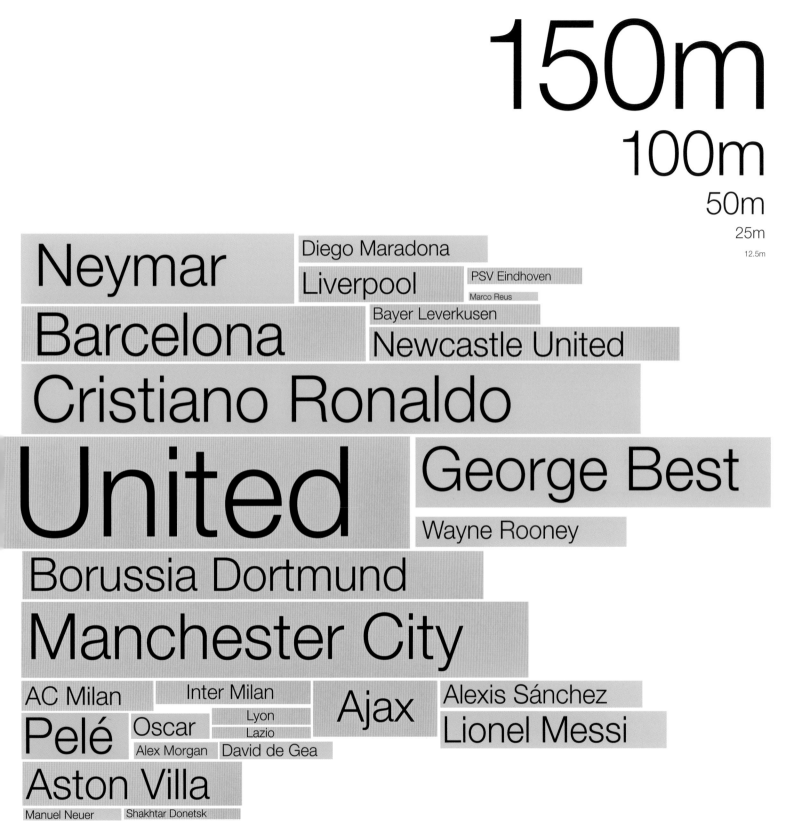

150m
100m
50m
25m
12.5m

Neymar
Diego Maradona
Liverpool
PSV Eindhoven
Marco Reus
Barcelona
Bayer Leverkusen
Newcastle United
Cristiano Ronaldo
United
George Best
Wayne Rooney
Borussia Dortmund
Manchester City
AC Milan
Inter Milan
Ajax
Alexis Sánchez
Pelé
Oscar
Lyon
Lazio
Lionel Messi
Alex Morgan
David de Gea
Aston Villa
Manuel Neuer
Shakhtar Donetsk

Source: Google (October 2015)

1970 WORLD CUP GOALS

Many pundits, players and fans still regard the 1970 World Cup in Mexico as the finest World Cup tournament of all. Reigning champions England played Brazil in a scintillating group game, Italy met Germany in the "Game of the Century" – Italy won 4–3 after five goals were scored in extra time, the only FIFA World Cup game when this has happened – and the final was a masterclass in demolition by the Brazilian squad. It was Carlos Alberto's perfect strike that was the nail in the coffin for Brazil's glorious 4–1 win over Italy in the final, arguably one of the greatest goals ever scored.

CARLOS ALBERTO – **Brazil** vs Italy

Brazil captain Carlos Alberto celebrates his team's 4th goal against Italy's goalkeeper Enrico Albertosi. Final score: Brazil 4 Italy 1, 21 June 1970.

1. Take on **Juliano**
2. Tackle **Brito**
3. Ball recovery **Tostão**
4. Pass **Tostão**
5. Pass **Piazza**
6. Pass **Clodoaldo**
7. Pass **Pelé**
8. Pass **Gérson**
9. Take on **Clodoaldo**
10. Good skill **Clodoaldo**
11. Challenge **Rivera**
12. Challenge **De Sisti**
13. Pass **Clodoaldo**
14. Pass **Rivelino**
15. Pass **Jairzinho**
16. Pass **Pelé**
17. Goal **Alberto**

KEY

Ball movement

Shot

Player with ball

Player without ball

24

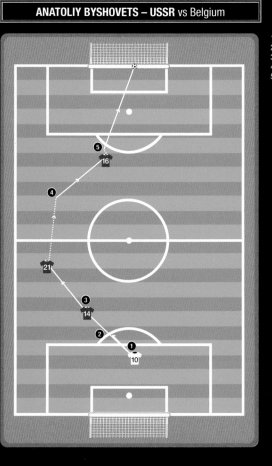

ANATOLIY BYSHOVETS – USSR vs Belgium

1. Lay-off **Van Himst**
2. Ball recovery **Muntyan**
3. Pass **Muntyan**
4. Pass **Khmelnytskyi**
5. Goal **Byshovets**

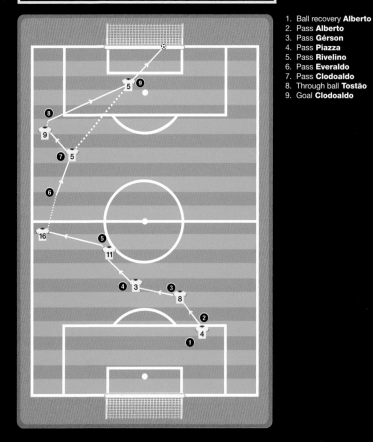

CLODOALDO – Brazil vs Uruguay

1. Ball recovery **Alberto**
2. Pass **Alberto**
3. Pass **Gérson**
4. Pass **Piazza**
5. Pass **Rivelino**
6. Pass **Everaldo**
7. Pass **Clodoaldo**
8. Through ball **Tostão**
9. Goal **Clodoaldo**

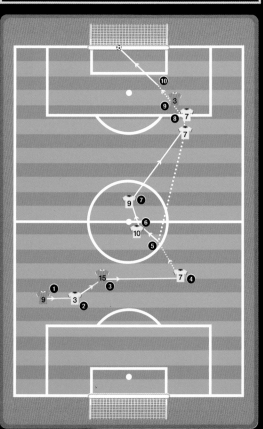

JAIRZINHO – Brazil vs Uruguay

1. Pass **Espárrago**
2. Interception **Piazza**
3. Pass **Fontes**
4. Ball recovery **Jairzinho**
5. Pass **Jairzinho**
6. Flick-on **Pelé**
7. Pass **Tostão**
8. Take on **Jairzinho**
9. Challenge **Matosas**
10. Goal **Jairzinho**

PELÉ – Brazil vs Czechoslovakia

1. Pass **Adamec**
2. Interception **Everaldo**
3. Ball recovery **Everaldo**
4. Pass **Everaldo**
5. Pass **Rivelino**
6. Turnover **Gérson**
7. Pass **Brito**
8. Pass **Alberto**
9. Pass **Rivelino**
10. Pass (chipped) **Gérson**
11. Goal **Pelé**

THE PERFECT WORLD CUP PENALTY

To place or to blast? That is the question facing World Cup penalty-takers under the intense pressure of the glaring floodlights, thousands of expectant fans and their teammates unable to look away. In a World Cup tie the hopes of a nation lie on the quality of the execution. Some, like Andreas Brehme in 1990, have the steady composure to help their sides lift the Jules Rimet, whereas others, such as England's Chris Waddle's high-and-wide miss in 1990, led only to the shattering of millions of hearts. So where would you aim *your* penalty kick?

TOP LEFT

96%
SCORED

49 GOALS SCORED
2 PENALTIES SAVED

HIGH CENTRE

94%
SCORED

BOTTOM LEFT

80%
SCORED

104 GOALS SCORED
26 PENALTIES SAVED

LOW CENTRE

69%
SCORED

68 Left-footed penalty goals

245 Right-footed penalty goals

313 Penalty goals in total
68 Penalty saves in total

Source: Opta (October 2015)
Percentages relate to penalties on target.

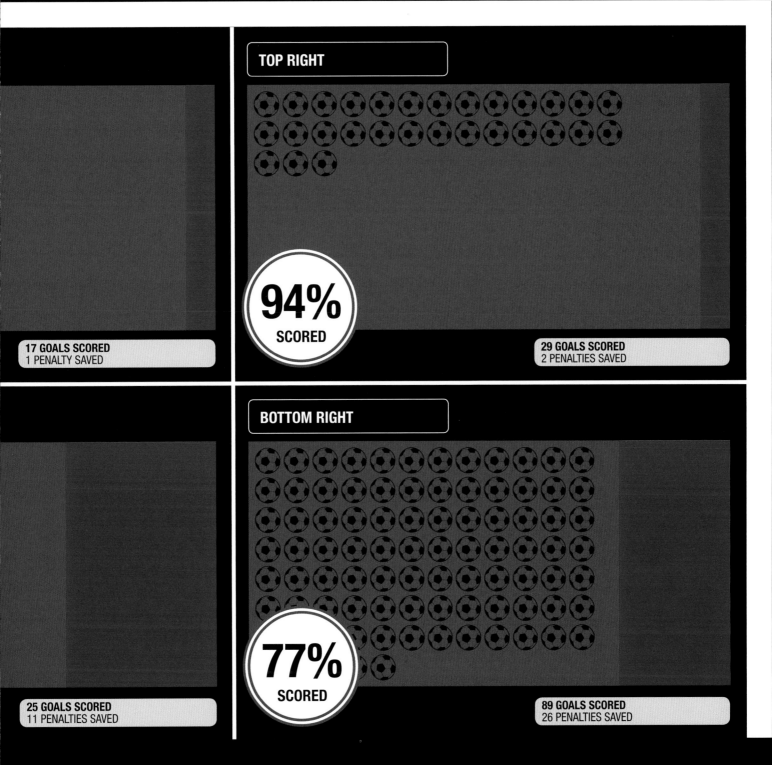

TOP RIGHT

94%
SCORED

17 GOALS SCORED
1 PENALTY SAVED

29 GOALS SCORED
2 PENALTIES SAVED

BOTTOM RIGHT

77%
SCORED

25 GOALS SCORED
11 PENALTIES SAVED

89 GOALS SCORED
26 PENALTIES SAVED

EVOLUTION OF FORMATIONS
1872–1967

Every team has ten outfield players. What has proved critical over the years is not just how those players perform, but where. Formation is a key tactical element and, as these diagrams show, it is continually evolving. We can see the attack-heavy teams that dominated the early years of the game gradually becoming more balanced, with stronger midfields and defence.

1872

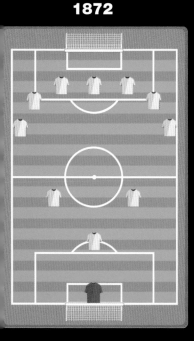

1-2-7 Formation
England

1889

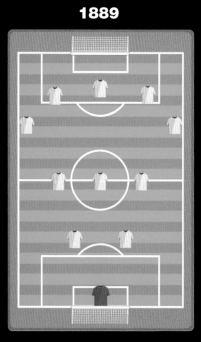

The Pyramid (2-3-5)
Preston North End

1930

The WM Formation
Arsenal

" **[Going behind] didn't bother us at all... We just knew we could turn the game around.** "

Djalma Santos, Brazil's
1958 FIFA World Cup defender

Brazil's employment of a 4-2-4 formation helped them to victory in the 1958 FIFA World Cup

1934

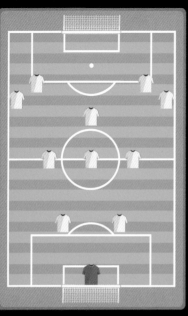

Danubian School

Austria

1938

The Metodo Formation

Italy

1953

The Diagonal Formation

Hungary

1958

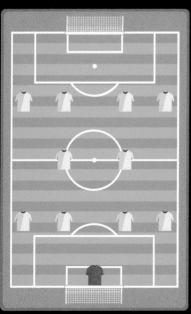

4-2-4 Formation

Brazil

1961

3-3-4 Formation

Tottenham Hotspur

1967

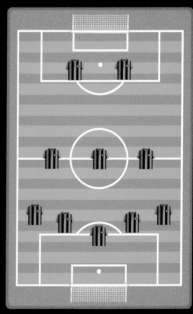

Catenaccio

Internazionale Milano

EVOLUTION OF FORMATIONS

1970–2016

From the 1970s onwards, the 4-4-2 formation became synonymous with the modern game. Here was a system that focused on passing and tackling in the central zones of the pitch and enabled increasingly fit midfielders to bolster both attacks and defences. It seemed the evolution had reached its conclusion. However, the search for any slight advantage meant coaches kept on tinkering. "Wingless wonder" teams and fluid "total football" line-ups were followed by wing-backs, "false 9s", pyramids and Christmas trees. Brazilian coach Carlos Alberto Parreira once predicted 4-6-0 as the "formation of the future" – and some might claim we are edging ever closer to that prophesy.

1971

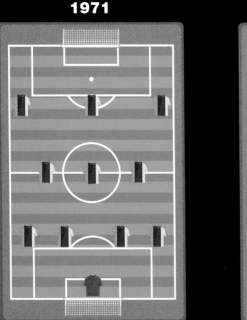

4-3-3 Formation
Ajax

1990

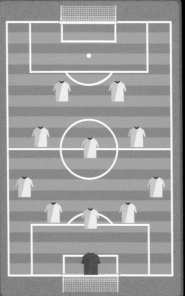

Wing-backs Formation
Germany

1998

4-4-2 Formation
Manchester United

"We know that's our way of playing, regardless of the score... It's very well defined, we have the right players and the right mentality… It doesn't mean we'll win in the future but we know how we'll try to win."

Midfielder Xabi Alonso on Spain's 2012 UEFA European Championship formation

2003

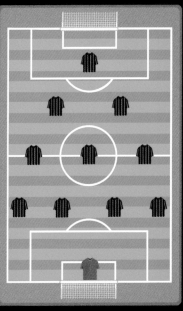

4-3-2-1 Christmas Tree
AC Milan

The Spanish national side's use of the "False 9" at the 2012 UEFA European Championships led to many other teams later employing the system.

2006

Diamond Formation
Ghana

2012

The "False 9" Formation
Spain

2014

4-5-1 Formation
Chelsea

LA LIGA TITLE WINS

La Liga, the elite league of Spanish football, was born in 1929 from a core group of teams playing for the national knockout competition, the Copa Del Rey. Sixty different teams have since competed in the league with nine different teams lifting the trophy. The league has been dominated by Barcelona and Real Madrid, the giants of Spanish football, with Athletic Bilbao, Atlético Madrid and Valencia deserving honourable mentions too. With its teams faring well in European competition, La Liga is currently rated the best league in Europe.

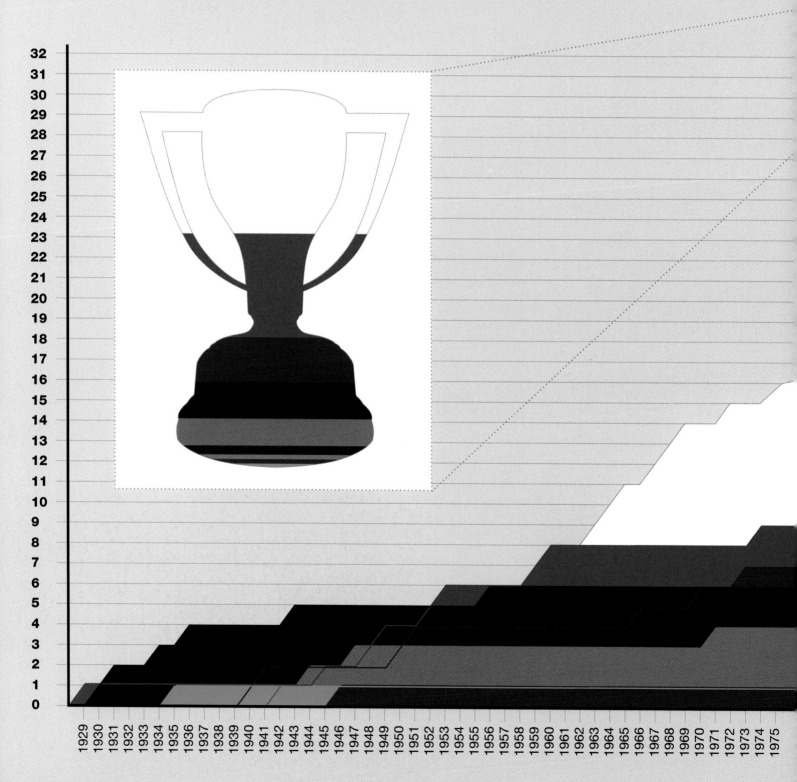

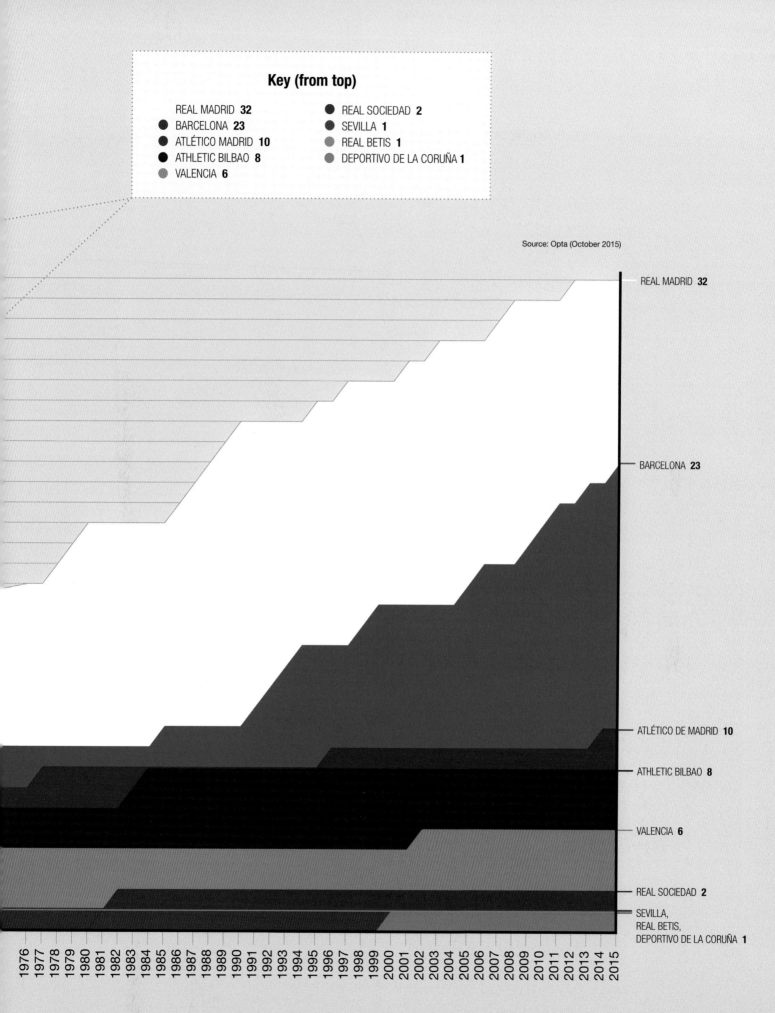

Key (from top)

REAL MADRID **32**
● BARCELONA **23**
● ATLÉTICO MADRID **10**
● ATHLETIC BILBAO **8**
◐ VALENCIA **6**

● REAL SOCIEDAD **2**
● SEVILLA **1**
● REAL BETIS **1**
● DEPORTIVO DE LA CORUÑA **1**

Source: Opta (October 2015)

REAL MADRID **32**

BARCELONA **23**

ATLÉTICO DE MADRID **10**

ATHLETIC BILBAO **8**

VALENCIA **6**

REAL SOCIEDAD **2**

SEVILLA,
REAL BETIS,
DEPORTIVO DE LA CORUÑA **1**

1976 1977 1978 1979 1980 1981 1982 1983 1984 1985 1986 1987 1988 1989 1990 1991 1992 1993 1994 1995 1996 1997 1998 1999 2000 2001 2002 2003 2004 2005 2006 2007 2008 2009 2010 2011 2012 2013 2014 2015

1974 WORLD CUP GOALS

In 1974 West Germany hosted (and won) a memorable World Cup that first gave us the Cruyff Turn, Zaire – the first African team to qualify – losing 3–0 to a below-par Brazil, a Cold War classic between East and West Germany and the "total football" displayed by the Netherlands. Goals came in all shapes and sizes, but we all remember the two belters from West Germany's Paul Breitner, Peter Lorimer's volley for Scotland against Zaire, Haiti's Emmanuel Sanon outpacing the Italian defence and Johan Cruyff's stunner against Brazil – a goal that crowned the Dutchman Player of the Tournament.

JOHAN CRUYFF – Netherlands vs Brazil

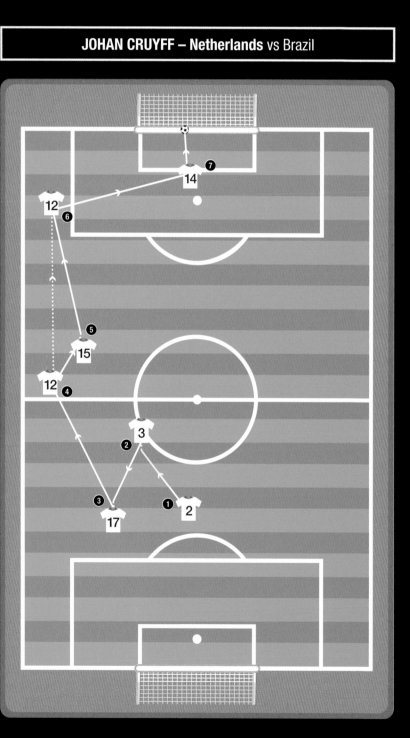

Fifty-two thousand fans watched Johan Cruyff score his second goal for the Netherlands against Brazil, 3 July 1974.

1. Free kick taken **Haan**
2. Pass **van Hanegem**
3. Pass (chipped) **Rijsbergen**
4. Pass **Krol**
5. Pass **Rensenbrink**
6. Pass (cross, chipped, long ball) **Krol**
7. Goal **Cruyff**

KEY

Ball movement	Player with ball
Shot	Player without ball

PAUL BREITNER – West Germany vs Chile

1. Take on **Rodríguez**
2. Tackle **Hoeneß**
3. Ball recovery **Hoeneß**
4. Pass **Hoeneß**
5. Pass **Overath**
6. Pass **Müller**
7. Pass **Hoeneß**
8. Pass **Breitner**
9. Pass **Hoeneß**
10. Pass **Overath**
11. Pass **Heynckes**
12. Pass **Hoeneß**
13. Pass **Beckenbauer**
14. Goal **Breitner**

JOHAN CRUYFF – Netherlands vs Argentina

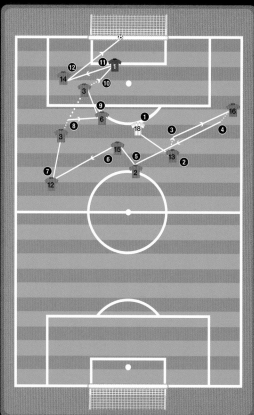

1. Pass **Telch**
2. Interception **Neeskens**
3. Pass **Neeskens**
4. Pass (chipped) **Rep**
5. Pass **Haan**
6. Lay-off **Rensenbrink**
7. Pass **Krol**
8. Pass **van Hanegem**
9. Pass **Jansen**
10. Attempt saved **van Hanegem**
11. Save (parried danger) **Carnevali**
12. Goal **Cruyff**

RIVELINO – Brazil vs Zaire

1. Pass **Jairzinho**
2. Pass (chipped) **Carpegiani**
3. Pass **Edu**
4. Pass **Marinho**
5. Pass **Jairzinho**
6. Goal **Rivelino**

JÜRGEN SPARWASSER – East Germany vs West Germany

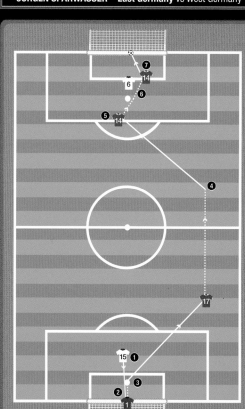

1. Head pass **Flohe**
2. Keeper pick-up **Croy**
3. Keeper throw **Croy**
4. Pass (long ball, chipped) **Hamann**
5. Take on **Sparwasser**
6. Challenge **Höttges**
7. Goal **Sparwasser**

SERIE A TITLE WINNERS

Serie A has been the top-flight tournament in Italian soccer since the 1929–30 season. Rated as one of the most entertaining and thrilling leagues in the world, Serie A has a reputation for highly tactical performances and players with virtuoso and prodigal technical ability. However, the league has also been rocked by controversy and scandal, such as the 2006 *Calciopoli*, as it became known, where some top teams were accused of rigging games by selecting biased referees. The winner of the league is awarded the *Scudetto*, a badge with the colours of the Italian flag, to be worn on the champions' shirts the following season.

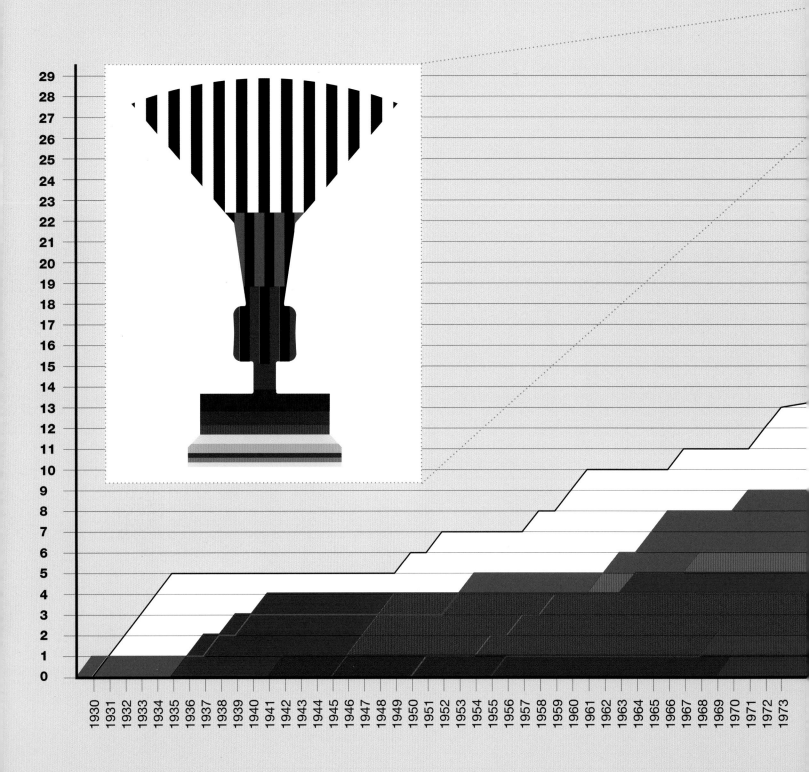

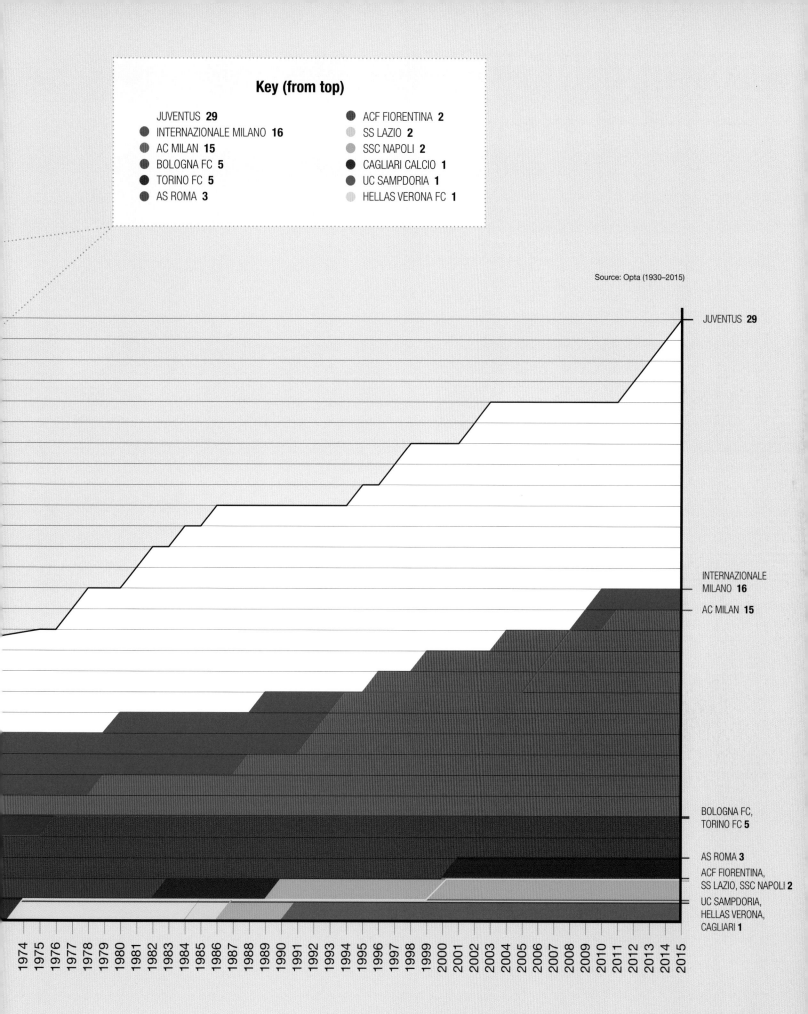

Key (from top)

JUVENTUS **29**
● INTERNAZIONALE MILANO **16**
● AC MILAN **15**
● BOLOGNA FC **5**
● TORINO FC **5**
● AS ROMA **3**

● ACF FIORENTINA **2**
● SS LAZIO **2**
● SSC NAPOLI **2**
● CAGLIARI CALCIO **1**
● UC SAMPDORIA **1**
● HELLAS VERONA FC **1**

Source: Opta (1930–2015)

JUVENTUS **29**

INTERNAZIONALE MILANO **16**

AC MILAN **15**

BOLOGNA FC, TORINO FC **5**

AS ROMA **3**

ACF FIORENTINA, SS LAZIO, SSC NAPOLI **2**

UC SAMPDORIA, HELLAS VERONA, CAGLIARI **1**

1974 1975 1976 1977 1978 1979 1980 1981 1982 1983 1984 1985 1986 1987 1988 1989 1990 1991 1992 1993 1994 1995 1996 1997 1998 1999 2000 2001 2002 2003 2004 2005 2006 2007 2008 2009 2010 2011 2012 2013 2014 2015

EUROPEAN CUP & CHAMPIONS LEAGUE RECORD GOALSCORERS

The talents of the game's greatest goalscorers have been showcased in the Champions League and its forerunner, the European Cup.

   The goalscorer table has been dominated by Real Madrid. Legendary striker Alfredo di Stefano led for many years before he had to give it up to Raúl in 2007. Barcelona's Lionel Messi took the record in November 2014, only to be equalled by Cristiano Ronaldo a day later. The great rivals continue to spar for the crown. Who will ultimately be victorious?

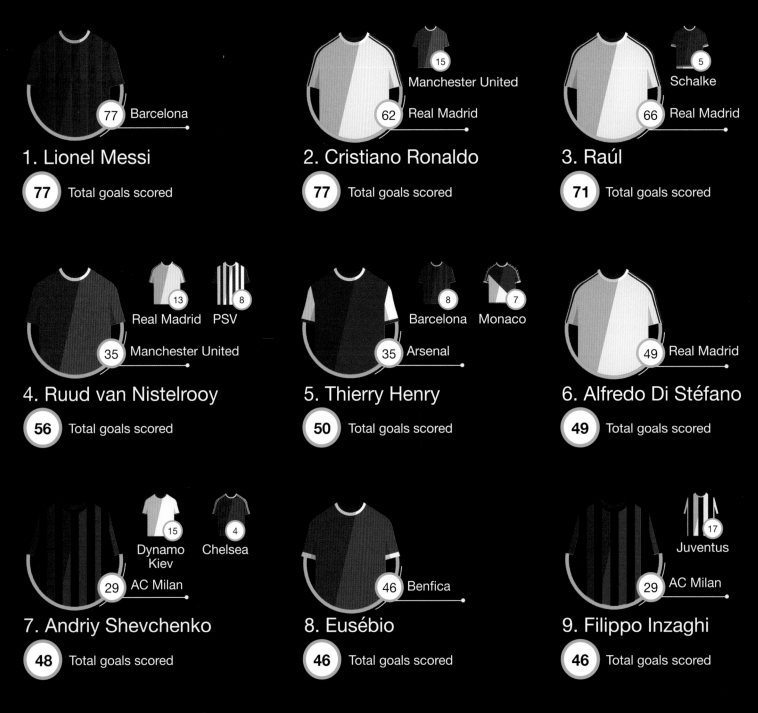

77 Barcelona

1. Lionel Messi

77 Total goals scored

15 Manchester United
62 Real Madrid

2. Cristiano Ronaldo

77 Total goals scored

5 Schalke
66 Real Madrid

3. Raúl

71 Total goals scored

13 Real Madrid **8** PSV
35 Manchester United

4. Ruud van Nistelrooy

56 Total goals scored

8 Barcelona **7** Monaco
35 Arsenal

5. Thierry Henry

50 Total goals scored

49 Real Madrid

6. Alfredo Di Stéfano

49 Total goals scored

15 Dynamo Kiev **4** Chelsea
29 AC Milan

7. Andriy Shevchenko

48 Total goals scored

46 Benfica

8. Eusébio

46 Total goals scored

17 Juventus
29 AC Milan

9. Filippo Inzaghi

46 Total goals scored

> **"I want to consistently play well and win titles...
> I'm only at the beginning."**
>
> Cristiano Ronaldo

5 Marseille 3 Galatasaray

36 Chelsea

10. Didier Drogba

44 Total goals scored

9 AC Milan 6 Inter 6 Ajax

15 Paris Saint-Germain

4 Barcelona

3 Juventus

11. Zlatan Ibrahimović

43 Total goals scored

42 Juventus

12. Alessandro Del Piero

42 Total goals scored

Source: Opta (1955 – August 2015)

EUROPEAN CUP & CHAMPIONS LEAGUE RECORD GOALSCORERS

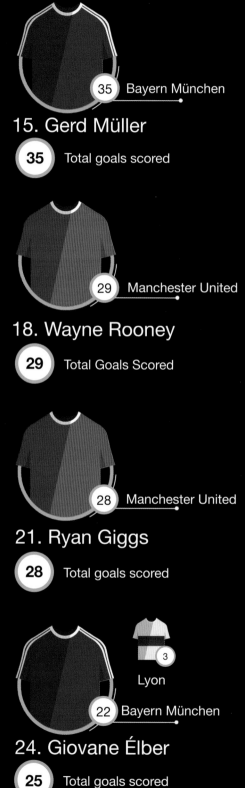

12 Lyon
30 Real Madrid

13. Karim Benzema
42 Total goals scored

1 Honvéd
35 Real Madrid

14. Ferenc Puskás
36 Total goals scored

35 Bayern München

15. Gerd Müller
35 Total goals scored

5 Real Madrid
25 AC Milan

16. Kaká
30 Total Goals Scored

30 Real Madrid

17. Paco Gento
30 Total Goals Scored

29 Manchester United

18. Wayne Rooney
29 Total Goals Scored

4 Monaco
25 Juventus

19. David Trezeguet
29 Total goals scored

28 Bayern München

20. Thomas Müller
28 Total goals scored

28 Manchester United

21. Ryan Giggs
28 Total goals scored

3 Olympiacos **2** AC Milan
22 Barcelona

22. Rivaldo
27 Total goals scored

3 Stuttgart
23 Bayern München

23. Mario Gómez
28 Total goals scored

3 Lyon
22 Bayern München

24. Giovane Élber
25 Total goals scored

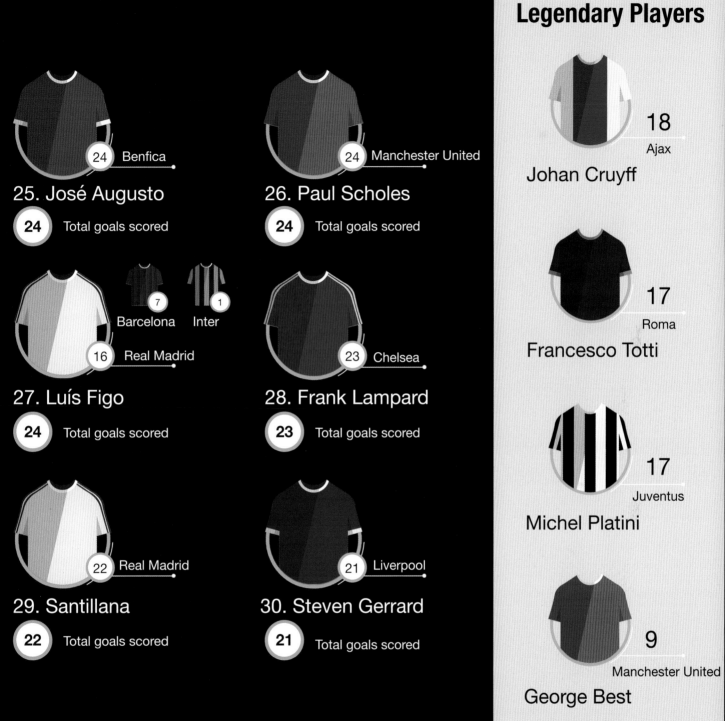

24   Benfica

25. José Augusto

24   Total goals scored

24   Manchester United

26. Paul Scholes

24   Total goals scored

7   Barcelona   1   Inter

16   Real Madrid

27. Luís Figo

24   Total goals scored

23   Chelsea

28. Frank Lampard

23   Total goals scored

22   Real Madrid

29. Santillana

22   Total goals scored

21   Liverpool

30. Steven Gerrard

21   Total goals scored

> **"Players today can only shoot with their laces. I could shoot with the inside, laces, and outside of both feet. In other words, I was six times better than today's players."**
>
> Johan Cruyff

Legendary Players

18   Ajax
Johan Cruyff

17   Roma
Francesco Totti

17   Juventus
Michel Platini

9   Manchester United
George Best

4   Bayern München
Franz Beckenbauer

Source: Opta (1955 – August 2015)

PREMIER LEAGUE TITLE WINNERS

The Premier League was formed in 1992. It is far and away the wealthiest league. It is also home to the richest clubs, nearly all of whom appear in the top 50 most well-off teams in the world. Premier League games are broadcast in more than 200 countries and since its formation it has been contested by 47 teams. But, as we all know, since the turn of the 21st century, the Premier League title is usually fought over by the same four elite teams – Manchester United, Chelsea, Arsenal and Liverpool, with Manchester City only becoming a serious contender within the past decade.

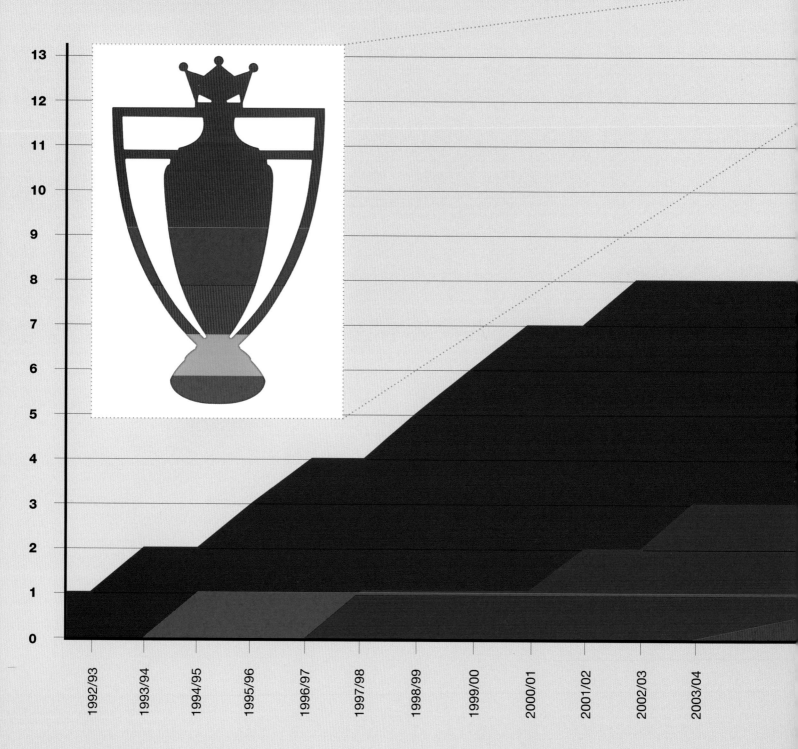

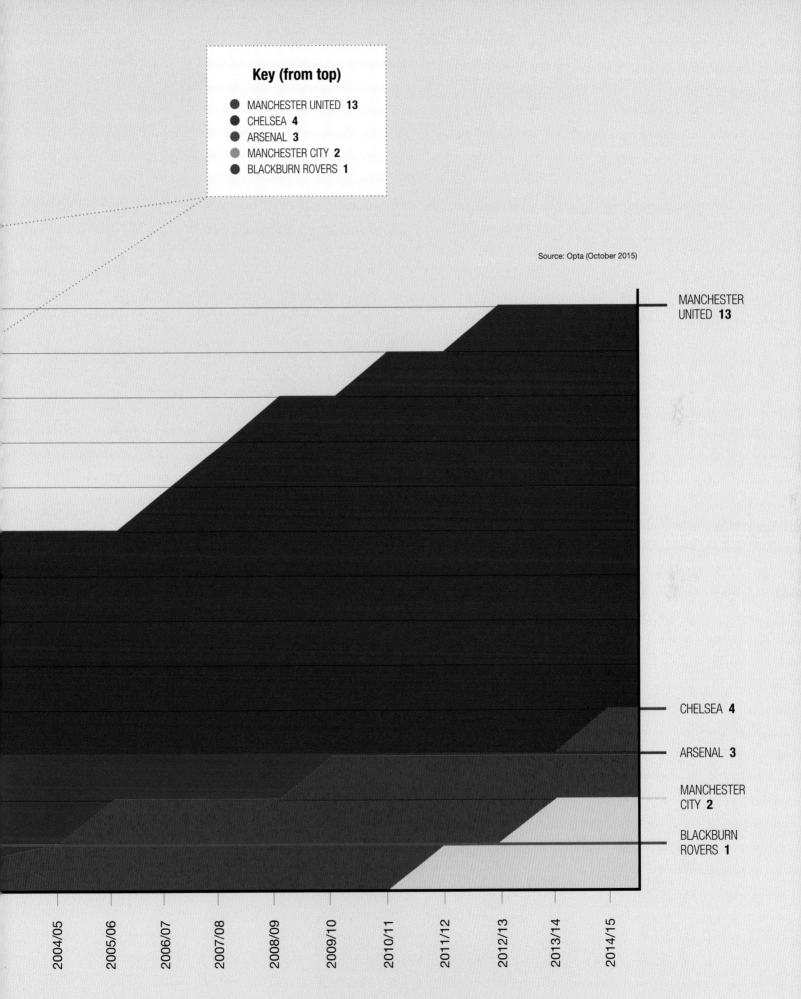

Key (from top)

- MANCHESTER UNITED **13**
- CHELSEA **4**
- ARSENAL **3**
- MANCHESTER CITY **2**
- BLACKBURN ROVERS **1**

MANCHESTER UNITED **13**

CHELSEA **4**

ARSENAL **3**

MANCHESTER CITY **2**

BLACKBURN ROVERS **1**

2004/05
2005/06
2006/07
2007/08
2008/09
2009/10
2010/11
2011/12
2012/13
2013/14
2014/15

1978 WORLD CUP GOALS

The "Tickertape Tournament" in 1978 was a bittersweet affair. It was set against an unsavoury political background, boycotted by Johan Cruyff (rated as the world's best player at the time) and disgraced by Scotland's Willie Johnston who was sent home after a positive drug test. However, the tournament also gave us some unforgettable goals, including a magical finish by Scotland's Archie Gemmill, screamers from the Netherland's Arie Haan and Brazil's Nelinho, and a much-needed morale-boosting triumph for the host nation, Argentina, when they defeated the Netherlands 3–1, thanks to the tournament's top scorer, Mario Kempes, and his second goal of the day.

ARIE HAAN – **Netherlands** vs West Germany

Arie Haan's goal against West Germany (18 June 1978) helped the Dutch national team reach the 1978 World Cup final, where they were beaten by Argentina 3–1 in extra time.

1. Goal kick (long ball) **Maier**
2. Head pass **Brandts**
3. Ball recovery **Haan**
4. Pass **Haan**
5. Pass **Willy van de Kerkhof**
6. Pass **René van de Kerkhof**
7. Goal **Haan**

KEY

Ball movement	▬▬▬	Player with ball ·············
Shot	▬▬⚽	Player without ball ··········

ARCHIE GEMMILL – Scotland vs Netherlands

1. Free kick taken **Rioch**
2. Pass **Kennedy**
3. Take on **Dalglish**
4. Take on **Gemmill**
5. Tackle **Krol**
6. Good skill **Gemmill**
7. Challenge **Krol**
8. Take on **Gemmill**
9. Goal **Gemmill**

LEOPOLDO LUQUE – Argentina vs France

1. Goal kick **Fillol**
2. Pass **Olguín**
3. Pass **Ardiles**
4. Pass **Gallego**
5. Pass **Kempes**
6. Pass **Ardiles**
7. Goal **Luque**

NELINHO – Brazil vs Italy

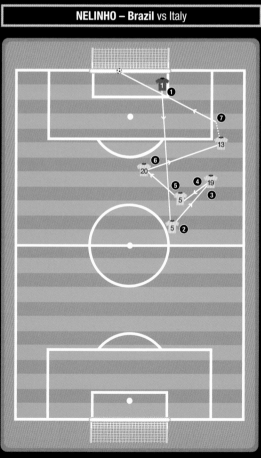

1. Goal kick (long ball) **Zoff**
2. Interception **Cerezo**
3. Ball recovery **Mendonça**
4. Pass **Mendonça**
5. Pass **Cerezo**
6. Pass **Dinamite**
7. Goal **Nelinho**

KARL-HEINZ RUMMENIGGE – West Germany vs Mexico

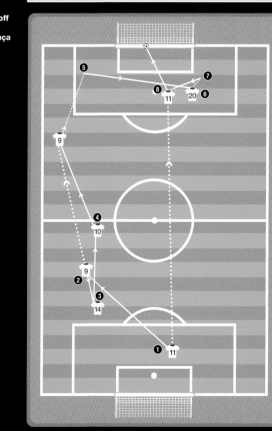

1. Clearance **Rummenigge**
2. Lay-off **Fischer**
3. Pass (chipped) **Dieter Müller**
4. Pass **Flohe**
5. Pass (cross, chipped, long ball) **Fischer**
6. Good skill **Hansi Müller**
7. Lay-off **Hansi Müller**
8. Goal **Rummenigge**

Source: Opta (October 2015)

BUNDESLIGA TITLE WINNERS

The Bundesliga was formed in 1963 to bring professionalism to the German game. The early years saw five different champions in five seasons before two promoted teams, Bayern München and Borussia Mönchengladbach, went on to dominate the league, both winning three successive titles. Bayern would continue to lead even after the league was revolutionized after 1989 at the unification of Germany. Various clubs – the latest being Borussia Dortmund – have risen to challenge Bayern's supremacy, but "FC Hollywood", as other teams' fans have continued to call them, remain the undisputed giants of the Bundesliga.

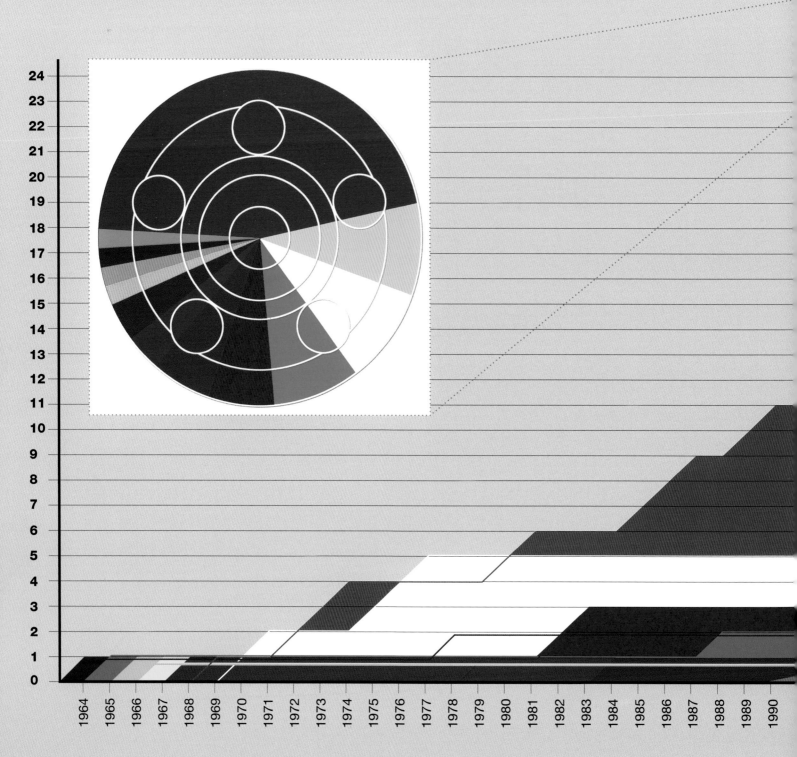

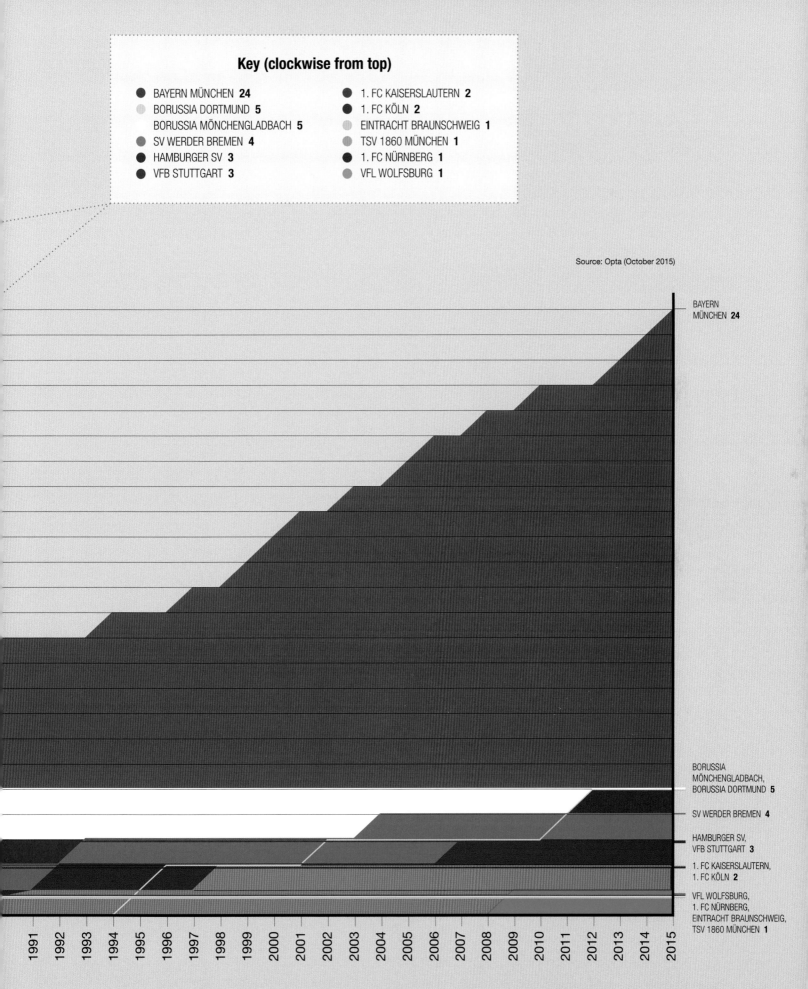

Key (clockwise from top)

- BAYERN MÜNCHEN **24**
- BORUSSIA DORTMUND **5**
- BORUSSIA MÖNCHENGLADBACH **5**
- SV WERDER BREMEN **4**
- HAMBURGER SV **3**
- VFB STUTTGART **3**

- 1. FC KAISERSLAUTERN **2**
- 1. FC KÖLN **2**
- EINTRACHT BRAUNSCHWEIG **1**
- TSV 1860 MÜNCHEN **1**
- 1. FC NÜRNBERG **1**
- VFL WOLFSBURG **1**

Source: Opta (October 2015)

BAYERN MÜNCHEN **24**

BORUSSIA MÖNCHENGLADBACH, BORUSSIA DORTMUND **5**

SV WERDER BREMEN **4**

HAMBURGER SV, VFB STUTTGART **3**

1. FC KAISERSLAUTERN, 1. FC KÖLN **2**

VFL WOLFSBURG, 1. FC NÜRNBERG, EINTRACHT BRAUNSCHWEIG, TSV 1860 MÜNCHEN **1**

1991 1992 1993 1994 1995 1996 1997 1998 1999 2000 2001 2002 2003 2004 2005 2006 2007 2008 2009 2010 2011 2012 2013 2014 2015

COPA AMÉRICA
RECORDS BY NATION

The Copa América is the oldest international continental football competition. It is now contested by the ten members of CONMEBOL, FIFA's South American region, with two invited guests. The first tournament took place in Argentina in 1916 and was annually (if sporadically) contested until 1967. The Copa América itself began in 1975 and continued in a four-year cycle. Since 1987 it has been hosted at irregular intervals of two, three or four years by a single nation and was contested by ten teams, enlarged to 12 in 1993 and 16 for 2016.

QUALIFICATION NOTES
Also competed: Mexico (9), Costa Rica (4), USA (3), Jamaica (1), Honduras (1), Japan (1). No host (3).

USA will host the 2016 tournament.

Chilean Alexis Sánchez lifts the trophy after winning the 2015 Copa América final between Chile and Argentina, Nacional Stadium, Santiago, Chile, 4 July 2015.

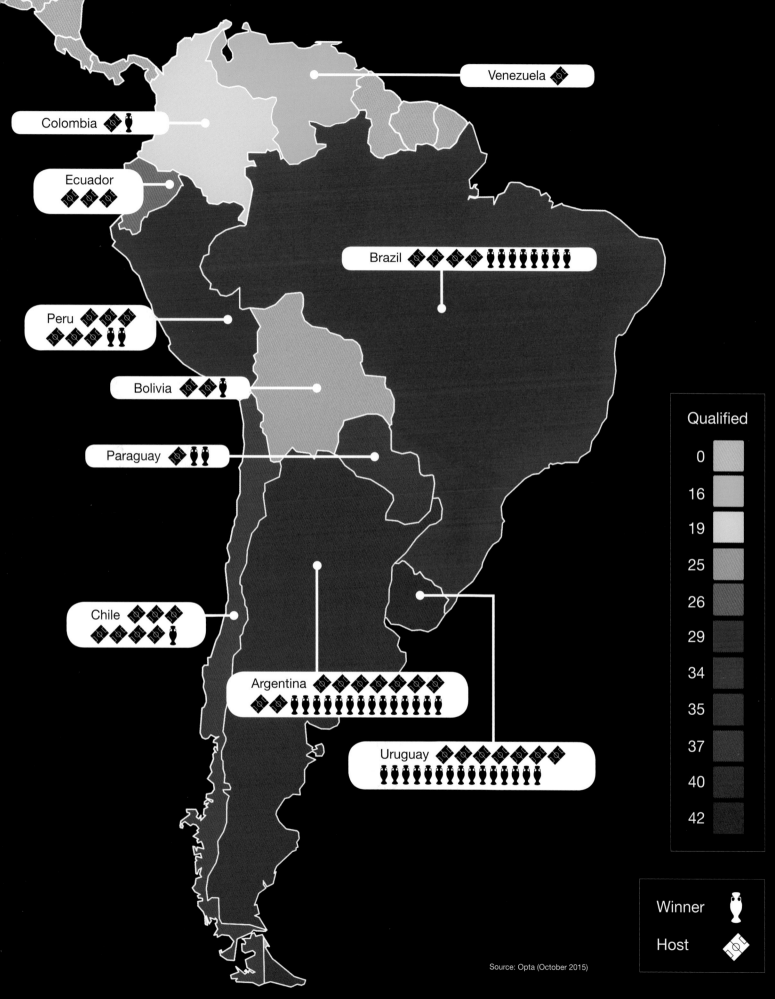

Venezuela

Colombia

Ecuador

Brazil

Peru

Bolivia

Paraguay

Chile

Argentina

Uruguay

Qualified

0

16

19

25

26

29

34

35

37

40

42

Winner

Host

Source: Opta (October 2015)

49

LONG RANGE WORLD CUP GOALS

Everyone loves a shot at goal from far out, especially if it's on target and struck with an awesome power to match. In particular, long range goals during World Cups are even more wondrous to behold as they instantly take on legendary status. Those long-rangers that live forever in the memory include Bobby Charlton's 25-yard strike against Mexico that fired up England's 1966 campaign, Arie Haan's 40-yard lightning-bolt as the Netherlands defeated Italy in 1978 and James Rodríguez's sensational chest and volley against Uruguay in 2014. All excellent goals, but where do they map in the long range pantheon?

ARIE HAAN

Netherlands
vs
Italy

36.71m

75:18

ROUND 2
21-06-1978

PAUL BREITNER

West Germany
vs
Chile

39.69m

15:50

GROUP STAGE
14-06-1974

Source: Opta (October 2015)

LOTHAR MATTHÄUS

West Germany
vs
Yugoslavia

31.93m

62:51

GROUP STAGE
10-06-1990

ARIE HAAN

Netherlands
vs
West Germany

31.41m

26:40

ROUND 2
18-06-1978

JOE COLE

England
vs
Sweden

33.2m

33:04

GROUP STAGE
20-06-2006

RONALDINHO

Brazil
vs
England

40.08m

49:02

QUARTER-FINAL
21-06-2002

NELINHO

Brazil
vs
Italy

31.86m

63:35

3RD PLACE MATCH
24-06-1978

WOMEN'S WORLD CUP TROPHIES AND GOALS

The first official Women's World Cup took place in China in 1991. There were 12 teams but no winners' prize money, no sponsor and the matches lasted just 80 minutes. Since then, the women's game and the competition have grown beyond recognition with eight four-yearly tournaments. In Canada, in 2015, the qualifying rounds saw 134 nations compete for 24 places; 26.7 million TV viewers made the final the most-watched soccer game in American history and the victorious US team won $2 million in prize money.

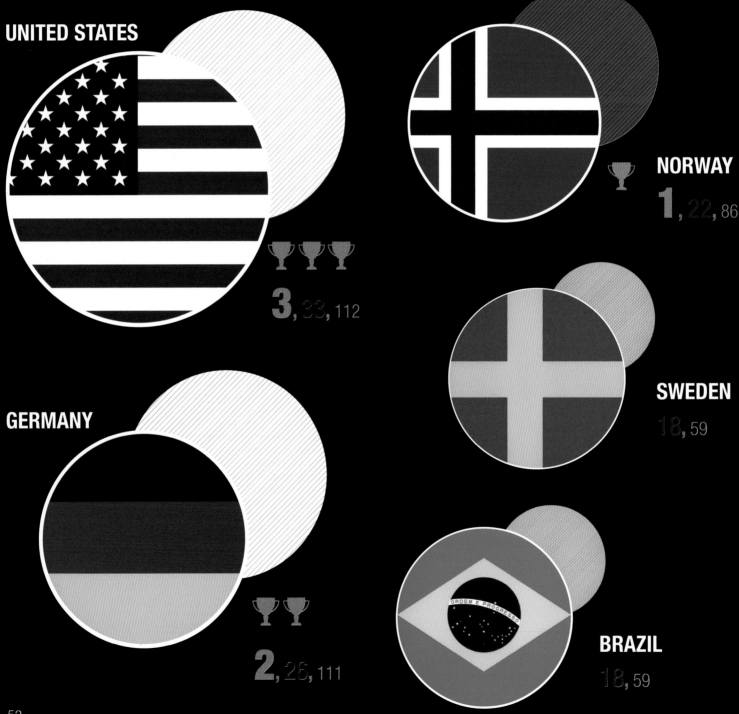

UNITED STATES

🏆🏆🏆 **3**, 33, 112

NORWAY

🏆 **1**, 22, 86

GERMANY

🏆🏆 **2**, 26, 111

SWEDEN

18, 59

BRAZIL

18, 59

CAMEROON
2, 9

FRANCE
6, 22

SWITZERLAND
1, 11

PR CHINA
15, 52

AUSTRALIA
5, 29

GHANA
1, 6

KOREA
REPUBLIC
1, 5

JAPAN
1, 13, 36

RUSSIA
4, 16

COLOMBIA
1, 4

ENGLAND
10, 30

DENMARK
3, 19

THAILAND
1, 3

NETHERLANDS
1, 3

NIGERIA
3, 18

CHINESE TAIPEI
1, 2

CANADA
6, 30

DPR KOREA
3, 12

TOURNAMENTS WON
MATCHES WON
GOALS SCORED

ITALY
3, 11

TICKET PRICES & AVERAGE STADIUM ATTENDANCES BY LEAGUE

What's the best league in the world? Don't just take the word of the commentator of whatever match you happen to be watching, this infographic maps out some of the variables at play, such as the cost of a matchday ticket, the size of the crowd and the quality of football on display. England's Premier League attracts big attendances at high prices to first-class action, but if you are seeking value for money then look no further than Germany's cut-price Bundesliga.

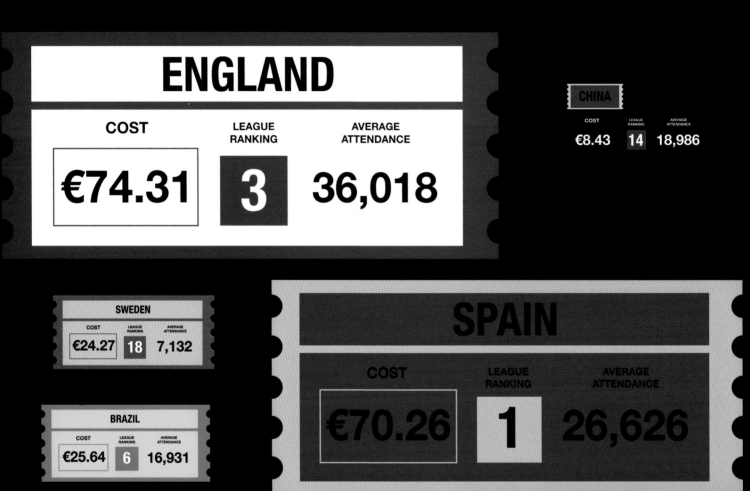

ENGLAND

COST	LEAGUE RANKING	AVERAGE ATTENDANCE
€74.31	3	36,018

CHINA

COST	LEAGUE RANKING	AVERAGE ATTENDANCE
€8.43	14	18,986

SWEDEN

COST	LEAGUE RANKING	AVERAGE ATTENDANCE
€24.27	18	7,132

SPAIN

COST	LEAGUE RANKING	AVERAGE ATTENDANCE
€70.26	1	26,626

BRAZIL

COST	LEAGUE RANKING	AVERAGE ATTENDANCE
€25.64	6	16,931

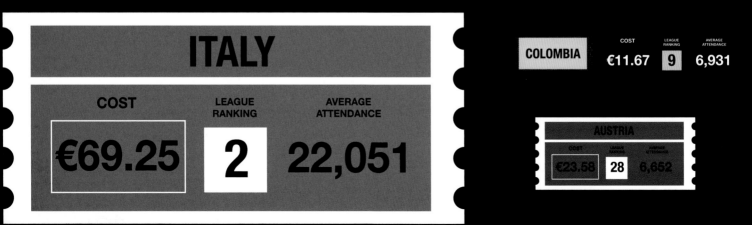

ITALY

COST	LEAGUE RANKING	AVERAGE ATTENDANCE
€69.25	2	22,051

COLOMBIA

COST	LEAGUE RANKING	AVERAGE ATTENDANCE
€11.67	9	6,931

AUSTRIA

COST	LEAGUE RANKING	AVERAGE ATTENDANCE
€23.58	28	6,652

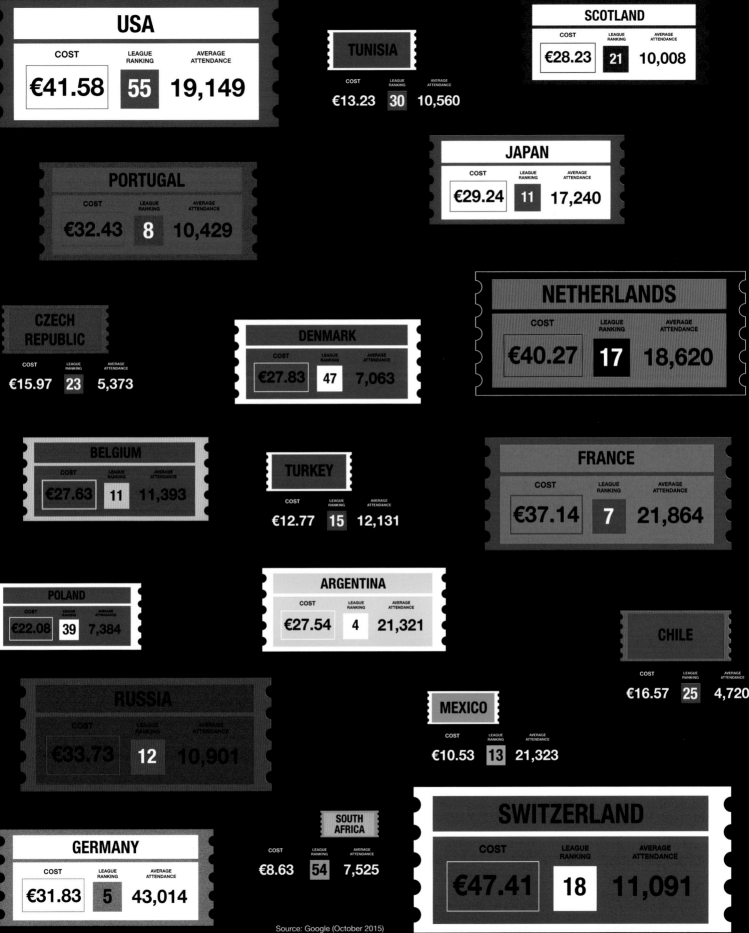

USA

COST	LEAGUE RANKING	AVERAGE ATTENDANCE
€41.58	55	19,149

TUNISIA

COST	LEAGUE RANKING	AVERAGE ATTENDANCE
€13.23	30	10,560

SCOTLAND

COST	LEAGUE RANKING	AVERAGE ATTENDANCE
€28.23	21	10,008

PORTUGAL

COST	LEAGUE RANKING	AVERAGE ATTENDANCE
€32.43	8	10,429

JAPAN

COST	LEAGUE RANKING	AVERAGE ATTENDANCE
€29.24	11	17,240

CZECH REPUBLIC

COST	LEAGUE RANKING	AVERAGE ATTENDANCE
€15.97	23	5,373

DENMARK

COST	LEAGUE RANKING	AVERAGE ATTENDANCE
€27.83	47	7,063

NETHERLANDS

COST	LEAGUE RANKING	AVERAGE ATTENDANCE
€40.27	17	18,620

BELGIUM

COST	LEAGUE RANKING	AVERAGE ATTENDANCE
€27.63	11	11,393

TURKEY

COST	LEAGUE RANKING	AVERAGE ATTENDANCE
€12.77	15	12,131

FRANCE

COST	LEAGUE RANKING	AVERAGE ATTENDANCE
€37.14	7	21,864

POLAND

COST	LEAGUE RANKING	AVERAGE ATTENDANCE
€22.08	39	7,384

ARGENTINA

COST	LEAGUE RANKING	AVERAGE ATTENDANCE
€27.54	4	21,321

CHILE

COST	LEAGUE RANKING	AVERAGE ATTENDANCE
€16.57	25	4,720

RUSSIA

COST	LEAGUE RANKING	AVERAGE ATTENDANCE
€33.73	12	10,901

MEXICO

COST	LEAGUE RANKING	AVERAGE ATTENDANCE
€10.53	13	21,323

SOUTH AFRICA

COST	LEAGUE RANKING	AVERAGE ATTENDANCE
€8.63	54	7,525

SWITZERLAND

COST	LEAGUE RANKING	AVERAGE ATTENDANCE
€47.41	18	11,091

GERMANY

COST	LEAGUE RANKING	AVERAGE ATTENDANCE
€31.83	5	43,014

Source: Google (October 2015)

1982 WORLD CUP GOALS

Spain's 1982 World Cup finals saw 24 teams play in a format involving two group stages. It was never used again. The tournament became the battleground for two of the greatest matches ever played in World Cup history. Italy's Paolo Rossi hit a hat-trick in an amazing 3–2 defeat of Brazil and, after a 3–3 draw, West Germany overcame France in the first ever World Cup penalty shoot-out. Memorable goals included an overhead bicycle kick by Germany's Klaus Fischer, a sublime chip from Brazil's Éder and a strike from his compatriot, Sócrates that proved completely unstoppable. However, it was Tardelli's goal (and his celebration) against West Germany in the final that we all remember the most.

MARCO TARDELLI – Italy vs West Germany

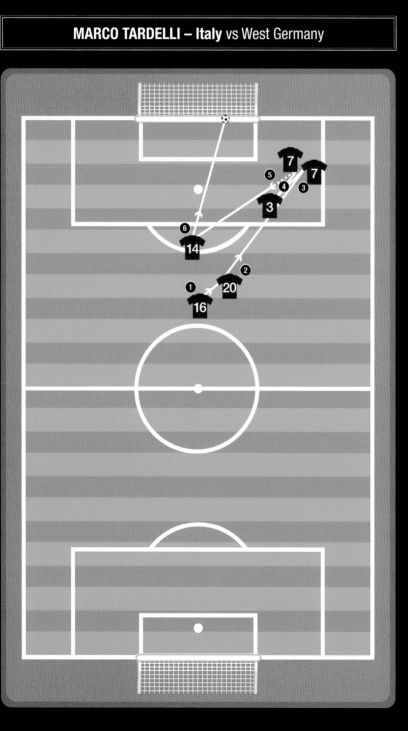

Italy's Marco Tardelli celebrates scoring his goal against West Germany during the 1982 World Cup final. Italy won the match 3–1, 11 July 1982.

1. Pass **Conti**
2. Pass **Rossi**
3. Pass **Scirea**
4. Pass **Bergomi**
5. Pass **Scirea**
6. Goal **Tardelli**

KEY

Ball movement ▬▬▬	Player with ball ··········
Shot ▬▬⚽	Player without ball ··········

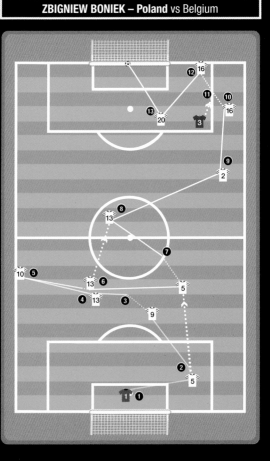

ZBIGNIEW BONIEK – Poland vs Belgium

1. Goal kick **Młynarczyk**
2. Pass **Janas**
3. Pass **Žmuda**
4. Pass **Buncol**
5. Pass **Majewski**
6. Pass (long ball) **Buncol**
7. Pass **Janas**
8. Pass (chipped, long ball) **Buncol**
9. Pass **Dziuba**
10. Take on **Lato**
11. Challenge **Millecamps**
12. Pull-back **Lato**
13. Goal **Boniek**

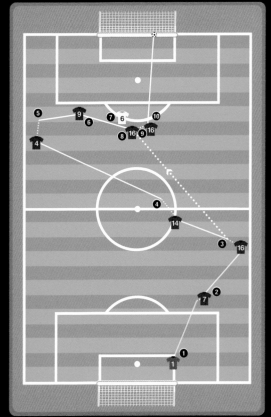

BRUNO CONTI – Italy vs Peru

1. Goal kick **Zoff**
2. Pass **Scirea**
3. Pass **Conti**
4. Pass (long ball, chipped) **Tardelli**
5. Pass **Cabrini**
6. Pass **Antognoni**
7. Challenge **Velásquez**
8. Good skill **Conti**
9. Take on **Conti**
10. Goal **Conti**

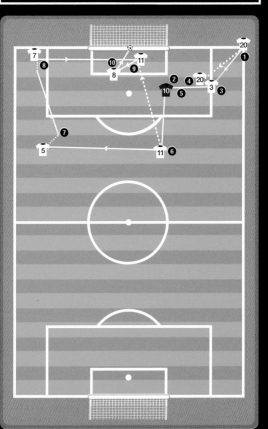

KLAUS FISCHER – West Germany vs France

1. Corner taken **Kaltz**
2. Clearance **Platini**
3. Pass **Breitner**
4. Pass (chipped, cross) **Kaltz**
5. Head pass **Kaltz**
6. Pass (long ball) **Rummenigge**
7. Pass **Förster**
8. Pass (chipped, cross, long ball) **Littbarski**
9. Head pass **Rummenigge**
10. Goal **Fischer**

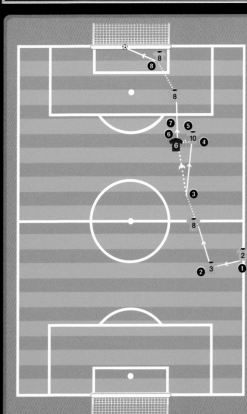

SÓCRATES – Brazil vs Italy

1. Throw in **Leandro**
2. Pass **Oscar**
3. Pass **Sócrates**
4. Good skill **Zico**
5. Take on **Zico**
6. Challenge **Gentile**
7. Through ball **Zico**
8. Goal **Sócrates**

STAR PLAYERS' TRANSFER FEES

The abolition of the maximum wage in English football and the rise of professionalism across Europe in the 1960s saw top players' wages skyrocket. They rose from 100 euros a week in the 1960s to 10,000 euros in the 1990s, and now to over one million euros every week. It was reported that, from the 2005–06 season, leading European football teams had agreed to cap their players' pay at 70 per cent of the team's income. This never materialized, and the wage debate continues to rage across the continent.

Real Madrid broke the world transfer record when they signed Gareth Bale. The Welsh player agreed a €402,000 per week, six-year deal after sealing a €100m move from Tottenham Hotspur in 2013.

GARETH BALE

ZLATAN IBRAHIMOVIĆ

LIONEL MESSI €134.6M

CRISTIANO RONALDO €145.1M

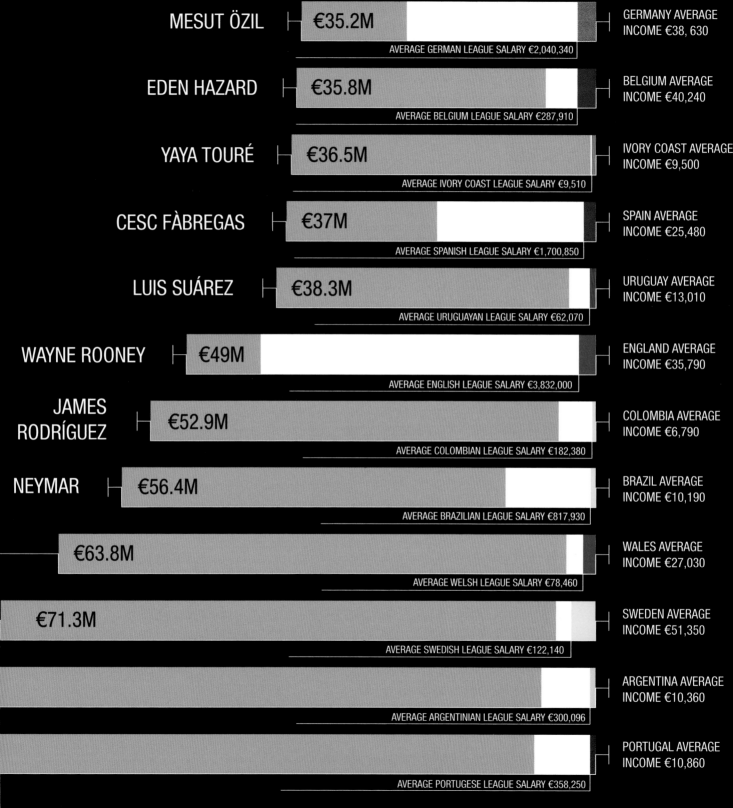

MESUT ÖZIL €35.2M
AVERAGE GERMAN LEAGUE SALARY €2,040,340
GERMANY AVERAGE INCOME €38, 630

EDEN HAZARD €35.8M
AVERAGE BELGIUM LEAGUE SALARY €287,910
BELGIUM AVERAGE INCOME €40,240

YAYA TOURÉ €36.5M
AVERAGE IVORY COAST LEAGUE SALARY €9,510
IVORY COAST AVERAGE INCOME €9,500

CESC FÀBREGAS €37M
AVERAGE SPANISH LEAGUE SALARY €1,700,850
SPAIN AVERAGE INCOME €25,480

LUIS SUÁREZ €38.3M
AVERAGE URUGUAYAN LEAGUE SALARY €62,070
URUGUAY AVERAGE INCOME €13,010

WAYNE ROONEY €49M
AVERAGE ENGLISH LEAGUE SALARY €3,832,000
ENGLAND AVERAGE INCOME €35,790

JAMES RODRÍGUEZ €52.9M
AVERAGE COLOMBIAN LEAGUE SALARY €182,380
COLOMBIA AVERAGE INCOME €6,790

NEYMAR €56.4M
AVERAGE BRAZILIAN LEAGUE SALARY €817,930
BRAZIL AVERAGE INCOME €10,190

€63.8M
AVERAGE WELSH LEAGUE SALARY €78,460
WALES AVERAGE INCOME €27,030

€71.3M
AVERAGE SWEDISH LEAGUE SALARY €122,140
SWEDEN AVERAGE INCOME €51,350

AVERAGE ARGENTINIAN LEAGUE SALARY €300,096
ARGENTINA AVERAGE INCOME €10,360

AVERAGE PORTUGESE LEAGUE SALARY €358,250
PORTUGAL AVERAGE INCOME €10,860

WORLD CUP GOALS BY BODY PART

"They all count!" It may be an old footballing cliché but it is as true in World Cup finals as it is anywhere else. For every exquisite shot curled in from the edge of the penalty area, there is a ricochet off the shin from 2 yards. For every perfectly-timed scissor-kick, there is a vicious and ugly toe-punt just to make sure the ball goes in. When it comes down to the wire in a World Cup match any goal will do.

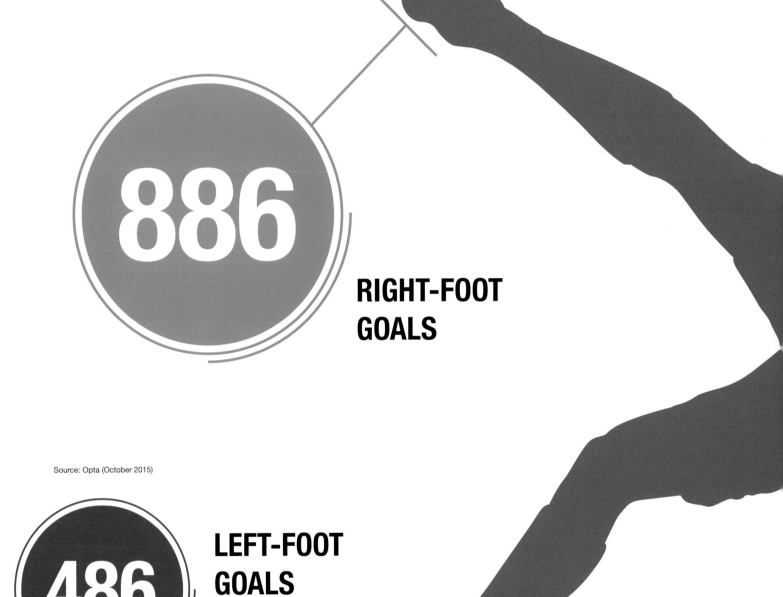

886

RIGHT-FOOT GOALS

Source: Opta (October 2015)

486

LEFT-FOOT GOALS

300 HEADED GOALS

10 OTHER GOALS

The most notorious scoring body part belongs to Maradona's "Hand of God", against England in 1986. Also worthy of a mention are Clint Dempsey's "Groin Goal" for the USA against Portugal in 2014 and the great Jairzinho "chesting" the ball in to score Brazil's second goal in the 1970 final.

30 OWN GOALS

Of the 1712 goals scored in the World Cup only 30 have been own goals – less than two per cent. Perhaps the strangest own goal ever scored, so far, belongs to Greece's Vasilis Torosidis during the World Cup qualifying game against Romania in 2014, whose intended left-foot clearance from inside the penalty box ended up being fished out from the back of his own net.

SERIE A GOALS

It is often stated that goals can be hard to come by in a defensively minded Serie A. The last five years' statistics bear this out with an average 2.6 goals being scored in each game, the lowest of the big four leagues. It wasn't a problem for 1930s star Silvio Piola whose record, set with Novara, Lazio, Juventus and others, looks unassailable. Udinese's Di Natale and Roma's Francesco Totti have him firmly in their sights, but both players are in the twilight of their careers.

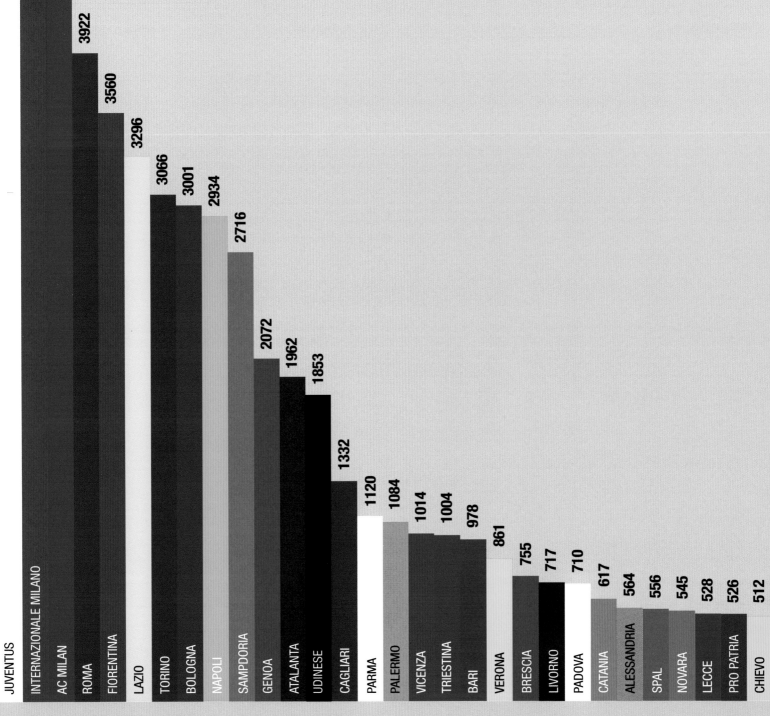

Team	Goals
JUVENTUS	4729
INTERNAZIONALE MILANO	4647
AC MILAN	4459
ROMA	3922
FIORENTINA	3560
LAZIO	3296
TORINO	3066
BOLOGNA	3001
NAPOLI	2934
SAMPDORIA	2716
GENOA	2072
ATALANTA	1962
UDINESE	1853
CAGLIARI	1332
PARMA	1120
PALERMO	1084
VICENZA	1014
TRIESTINA	1004
BARI	978
VERONA	861
BRESCIA	755
LIVORNO	717
PADOVA	710
CATANIA	617
ALESSANDRIA	564
SPAL	556
NOVARA	545
LECCE	528
PRO PATRIA	526
CHIEVO	512

FRANCESCO TOTTI 243

FILIPPO INZAGHI 156

MARCO DI VAIO 143

GIUSEPPE SIGNORI 128

CRISTIANO LUCARELLI 120

FABRIZIO MICCOLI 103

OLIVER BIERHOFF 100

ANTONIO DI NATALE 207

GABRIEL BATISTUTA 155

CHRISTIAN VIERI 141

ANDRIY SHEVCHENKO 127

EDINSON CAVANI 112

ADRIAN MUTU 103

ALESSANDRO DEL PIERO 183

HERNÁN CRESPO 153

VINCENZO MONTELLA 141

DAVID TREZEGUET 123

ANTONIO CASSANO 111

TOMMASO ROCCHI 102

ALBERTO GILARDINO 178

LUCA TONI 151

ENRICO CHIESA 137

ZLATAN IBRAHIMOVIĆ 122

NICOLA AMORUSO 110

GIAMPAOLO PAZZINI 101

Source: Opta (August 2015)
Player data: 1994–95 to August 2015.
Colour relates to the team the player scored the highest number of goals for.

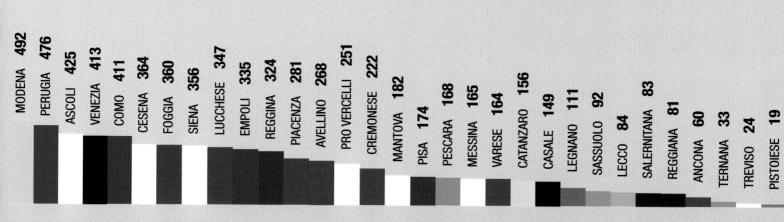

MODENA 492
PERUGIA 476
ASCOLI 425
VENEZIA 413
COMO 411
CESENA 364
FOGGIA 360
SIENA 356
LUCCHESE 347
EMPOLI 335
REGGINA 324
PIACENZA 281
AVELLINO 268
PRO VERCELLI 251
CREMONESE 222
MANTOVA 182
PISA 174
PESCARA 168
MESSINA 165
VARESE 164
CATANZARO 156
CASALE 149
LEGNANO 111
SASSUOLO 92
LECCO 84
SALERNITANA 83
REGGIANA 81
ANCONA 60
TERNANA 33
TREVISO 24
PISTOIESE 19

GAMES TO REACH 100 GOALS

It's true that you need more than star power in order to consistently score goals. You need a little luck, talented teammates and a crumbling opposition too. But when it comes to scoring a century (and more) for their club, the Premier League players below have shown they've got what it takes to become truly magical and, as a result, have joined an elite squad of top-scoring centurions. For all strikers, this is the benchmark worth getting out of bed for.

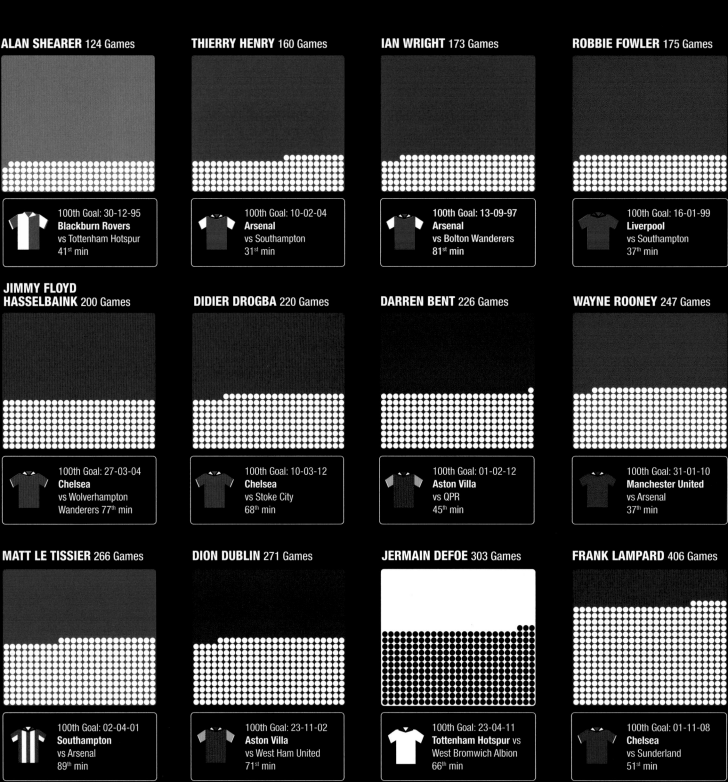

ALAN SHEARER 124 Games

100th Goal: 30-12-95
Blackburn Rovers
vs Tottenham Hotspur
41st min

THIERRY HENRY 160 Games

100th Goal: 10-02-04
Arsenal
vs Southampton
31st min

IAN WRIGHT 173 Games

100th Goal: 13-09-97
Arsenal
vs Bolton Wanderers
81st min

ROBBIE FOWLER 175 Games

100th Goal: 16-01-99
Liverpool
vs Southampton
37th min

JIMMY FLOYD HASSELBAINK 200 Games

100th Goal: 27-03-04
Chelsea
vs Wolverhampton
Wanderers 77th min

DIDIER DROGBA 220 Games

100th Goal: 10-03-12
Chelsea
vs Stoke City
68th min

DARREN BENT 226 Games

100th Goal: 01-02-12
Aston Villa
vs QPR
45th min

WAYNE ROONEY 247 Games

100th Goal: 31-01-10
Manchester United
vs Arsenal
37th min

MATT LE TISSIER 266 Games

100th Goal: 02-04-01
Southampton
vs Arsenal
89th min

DION DUBLIN 271 Games

100th Goal: 23-11-02
Aston Villa
vs West Ham United
71st min

JERMAIN DEFOE 303 Games

100th Goal: 23-04-11
Tottenham Hotspur vs
West Bromwich Albion
66th min

FRANK LAMPARD 406 Games

100th Goal: 01-11-08
Chelsea
vs Sunderland
51st min

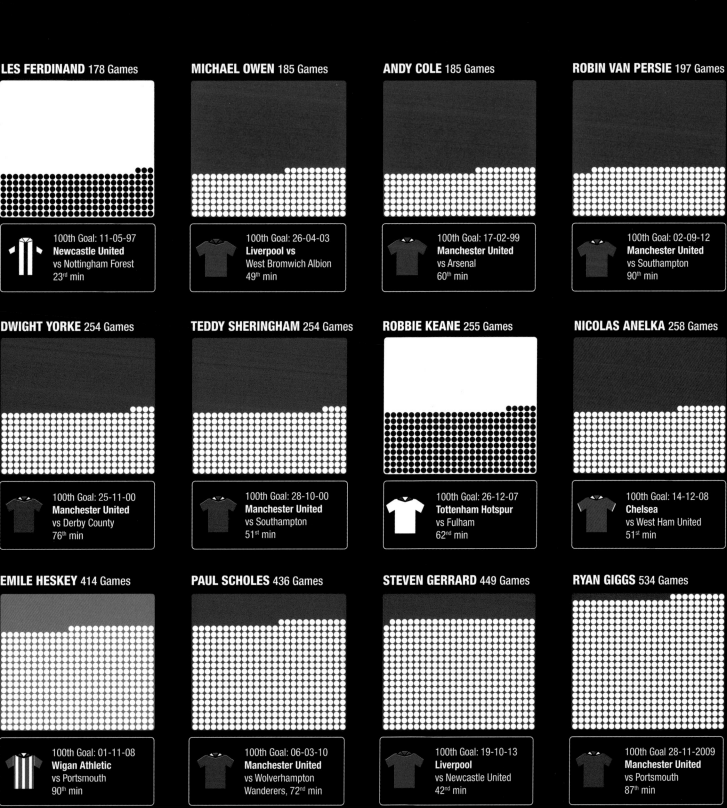

LES FERDINAND 178 Games

100th Goal: 11-05-97
Newcastle United
vs Nottingham Forest
23rd min

MICHAEL OWEN 185 Games

100th Goal: 26-04-03
Liverpool vs
West Bromwich Albion
49th min

ANDY COLE 185 Games

100th Goal: 17-02-99
Manchester United
vs Arsenal
60th min

ROBIN VAN PERSIE 197 Games

100th Goal: 02-09-12
Manchester United
vs Southampton
90th min

DWIGHT YORKE 254 Games

100th Goal: 25-11-00
Manchester United
vs Derby County
76th min

TEDDY SHERINGHAM 254 Games

100th Goal: 28-10-00
Manchester United
vs Southampton
51st min

ROBBIE KEANE 255 Games

100th Goal: 26-12-07
Tottenham Hotspur
vs Fulham
62nd min

NICOLAS ANELKA 258 Games

100th Goal: 14-12-08
Chelsea
vs West Ham United
51st min

EMILE HESKEY 414 Games

100th Goal: 01-11-08
Wigan Athletic
vs Portsmouth
90th min

PAUL SCHOLES 436 Games

100th Goal: 06-03-10
Manchester United
vs Wolverhampton
Wanderers, 72nd min

STEVEN GERRARD 449 Games

100th Goal: 19-10-13
Liverpool
vs Newcastle United
42nd min

RYAN GIGGS 534 Games

100th Goal 28-11-2009
Manchester United
vs Portsmouth
87th min

CONCACAF GOLD CUP RECORDS BY NATION

The CONCACAF Gold Cup is a biennial competition for nations from North and Central America and the Caribbean. The six-team tournament was first held in 1963 and then every two years. Between 1973 and 1989, the competition was held every four years and doubled as a World Cup qualifying process. In 1991 it was expanded to eight teams and reverted to a biennial format and in 2001 it was enlarged to 12 nations. Between 1997 and 2003 guest teams, including Brazil and Colombia, also competed in the tournament.

QUALIFICATION NOTES
The colour coding and winners and hosts icons are based only on the Gold Cup since 1991.

Mexico have won the CONCACAF
Gold Cup a record ten times.

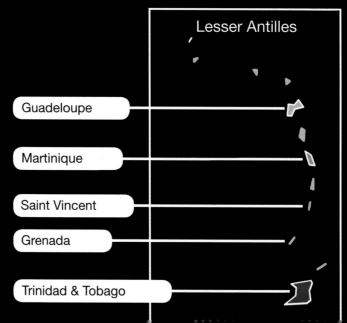

Lesser Antilles

Guadeloupe

Martinique

Saint Vincent

Grenada

Trinidad & Tobago

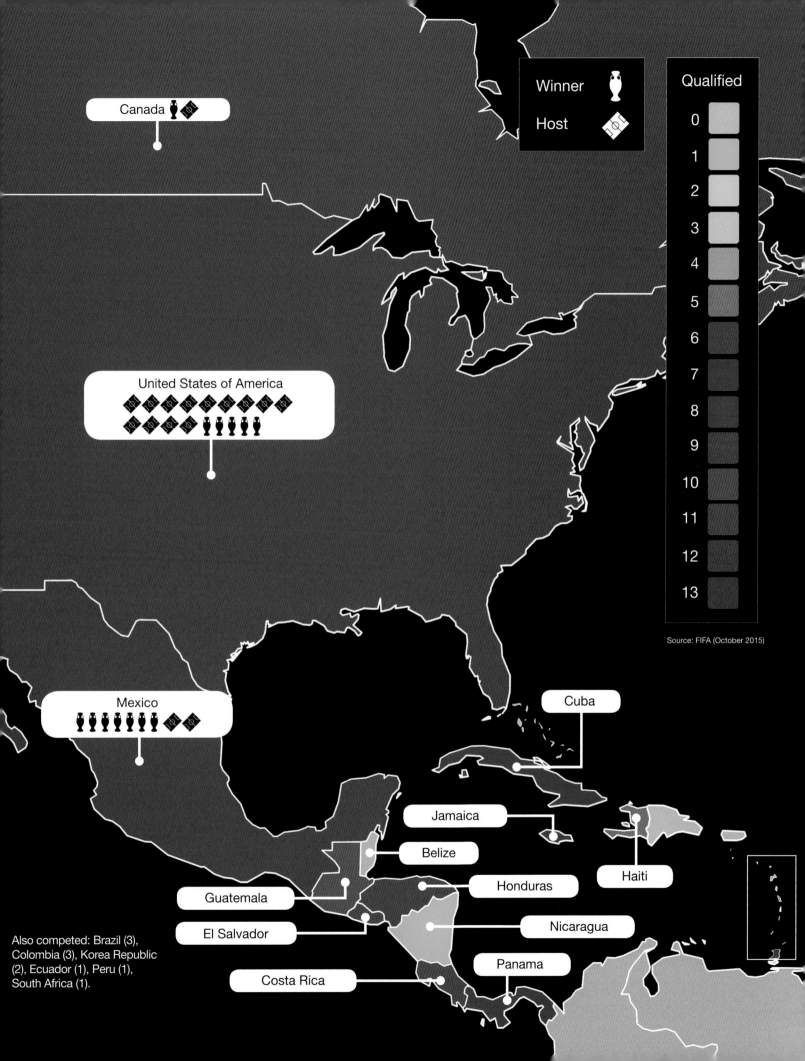

Canada

Winner
Host

Qualified
0
1
2
3
4
5
6
7
8
9
10
11
12
13

Source: FIFA (October 2015)

United States of America

Mexico

Cuba

Jamaica

Belize

Haiti

Honduras

Guatemala

Nicaragua

El Salvador

Panama

Costa Rica

Also competed: Brazil (3),
Colombia (3), Korea Republic
(2), Ecuador (1), Peru (1),
South Africa (1).

SPANISH LA LIGA SHIRT COLOURS

There can be few football kits as iconic and renowned around the world as the stylish all-white of Real Madrid, first made famous by the all-conquering side of the 1950s. Of course, Barcelona would claim equal status for their red and blue, with the club widely known as the "Blaugrana" (the names of these colours in the Catalan language). Also recognizable, though not as famous, are the "Yellow Submarines" of Villarreal, who have sported their all-yellow kit since 2003.

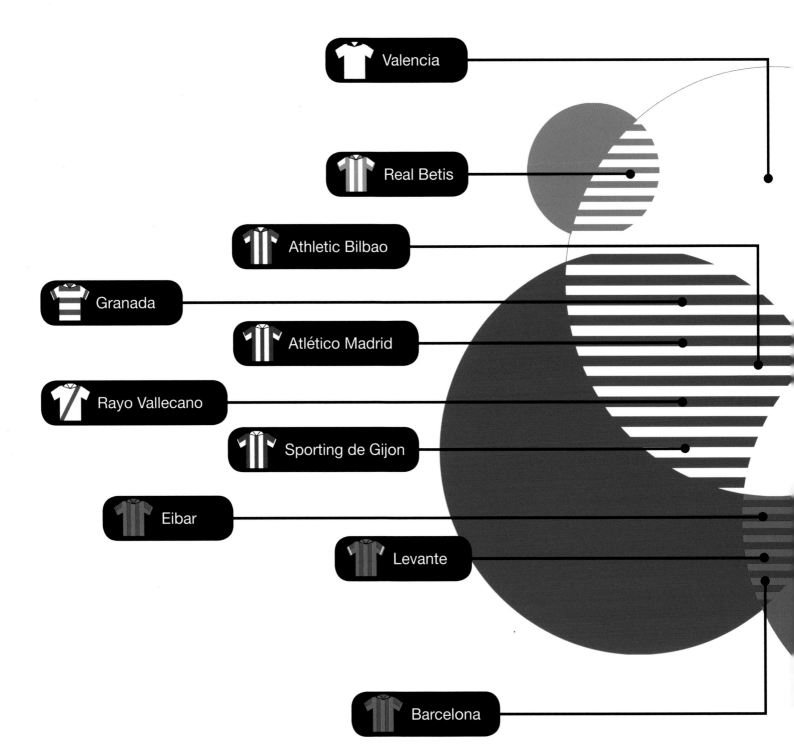

Valencia

Real Betis

Athletic Bilbao

Granada

Atlético Madrid

Rayo Vallecano

Sporting de Gijon

Eibar

Levante

Barcelona

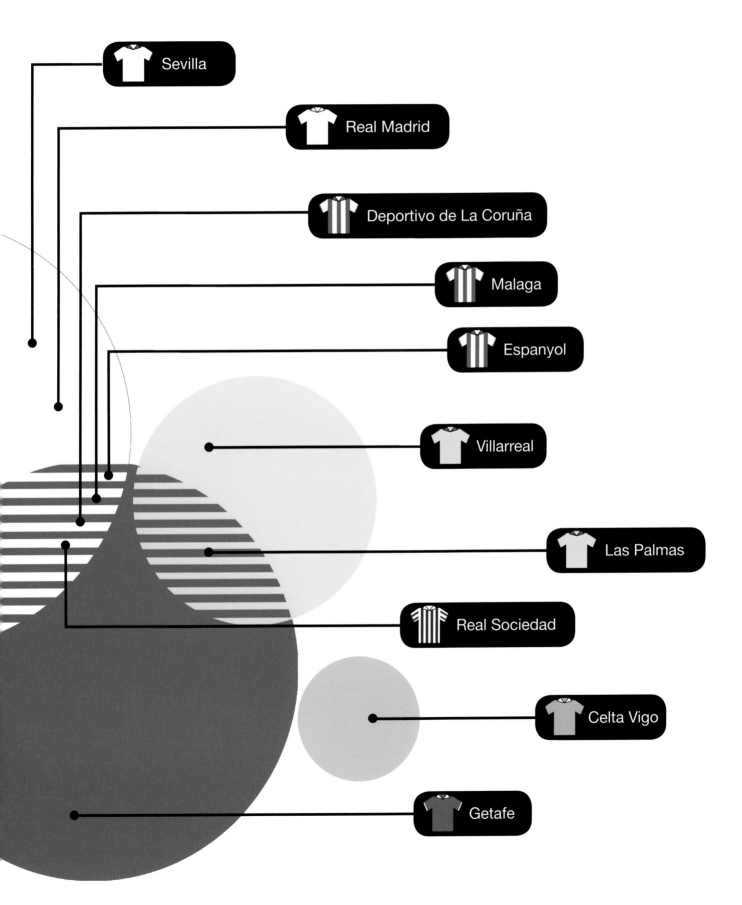

1986 WORLD CUP GOALS

Mexico may have hosted the 1986 World Cup, but the tournament was all about one man – Argentina's Diego Maradona. The 25-year-old's goals against England and Belgium were described by many pundits, players and fans alike as "pure genius". In the now famous quarter-final match against England, Maradona's unforgettable "Hand of God" goal was (almost) forgotten when he scored his "Goal of the Century" just four minutes later. His achievements would dwarf the World Cup's other magical moments, which included six goals from England's Gary Lineker (the tournament's top scorer), a screamer from Brazil's Josimar and an ambitious scissor-kick from the Mexican player Manuel Negrete.

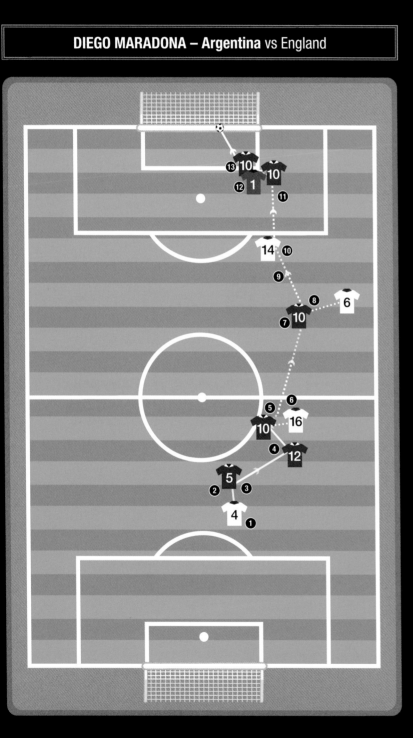

DIEGO MARADONA – Argentina vs England

Diego Maradona dribbles the ball beyond England goalkeeper Peter Shilton to score the "Goal of the Century". Argentina won 2–1, 22 June 1986.

1. Pass **Hoddle**
2. Pass **Brown**
3. Ball recovery **Brown**
4. Pass **Enrique**
5. Take on **Maradona**
6. Challenge **Reid**
7. Take on **Maradona**
8. Challenge **Butcher**
9. Take on **Maradona**
10. Challenge **Fenwick**
11. Take on **Maradona**
12. Challenge **Shilton**
13. Goal **Maradona**

KEY

Ball movement ——————

Shot ——————

Player with ball ·············

Player without ball ·············

CARECA – Brazil vs France

1. Keeper pick-up **Bats**
2. Keeper kick from hands (long ball) **Bats**
3. Clearance **César**
4. Ball recovery **Josimar**
5. Pass (chipped) **Josimar**
6. Pass **Sócrates**
7. Pass **Alemão**
8. Pass **Josimar**
9. Pass **Sócrates**
10. Pass **Müller**
11. Pass **Müller**
12. Pass **Júnior**
13. Goal **Careca**

MICHAEL LAUDRUP – Denmark vs Uruguay

1. Pass **Lerby**
2. Pass **Andersen**
3. Pass **Bertelsen**
4. Pass **Andersen**
5. Good skill **Laudrup**
6. Pass **Laudrup**
7. Pass **Andersen**
8. Pass **Laudup**
9. Pass **Olsen**
10. Pass (crossed, chipped) **Arnesen**
11. Pass (chipped) **Lerby**
12. Clearance **Batista**
13. Pass **Busk**
14. Pass **Lerby**
15. Take on **Laudrup**
16. Take on **Laudrup**
17. Take on **Laudrup**
18. Good skill **Laudrup**
19. Goal **Laudrup**

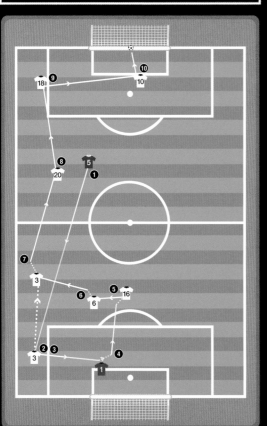

GARY LINEKER – England vs Poland

1. Pass (chipped, long ball) **Wójcicki**
2. Ball recovery **Sansom**
3. Pass **Sansom**
4. Pass **Shilton**
5. Pass **Reid**
6. Pass **Butcher**
7. Pass **Sansom**
8. Pass **Beardsley**
9. Pass (cross, long ball) **Hodge**
10. Goal **Lineker**

JEAN TIGANA – France vs Hungary

1. Pass **Rocheteau**
2. Pass **Amoros**
3. Pass **Rocheteau**
4. Pass **Tigana**
5. Pass **Platini**
6. Pass **Tigana**
7. Through ball **Rocheteau**
8. Goal **Tigana**

EUROPEAN CHAMPIONSHIP TROPHIES AND GOALS

It's an old football cliché, but it is certainly true that there have been no easy games in the European Championship. The format of this much-revered event has historically led to a select and elite group of nations reaching the finals, so this data is not distorted by easy wins and goal feasts. While Germany are top in the all-time Euro table, the other leading nations have similar records – except for England, whose lack of success in the competition is starkly obvious.

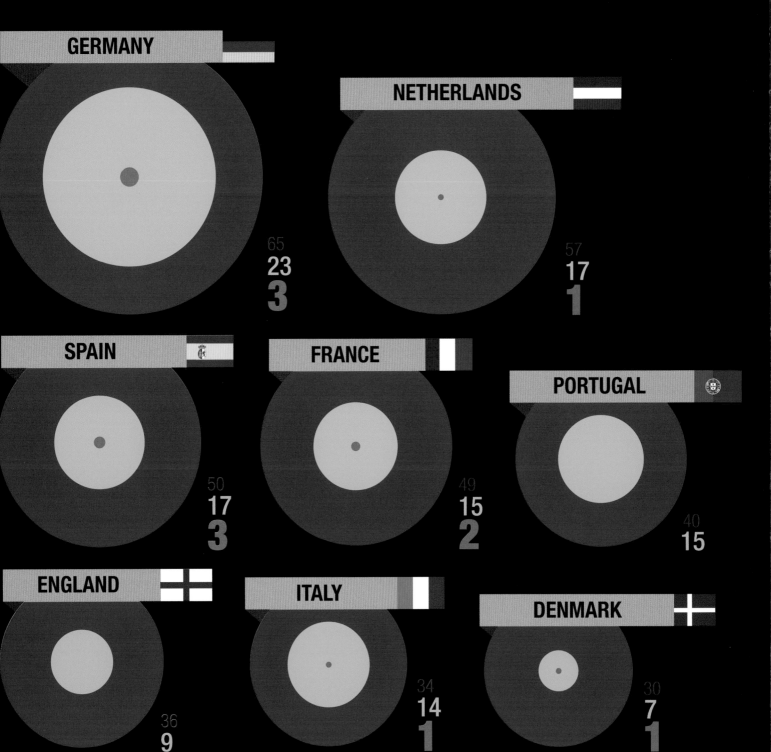

GERMANY
65
23
3

NETHERLANDS
57
17
1

SPAIN
50
17
3

FRANCE
49
15
2

PORTUGAL
40
15

ENGLAND
36
9

ITALY
34
14
1

DENMARK
30
7
1

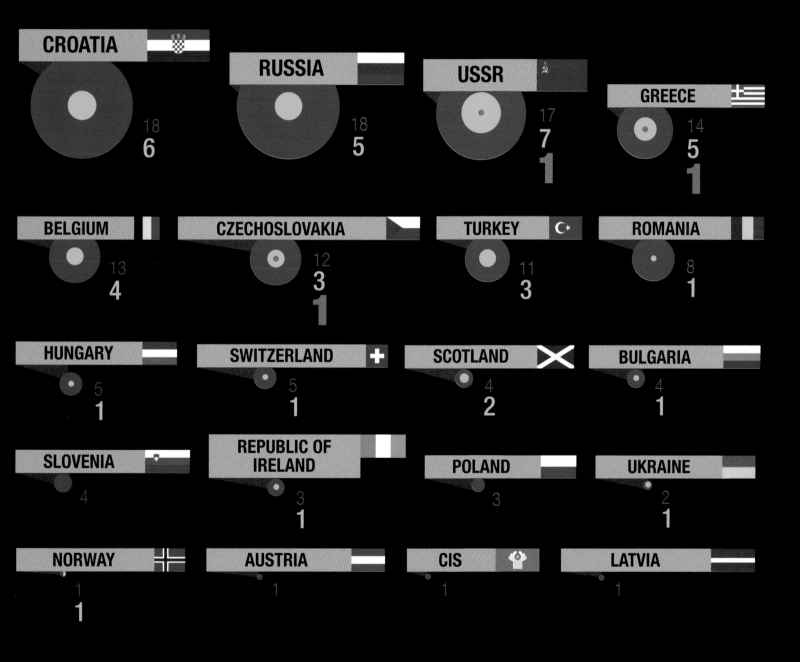

CZECH REPUBLIC

28
10

SWEDEN

24
5

YUGOSLAVIA

21
3

CROATIA

18
6

RUSSIA

18
5

USSR

17
7
1

GREECE

14
5
1

BELGIUM

13
4

CZECHOSLOVAKIA

12
3
1

TURKEY

11
3

ROMANIA

8
1

HUNGARY

5
1

SWITZERLAND

5
1

SCOTLAND

4
2

BULGARIA

4
1

SLOVENIA

4

REPUBLIC OF IRELAND

3
1

POLAND

3

UKRAINE

2
1

NORWAY

1
1

AUSTRIA

1

CIS

1

LATVIA

1

● **TOURNAMENTS WON**
● **MATCHES WON**
● **GOALS SCORED**

Source: Opta (August 2015)

UEFA CHAMPIONS LEAGUE DECADE BY DECADE PERFORMANCE

Though the UEFA Champions League is seen as the province of Europe's powerhouse teams, the 78 clubs taking part (including the qualifying stages) hail from 53 different nations. Teams from 32 countries have been represented in the group stages since it was rebranded from the European Cup in 1992. The competition has come a long way since the first European Cup finals of 1955–56 (Real Madrid won that year), which included teams from just 16 different nations, including the French protectorate Saar but, strangely, not Chelsea (England). The FA, at the time, saw the European Cup as a distraction to domestic football.

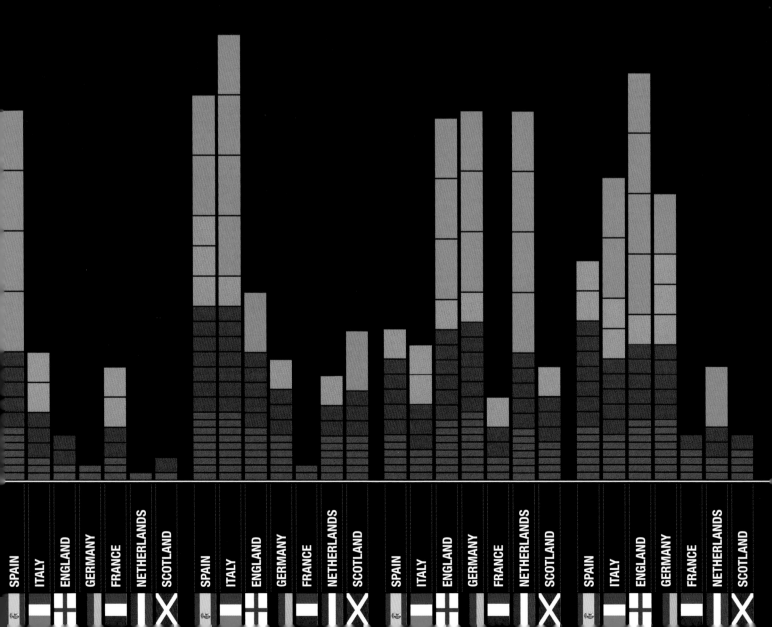

SPAIN ITALY ENGLAND GERMANY FRANCE NETHERLANDS SCOTLAND SPAIN ITALY ENGLAND GERMANY FRANCE NETHERLANDS SCOTLAND SPAIN ITALY ENGLAND GERMANY FRANCE NETHERLANDS SCOTLAND SPAIN ITALY ENGLAND GERMANY FRANCE NETHERLANDS SCOTLAND

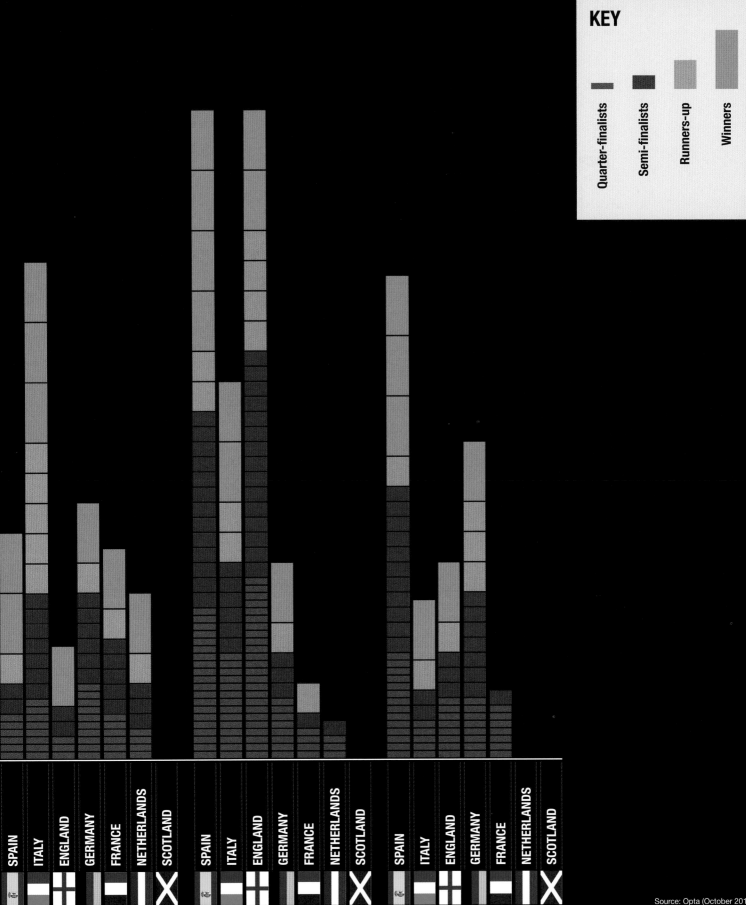

KEY

Quarter-finalists
Semi-finalists
Runners-up
Winners

SPAIN ITALY ENGLAND GERMANY FRANCE NETHERLANDS SCOTLAND
SPAIN ITALY ENGLAND GERMANY FRANCE NETHERLANDS SCOTLAND
SPAIN ITALY ENGLAND GERMANY FRANCE NETHERLANDS SCOTLAND

Source: Opta (October 2015)

FIFA WORLD CUP WINS BY COUNTRY

Brazil truly are the World Cup kings. Not only are they the most successful nation, they also top the chart of World Cup wins, have registered the most consecutive wins (vs Turkey in 2002 to Ghana in 2006) and they are the only team to have won all their matches in two tournaments (1970 and 2002). At the other end of the scale, Bulgaria failed to win in five finals from 1962 to 1986, before finally beating Greece in their second game in 1994.

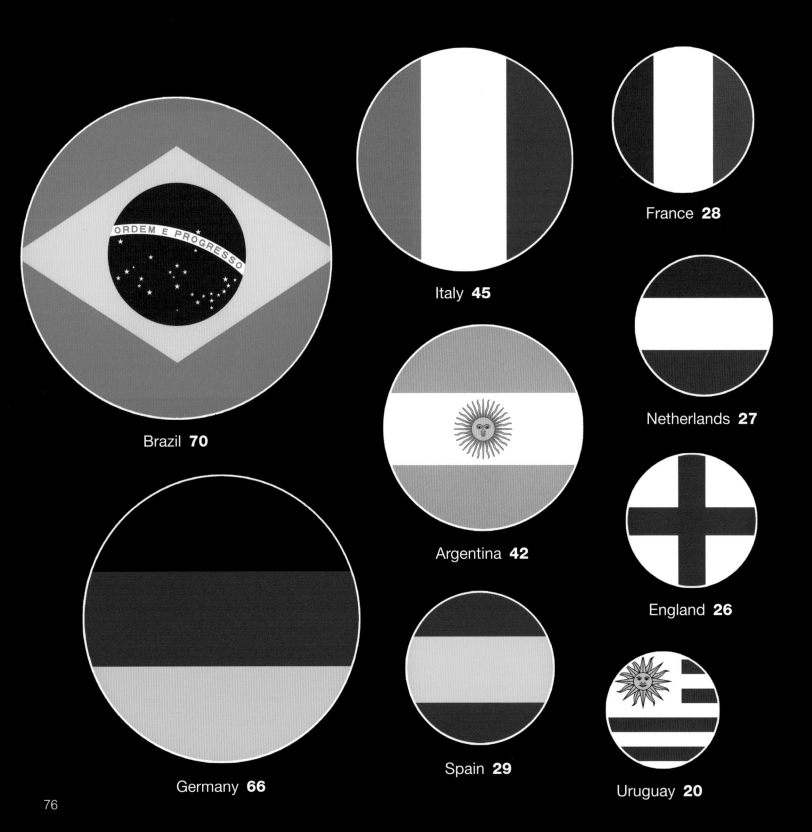

Brazil **70**

Italy **45**

France **28**

Netherlands **27**

Argentina **42**

England **26**

Germany **66**

Spain **29**

Uruguay **20**

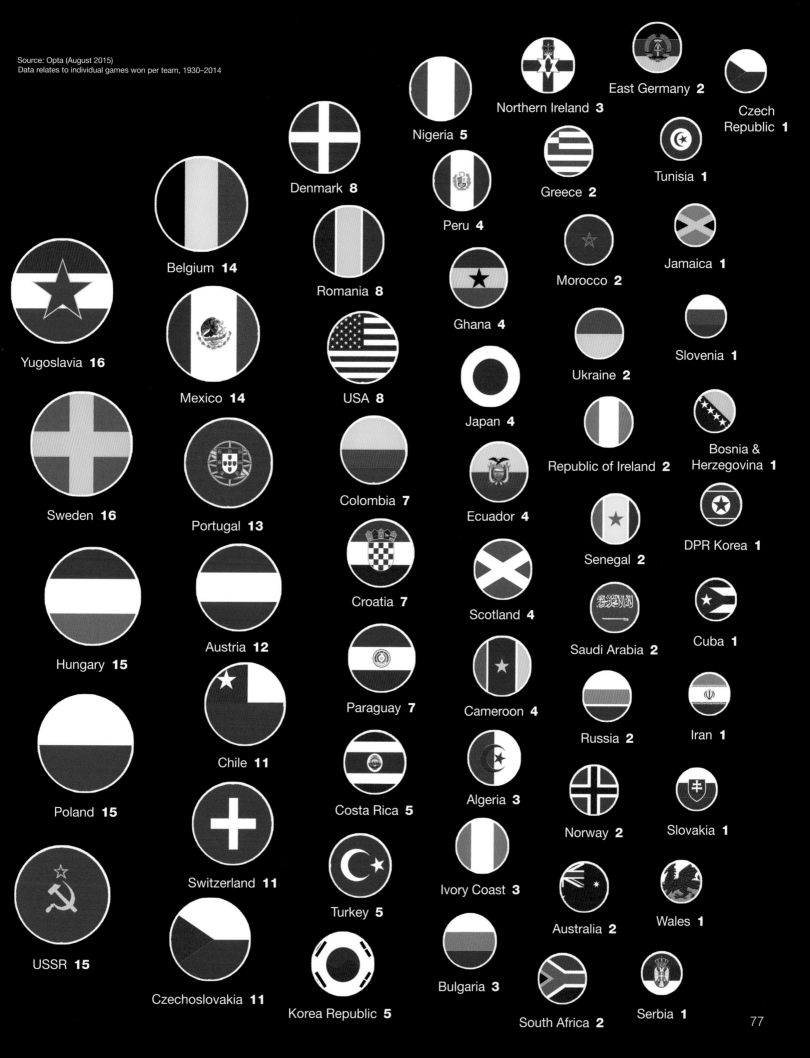

Source: Opta (August 2015)
Data relates to individual games won per team, 1930–2014

Yugoslavia **16**

Belgium **14**

Denmark **8**

Nigeria **5**

Northern Ireland **3**

East Germany **2**

Czech Republic **1**

Sweden **16**

Mexico **14**

Romania **8**

Peru **4**

Greece **2**

Tunisia **1**

Hungary **15**

Portugal **13**

USA **8**

Ghana **4**

Morocco **2**

Jamaica **1**

Poland **15**

Austria **12**

Colombia **7**

Japan **4**

Ukraine **2**

Slovenia **1**

USSR **15**

Chile **11**

Croatia **7**

Ecuador **4**

Republic of Ireland **2**

Bosnia & Herzegovina **1**

Switzerland **11**

Paraguay **7**

Scotland **4**

Senegal **2**

DPR Korea **1**

Czechoslovakia **11**

Costa Rica **5**

Cameroon **4**

Saudi Arabia **2**

Cuba **1**

Korea Republic **5**

Turkey **5**

Algeria **3**

Russia **2**

Iran **1**

Ivory Coast **3**

Norway **2**

Slovakia **1**

Bulgaria **3**

Australia **2**

Wales **1**

South Africa **2**

Serbia **1**

FRENCH LIGUE 1 SHIRT COLOURS

The all-white kit of Olympique Lyonnais (Lyon) became familiar after they dominated French football in the first decade of the 21st century; Saint-Étienne wear the green of the Casino supermarket because the club was founded by some of their employees in 1919; AS Monaco wear the heraldic red and white colours of their prince's House of Grimaldi and PSG's Eiffel Tower design is the work of fashion designer Daniel Hechter, PSG president from 1973–1978.

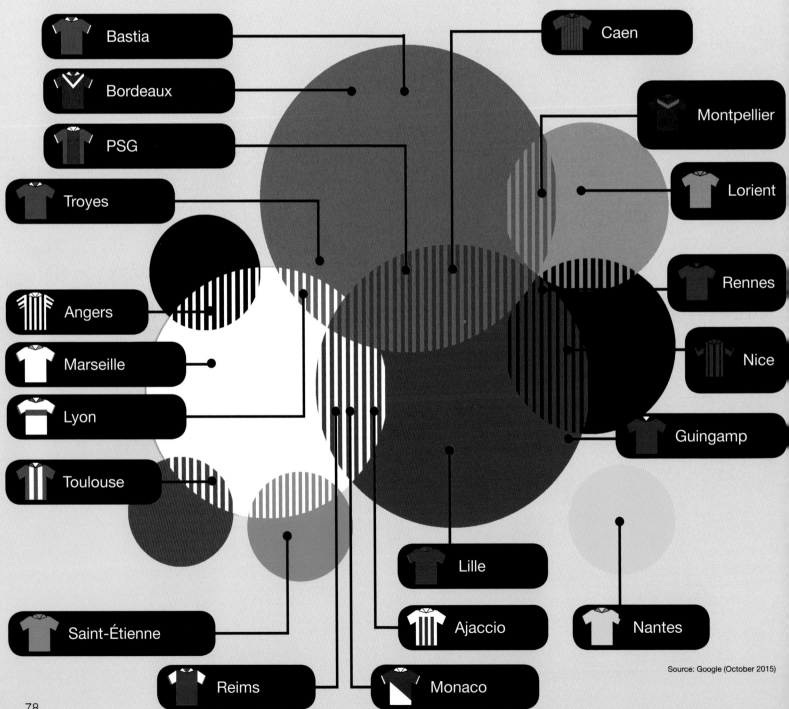

Bastia
Bordeaux
PSG
Troyes
Angers
Marseille
Lyon
Toulouse
Saint-Étienne
Reims
Monaco
Ajaccio
Lille
Nantes
Guingamp
Nice
Rennes
Lorient
Montpellier
Caen

Source: Google (October 2015)

SCOTTISH PREMIER LEAGUE SHIRT COLOURS

Their 1967 European Cup triumph made the strip of Glasgow Celtic recognizable around the world. Their green hoops signified their roots in the city's Irish community, a link shared in Edinburgh by the green shirts of Hibernian. Similarly, Glasgow Rangers acknowledge their loyal tradition in their wearing of "British" red, white and (mainly) blue. A more fun fact lies in the orange and black of Dundee United, who adopted the colours after wearing a similar strip as Dallas Tornado in the USA in 1967.

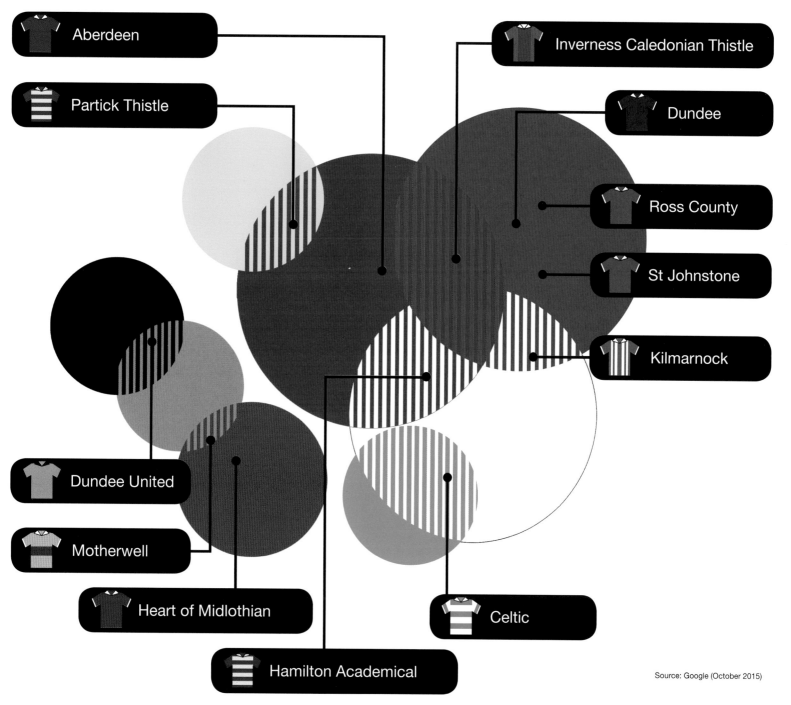

Aberdeen

Partick Thistle

Inverness Caledonian Thistle

Dundee

Ross County

St Johnstone

Kilmarnock

Dundee United

Motherwell

Heart of Midlothian

Celtic

Hamilton Academical

Source: Google (October 2015)

PREMIER LEAGUE GAME WINS

The Premier League thrives on the ability of any of its teams to beat another. Although the elite teams generally dominate the top of the table they cannot be sure of winning every game. The league winners collect around 27 wins, on average, in a season with Chelsea holding the record with 29 wins on two occasions (2004–05, 2005–06). Consecutive runs of eight or more victories are rare, with Arsenal setting the bar at 14 in 2002.

WOLVERHAMPTON WANDERERS **32**
READING **32**
HULL CITY **32**
SHEFFIELD UNITED **32**
SWANSEA CITY **50**
IPSWICH TOWN **57**
NOTTINGHAM FOREST **60**
CRYSTAL PALACE **63**
DERBY COUNTY **68**
BIRMINGHAM CITY **73**
PORTSMOUTH **79**
NORWICH CITY **80**
QUEENS PARK RANGERS **81**
STOKE CITY **84**
WEST BROMWICH ALBION **84**
WIGAN ATHLETIC **85**
CHARLTON ATHLETIC **93**
LEICESTER CITY **95**
WIMBLEDON **99**
COVENTRY CITY **99**
SHEFFIELD WEDNESDAY **101**
SUNDERLAND **138**
BOLTON WANDERERS **149**
FULHAM **150**
MIDDLESBROUGH **160**
LEEDS UNITED **189**
SOUTHAMPTON **192**
WEST HAM UNITED **237**
BLACKBURN ROVERS **262**
MANCHESTER CITY **285**

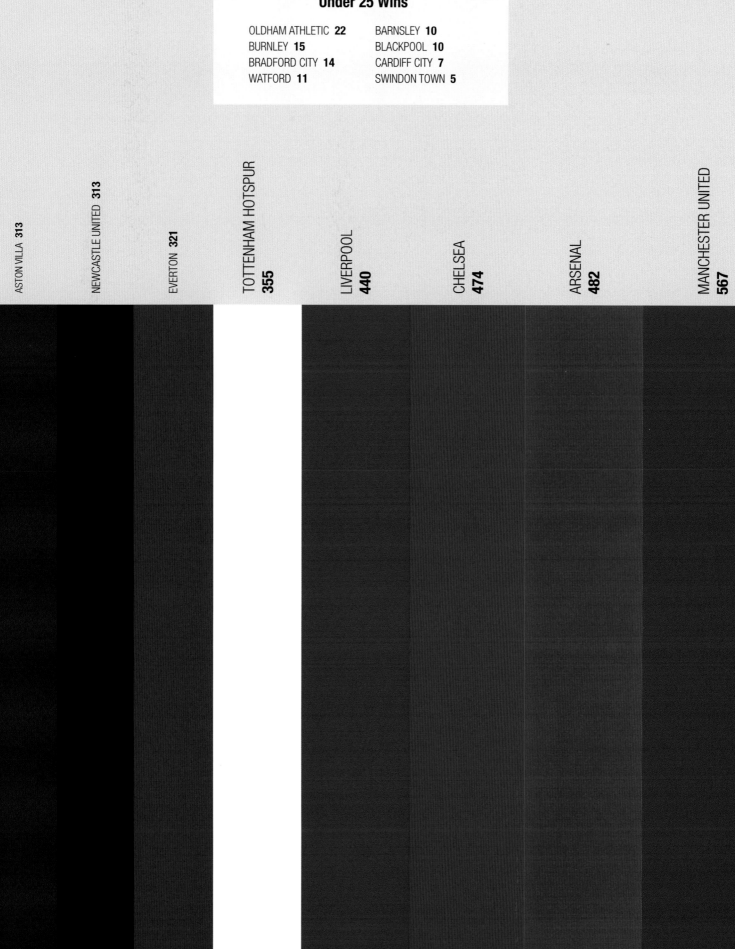

Source: Opta (August 2015)

Under 25 Wins

OLDHAM ATHLETIC **22**	BARNSLEY **10**
BURNLEY **15**	BLACKPOOL **10**
BRADFORD CITY **14**	CARDIFF CITY **7**
WATFORD **11**	SWINDON TOWN **5**

ASTON VILLA **313**

NEWCASTLE UNITED **313**

EVERTON **321**

TOTTENHAM HOTSPUR **355**

LIVERPOOL **440**

CHELSEA **474**

ARSENAL **482**

MANCHESTER UNITED **567**

FOOTBALL RIVALRIES, PART 2

"The Derby" is an unofficial competition recognized across the football world. It signifies a two-match battle between two rival teams each season, where the victorious side wins hometown pride and temporary bragging rights over the other. Italy plays host to some of the sport's more heated rivalries, the oldest being the *Derby della Lanterna* in which Genoa duel Sampdoria, while *Derby d'Italia* brings together Internazionale Milano and Juventus. Meanwhile, in Spain's La Liga, the dominance of powerhouses Barcelona and Real Madrid has fired *El Clásico*, a rivalry constantly simmering through decades of interconnected history, politics and geography.

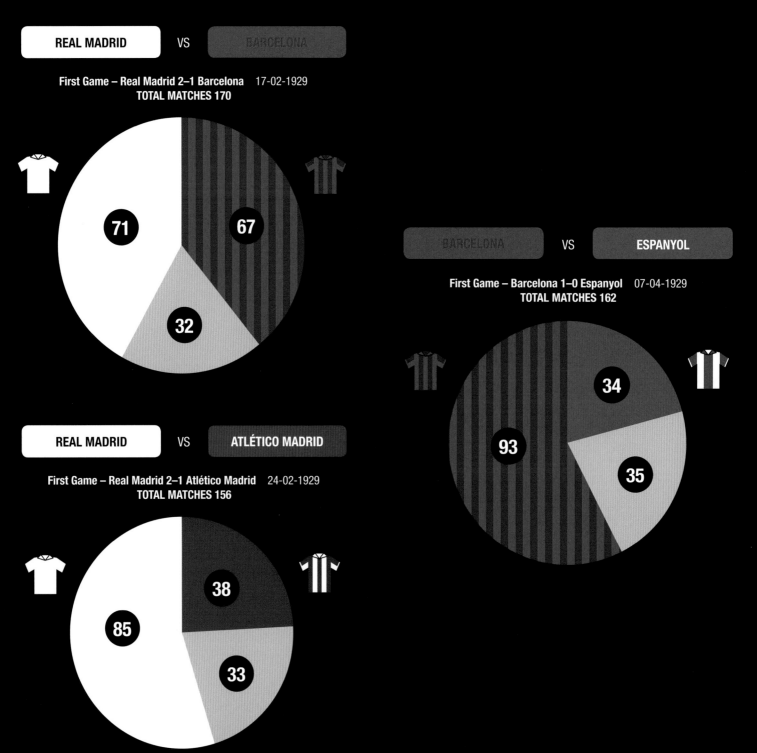

REAL MADRID VS BARCELONA

First Game – Real Madrid 2–1 Barcelona   17-02-1929
TOTAL MATCHES 170

71   67   32

BARCELONA VS **ESPANYOL**

First Game – Barcelona 1–0 Espanyol   07-04-1929
TOTAL MATCHES 162

34   93   35

REAL MADRID VS **ATLÉTICO MADRID**

First Game – Real Madrid 2–1 Atlético Madrid   24-02-1929
TOTAL MATCHES 156

38   85   33

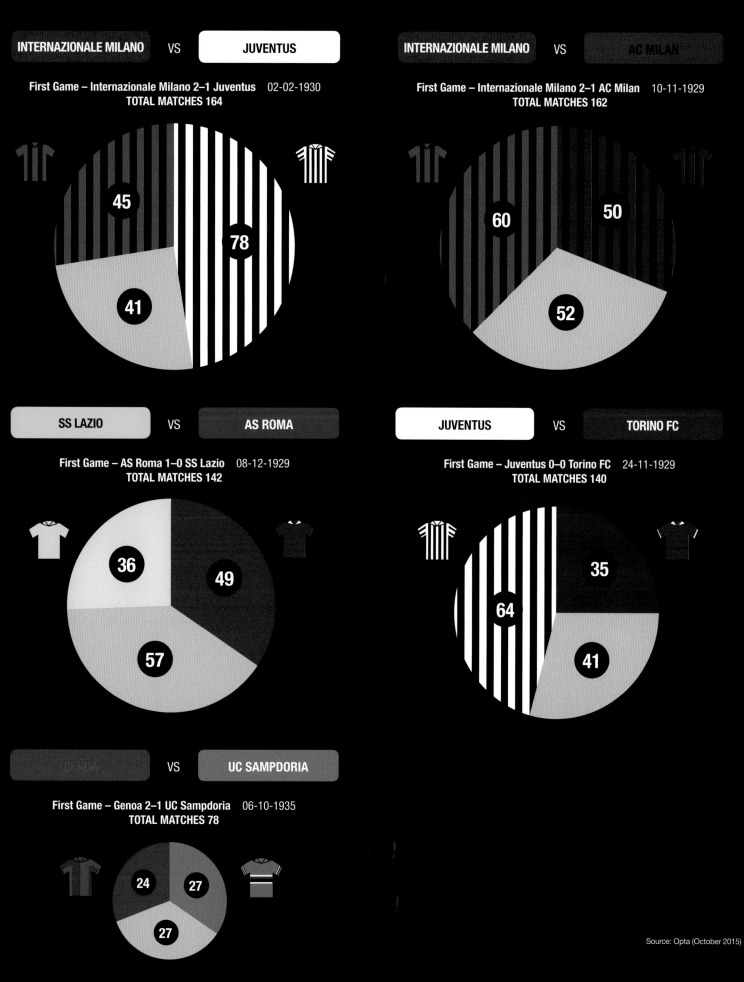

INTERNAZIONALE MILANO VS **JUVENTUS**

First Game – Internazionale Milano 2–1 Juventus   02-02-1930
TOTAL MATCHES 164

45
78
41

INTERNAZIONALE MILANO VS **AC MILAN**

First Game – Internazionale Milano 2–1 AC Milan   10-11-1929
TOTAL MATCHES 162

60   50
52

SS LAZIO VS **AS ROMA**

First Game – AS Roma 1–0 SS Lazio   08-12-1929
TOTAL MATCHES 142

36
49
57

JUVENTUS VS **TORINO FC**

First Game – Juventus 0–0 Torino FC   24-11-1929
TOTAL MATCHES 140

35
64
41

GENOA VS **UC SAMPDORIA**

First Game – Genoa 2–1 UC Sampdoria   06-10-1935
TOTAL MATCHES 78

24   27
27

Source: Opta (October 2015)

83

FIFA WORLD PLAYER OF THE YEAR WINNERS

In 2010, the Ballon d'Or merged with FIFA's World Footballer of the Year award, the two competitions having run concurrently since 1991. The Ballon d'Or (Golden Ball) is the award given to the footballer rated by FIFA as the best player in the world. The coach, team captain and a media representative of every nation selects their top three players (awarded five, three and one point, respectively) from a 23-man shortlist devised by FIFA. The top three players in the world are decided by combining all of the points awarded.

LIONEL MESSI (2009, 2010, 2011, 2012)

CRISTIANO RONALDO (2008, 2013, 2014)

ZINEDINE ZIDANE (1998, 2000, 2003)

RONALDO (1996, 1997, 2002)

RONALDINHO (2004, 2005)

KAKÁ (2007)

FABIO CANNAVARO (2006)

LUÍS FIGO (2001)

RIVALDO (1999)

GEORGE WEAH (1995)

ROMÁRIO (1994)

ROBERTO BAGGIO (1993)

MARCO VAN BASTEN (1992)

LOTHAR MATTHÄUS (1991)

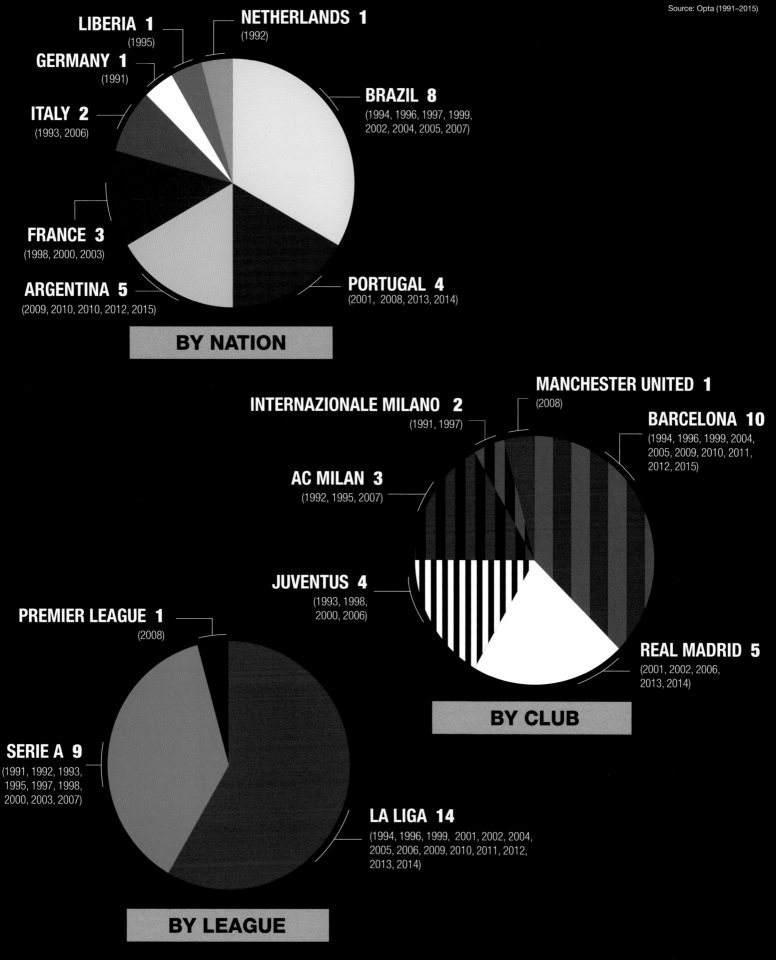

LIBERIA 1
(1995)

NETHERLANDS 1
(1992)

GERMANY 1
(1991)

ITALY 2
(1993, 2006)

BRAZIL 8
(1994, 1996, 1997, 1999,
2002, 2004, 2005, 2007)

FRANCE 3
(1998, 2000, 2003)

ARGENTINA 5
(2009, 2010, 2010, 2012, 2015)

PORTUGAL 4
(2001, 2008, 2013, 2014)

BY NATION

INTERNAZIONALE MILANO 2
(1991, 1997)

MANCHESTER UNITED 1
(2008)

BARCELONA 10
(1994, 1996, 1999, 2004,
2005, 2009, 2010, 2011,
2012, 2015)

AC MILAN 3
(1992, 1995, 2007)

JUVENTUS 4
(1993, 1998,
2000, 2006)

PREMIER LEAGUE 1
(2008)

REAL MADRID 5
(2001, 2002, 2006,
2013, 2014)

BY CLUB

SERIE A 9
(1991, 1992, 1993,
1995, 1997, 1998,
2000, 2003, 2007)

LA LIGA 14
(1994, 1996, 1999, 2001, 2002, 2004,
2005, 2006, 2009, 2010, 2011, 2012,
2013, 2014)

BY LEAGUE

85

LA LIGA GOALS PER CLUB

The history of La Liga is filled with great coaches whose dynamic team engineering has helped squads amass huge goalscoring tallies. From the bowler-hatted Englishman, Fred Penland, whose 1930s' Athletic Bilbao conquered any team that stood before them, to the star-studded era of Miguel Muñoz at Real Madrid in the 1960s and 1970s. Johan Cruyff, and his successor Louis van Gaal, brought success back to Barcelona in the '90s. Leo Beenhakker, Vicente del Bosque and Carlo Ancelotti have brought glory to Real Madrid in recent years, while Frank Rijkaard and Pep Guardiola made Barcelona the most feared team in Europe – though judging by the goal totals between those two teams now, there's still everything to play for...

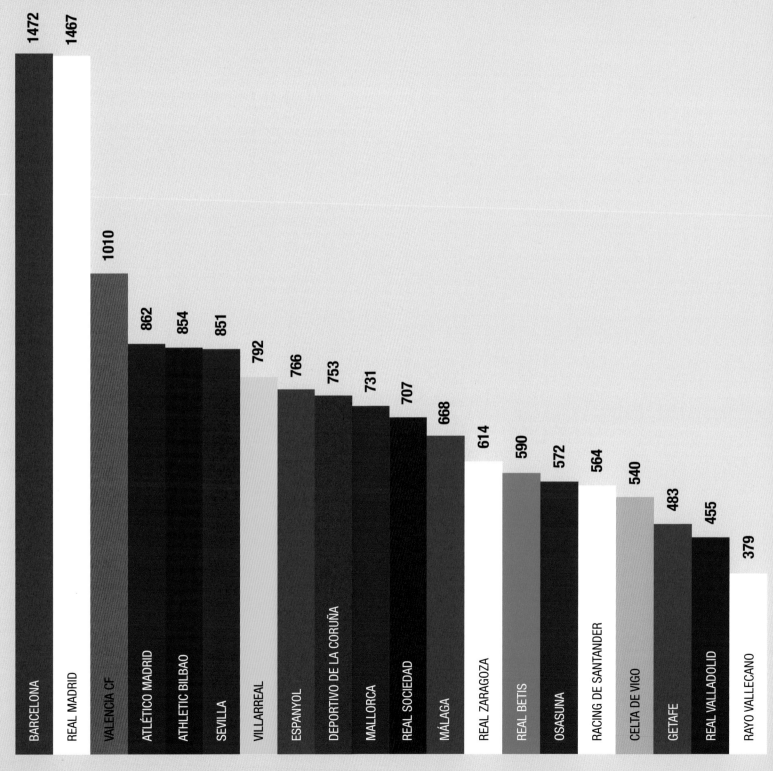

Club	Goals
BARCELONA	1472
REAL MADRID	1467
VALENCIA CF	1010
ATLÉTICO MADRID	862
ATHLETIC BILBAO	854
SEVILLA	851
VILLARREAL	792
ESPANYOL	766
DEPORTIVO DE LA CORUÑA	753
MALLORCA	731
REAL SOCIEDAD	707
MÁLAGA	668
REAL ZARAGOZA	614
REAL BETIS	590
OSASUNA	572
RACING DE SANTANDER	564
CELTA DE VIGO	540
GETAFE	483
REAL VALLADOLID	455
RAYO VALLECANO	379

*The red and blue of Ronaldo's Barcelona takes
on the all-white Real Madrid, 6 February 1997.*

Source: Opta (August 2015)

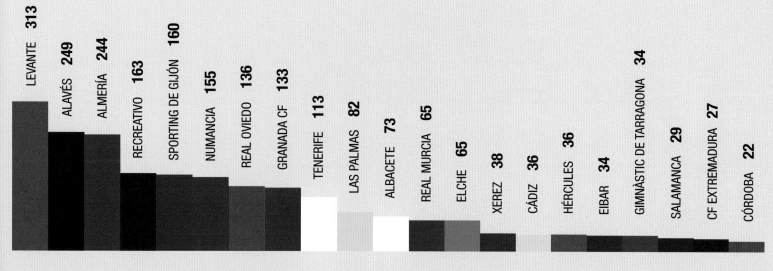

LEVANTE **313**
ALAVÉS **249**
ALMERÍA **244**
RECREATIVO **163**
SPORTING DE GIJÓN **160**
NUMANCIA **155**
REAL OVIEDO **136**
GRANADA CF **133**
TENERIFE **113**
LAS PALMAS **82**
ALBACETE **73**
REAL MURCIA **65**
ELCHE **65**
XEREZ **38**
CÁDIZ **36**
HÉRCULES **36**
EIBAR **34**
GIMNÀSTIC DE TARRAGONA **34**
SALAMANCA **29**
CF EXTREMADURA **27**
CÓRDOBA **22**

1990 WORLD CUP GOALS

The negativity surrounding the football performances of the 1990 World Cup finals in Italy was alleviated by Luciano Pavarotti's singing of the tournament anthem "Nessun Dorma", the energy and spirit of Roger Milla and his Cameroon teammates, the passion and drama of England's Paul Gascoigne and the superboots of Italy's Salvatore "Totò" Schillaci. There were outstanding goals galore too, including a surging run and knockout shot from Germany's Lothar Matthäus, an over-the-shoulder volley from England's David Platt and virtuoso brilliance by Italy's one-and-only *Il Divin Codino* ("The Divine Ponytail") – Roberto Baggio.

ROBERTO BAGGIO – **Italy** vs Czechoslovakia

Roberto Baggio on his way to scoring Italy's second goal. Italy won 2–0 against Czechoslovakia, 19 June 1990.

1. Take on **Schillaci**
2. Tackle **Hašek**
3. Pass **Giannini**
4. Pass **Baggio**
5. Pass **Giannini**
6. Take on **Baggio**
7. Challenge **Hašek**
8. Goal **Baggio**

KEY

Ball movement	——	Player with ball	··············
Shot	——⚽	Player without ball	················

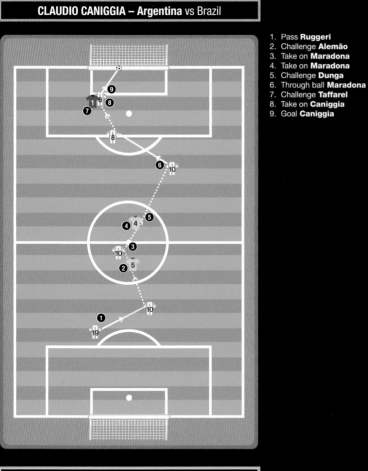

CLAUDIO CANIGGIA – Argentina vs Brazil

1. Pass **Ruggeri**
2. Challenge **Alemão**
3. Take on **Maradona**
4. Take on **Maradona**
5. Challenge **Dunga**
6. Through ball **Maradona**
7. Challenge **Taffarel**
8. Take on **Caniggia**
9. Goal **Caniggia**

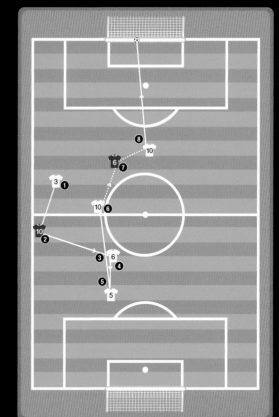

LOTHAR MATTHÄUS – Germany vs Yugoslavia

1. Challenge **Brehme**
2. Pass **Stojković**
3. Ball recovery **Buchwald**
4. Pass **Buchwald**
5. Pass **Augenthaler**
6. Take on **Matthäus**
7. Challenge **Jozić**
8. Goal **Matthäus**

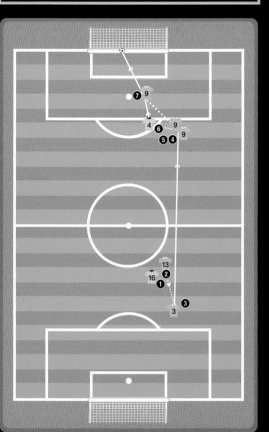

ROGER MILLA – Cameroon vs Romania

1. Dispossesed **Timofte**
2. Tackle **Pagal**
3. Launch (long ball) **Onana**
4. Aerial **Andone**
5. Aerial **Milla**
6. Error **Andone**
7. Goal **Milla**

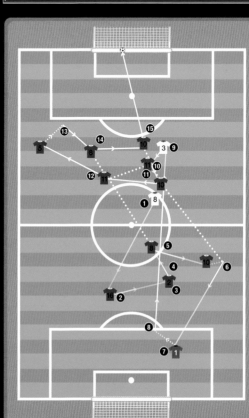

ENZO SCIFO – Belgium vs Uruguay

1. Pass (chipped) **Ostolaza**
2. Clearance **De Wolf**
3. Ball recovery **Gerets**
4. Pass **Gerets**
5. Pass **Van der Elst**
6. Pass **Scifo**
7. Keeper pick-up **Preud'homme**
8. Keeper kick from hands (long ball) **Preud'homme**
9. Clearance **de León**
10. Pass **Ceulemans**
11. Pass **Scifo**
12. Pass **Ceulemans**
13. Pass **Versavel**
14. Pass **Van der Elst**
15. Goal **Scifo**

STAYING POWER

Promotion to the top league presents a wonderful opportunity to establish a club in the top flight. The lucky ones such as TSG 1899 Hoffenheim in the Bundesliga or AC Monaco in Ligue 1 thrive, usually helped by big money backers. Some, like US Pistoiese 1921 (Serie A 1980–81), or Barnsley (Premier League, 1998–99) are immediately relegated and never seen again. More often they are "yo-yo" teams like FC Nürnberg, Middlesbrough, Real Betis or FC Bari 1908, doomed to eternally oscillate between promotion and relegation.

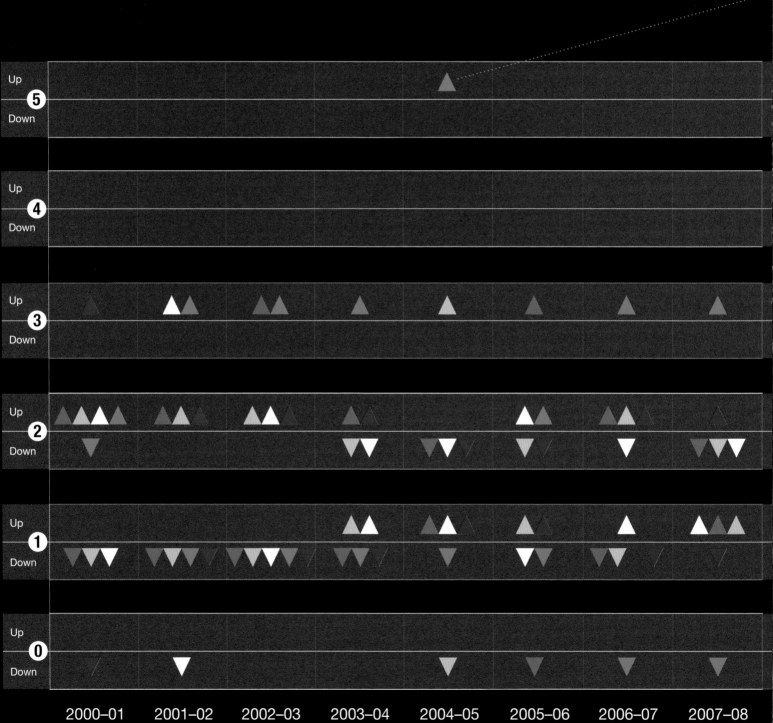

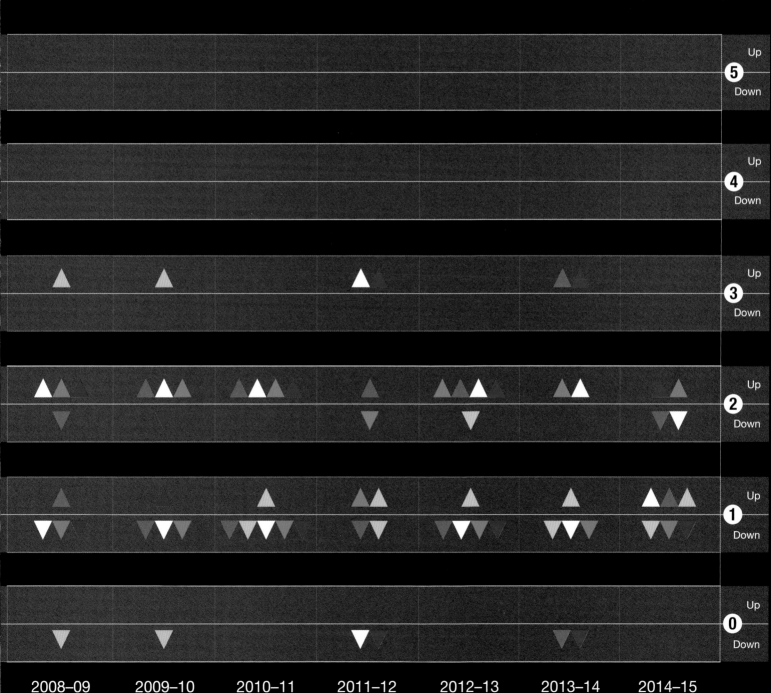

Source: Opta (August 2015)

	ENGLISH PREMIER LEAGUE
	ITALIAN SERIE A
	GERMAN BUNDESLIGA
	FRENCH LIGUE 1
	SPANISH LA LIGA

This anomaly in the data highlights the May 2006 Italian football scandal, where Italian police implicated many Serie A teams' managers and league referees for their creation of a highly organized match-fixing network.

Against all predictions, there is not one occasion in this time period when all promoted teams are immediately relegated the following season.

Up
5
Down

Up
4
Down

Up
3
Down

Up
2
Down

Up
1
Down

Up
0
Down

2008–09   2009–10   2010–11   2011–12   2012–13   2013–14   2014–15

SOCIAL MEDIA CHAMPIONS

Supporter club numbers, shirt sales, season ticket waiting lists – there are many ways of measuring the popularity of football clubs, but the size of their social media presence is now a massive indicator of a club's global reach.

Over the last ten years, clubs across the globe have realized that the use of social media is vital in growing their business and increasing their fan base. Most clubs have official profiles on Facebook, Instagram and Twitter and regularly communicate with fans around the world, providing news, videos and chat-based forums. This infographic compares their social media followings.

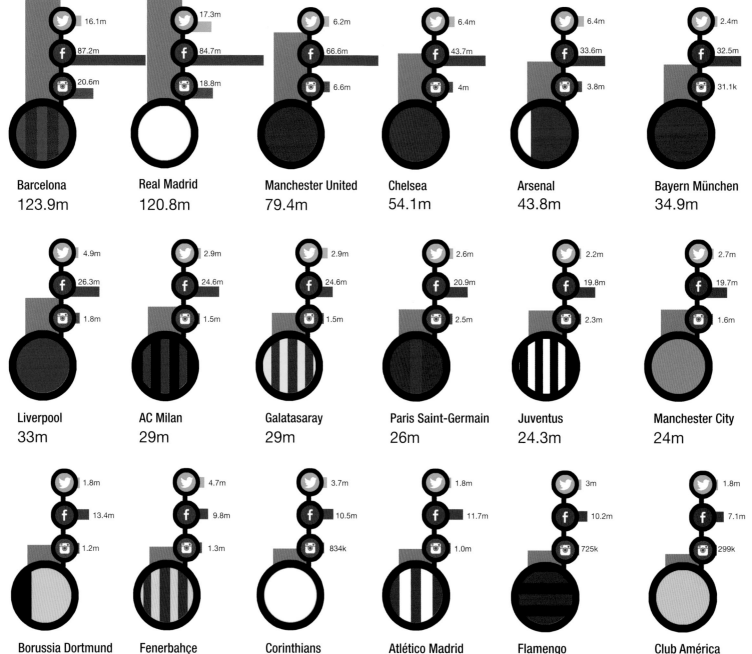

Barcelona
123.9m

Real Madrid
120.8m

Manchester United
79.4m

Chelsea
54.1m

Arsenal
43.8m

Bayern München
34.9m

Liverpool
33m

AC Milan
29m

Galatasaray
29m

Paris Saint-Germain
26m

Juventus
24.3m

Manchester City
24m

Borussia Dortmund
16.4m

Fenerbahçe
15.8m

Corinthians
15m

Atlético Madrid
14.5m

Flamengo
13.9m

Club América
9.2m

Tottenham Hotspur
1.2m · 7m · 395k
8.6m

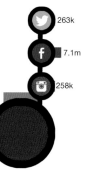
River Plate
1.3m · 6m · 375k
7.7m

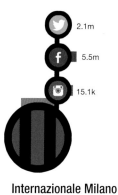

Al-Ahly
263k · 7.1m · 258k
7.6m

Internazionale Milano
2.1m · 5.5m · 15.1k
7.6m

Besiktas
1.3k · 5.6m · 354k
7.3m

Olympique Marseilles
2.1m · 4.3m · 15.1k
6.4m

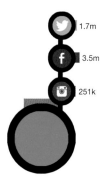
Palmeiras
1.7m · 3.5m · 251k
5.5m

Santos
1.8m · 3.3m · 213k
5.3m

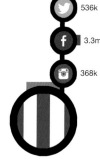
Zamalek
312k · 4.3m · 167k
4.8m

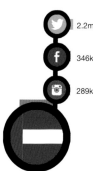
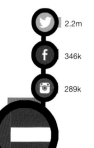

Porto
536k · 3.3m · 368k
4.2m

Nacional (Uruguay)
86.7k · 4m · 49.6k
4.1m

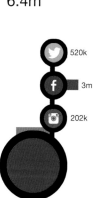
Benfica
520k · 3m · 202k
3.7m

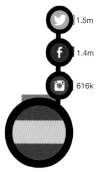
Boca Juniors
1.5m · 1.4m · 616k
3.5m

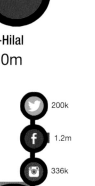
Al-Hilal
2.3m · 55.5k · 632k
3.0m

Colo-Colo
466k · 2.2m · 130k
2.8m

Chivas Guadalajara
2.2m · 346k · 289k
2.8m

Ajax
584k · 2.0m · 172k
2.7m

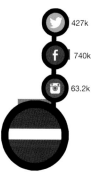
Sporting Lisbon
341k · 2.0m · 82.9k
2.4m

LA Galaxy
253k · 1.6m · 336k
2.2m

New York City
200k · 1.2m · 336k
1.7m

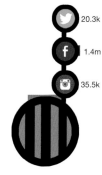
Celtic
299k · 1.4m · 31.6k
1.7m

Shakhtar Donetsk
20.3k · 1.4m · 35.5k
1.5m

FC Zenit
487k · 965k · 6.5k
1.4m

Spartak Moscow
427k · 740k · 63.2k
1.2m

Source: Facebook, Instagram, Twitter (October 2015)

MLS GOALS PER CLUB

Thierry Henry, David Villa, Robbie Keane and Didier Drogba have all scored freely in the United States, but the MLS record books are topped by home-grown heroes like Landon Donovan, Jeff Cunningham and Chris Wondolowski. All the goals from the MLS's short history are recorded below, including such celebrated goals as Marco Etcheverry's strike from the halfway line for D.C. United, Metrostars' Clint Mathis' 50-yard run to score the 2001 MLS Goal of the Year and a magnificent flick and volley from the Vancouver Whitecaps' Eric Hassli.

Source: mlssoccer.com (December 2015)

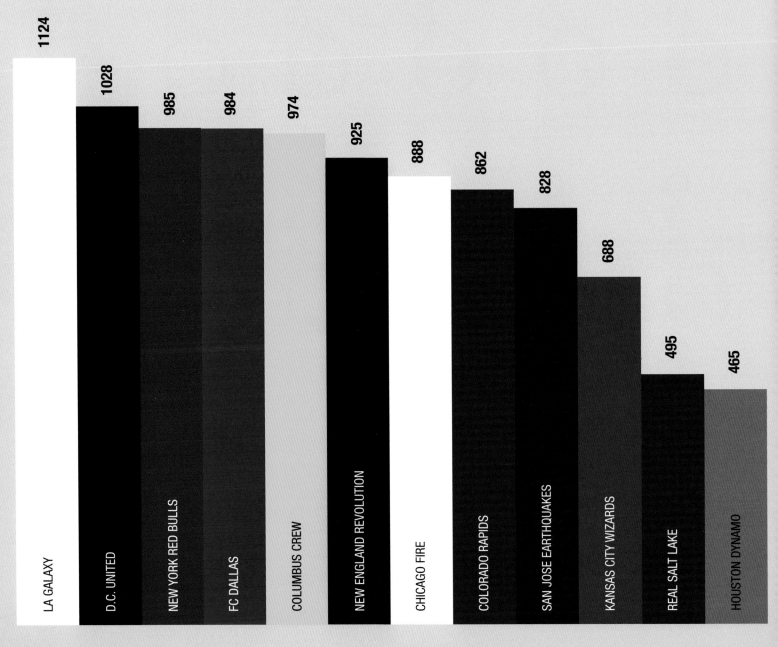

Club	Goals
LA GALAXY	1124
D.C. UNITED	1028
NEW YORK RED BULLS	985
FC DALLAS	984
COLUMBUS CREW	974
NEW ENGLAND REVOLUTION	925
CHICAGO FIRE	888
COLORADO RAPIDS	862
SAN JOSE EARTHQUAKES	828
KANSAS CITY WIZARDS	688
REAL SALT LAKE	495
HOUSTON DYNAMO	465

LANDON DONOVAN **144**

CHRIS WONDOLOWKSI **109**

EDSON BUDDLE **100**

RAÚL DÍAZ ARCE **82**

STEVE RALSTON **76**

JUAN PABLO ÁNGEL **72**

COBI JONES **70**

MARK CHUNG **61**

CHAD BARRETT **56**

ALEJANDRO MORENO **52**

THIERRY HENRY **51**

JEFF CUNNINGHAM **134**

JASON KREIS **108**

ROY LASSITER **88**

BRIAN MCBRIDE **80**

KENNY COOPER **75**

RONALD CERRITOS **71**

ÁLVARO SABORÍO **67**

CLINT MATHIS **61**

DOMINIC ODURO **56**

DANTE WASHINGTON **52**

EDDIE GAVEN **51**

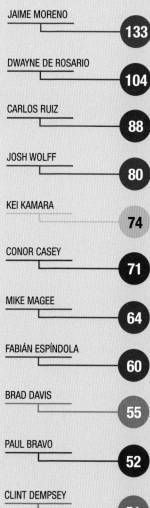

JAIME MORENO **133**

DWAYNE DE ROSARIO **104**

CARLOS RUIZ **88**

JOSH WOLFF **80**

KEI KAMARA **74**

CONOR CASEY **71**

MIKE MAGEE **64**

FABIÁN ESPÍNDOLA **60**

BRAD DAVIS **55**

PAUL BRAVO **52**

CLINT DEMPSEY **51**

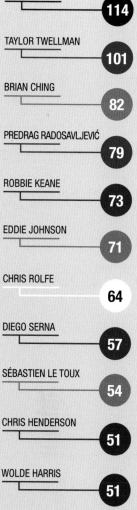

ANTE RAZOV **114**

TAYLOR TWELLMAN **101**

BRIAN CHING **82**

PREDRAG RADOSAVLJEVIĆ **79**

ROBBIE KEANE **73**

EDDIE JOHNSON **71**

CHRIS ROLFE **64**

DIEGO SERNA **57**

SÉBASTIEN LE TOUX **54**

CHRIS HENDERSON **51**

WOLDE HARRIS **51**

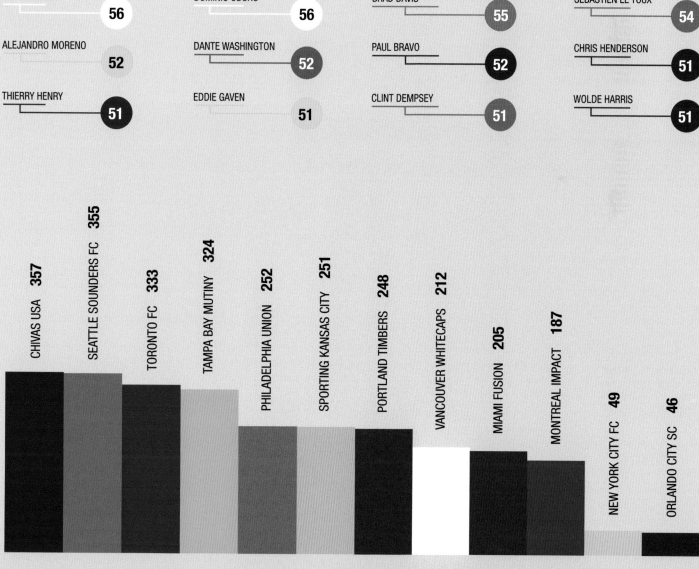

CHIVAS USA **357**

SEATTLE SOUNDERS FC **355**

TORONTO FC **333**

TAMPA BAY MUTINY **324**

PHILADELPHIA UNION **252**

SPORTING KANSAS CITY **251**

PORTLAND TIMBERS **248**

VANCOUVER WHITECAPS **212**

MIAMI FUSION **205**

MONTREAL IMPACT **187**

NEW YORK CITY FC **49**

ORLANDO CITY SC **46**

RONALDO vs MESSI

Future generations might well consider us blessed to have seen the two greatest players in the history of the game. In 2008, Cristiano Ronaldo received the Ballon D'Or with the Argentinian, Lionel Messi, as his runner-up. Since then they have occupied the top two positions in every year except one – 2010. Both players have scored in two UEFA Champions League finals, have regularly scored more than 50 goals in a single season, and have amassed more than 400 goals each for club and country.

CRISTIANO RONALDO

Club Record

Matches won	407
Goals scored	436
Games played	622

0   650

International Record

Matches won	74
Goals scored	55
Games played	120

0   650

League Championships	🏆🏆🏆🏆
National Cups	🏆🏆🏆
National League Cups	🏆🏆
Comm Shield/Super Cup	🏆🏆
Champions League	🏆🏆
UEFA Super Cup	🏆
Club World Cup	🏆🏆

Total	**16**

Comm Shield = FA Community Shield / Super Cup = Spanish Super Cup

LIONEL MESSI

Club Record

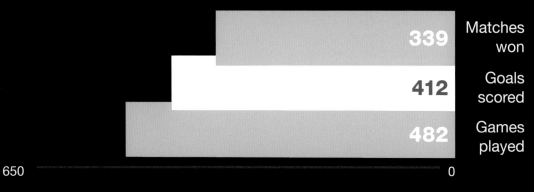

339	Matches won
412	Goals scored
482	Games played

650   0

International Record

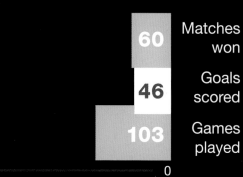

60	Matches won
46	Goals scored
103	Games played

650   0

Trophies	Category
🏆🏆🏆🏆🏆🏆	League Championships
🏆🏆🏆	National Cups
	National League Cups
🏆🏆🏆🏆🏆🏆	Comm Shield/Super Cup
🏆🏆🏆🏆	Champions League
🏆🏆	UEFA Super Cup
🏆🏆	Club World Cup
🏆	Olympic Gold Medal
25	**Total**

Source: Opta (August 2015)

1994 WORLD CUP GOALS

Despite America's lack of a national top-level league, the 1994 World Cup is remembered for breaking average attendance records with almost 70,000 fans per game – a feat that still stands today. Played in nine cities across the US, this World Cup saw Italy lose 3–2 to Brazil in a penalty shoot-out – the first ever World Cup final to be decided by penalties. Roberto Baggio's wild penalty miss will long be remembered. Germany's Jürgen Klinsmann's flick, spin and volley, Saudi Arabia's Saeed Al-Owairan's 65-yard run to score and Bulgaria's Yordan Letchkov's diving header were all wonderful goals, but it's Hagi's strike against Colombia that we'll never forget...

GHEORGHE HAGI – Romania vs Colombia

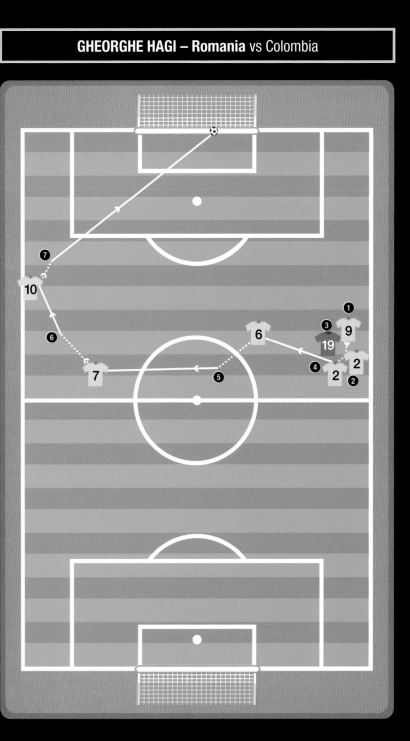

Romania's Gheorghe Hagi celebrates after scoring his unforgettable left-foot lob over the top of Colombian keeper Óscar Córdoba, 18 June 1994.

1. Tackle **Râducioiu**
2. Ball recovery **Petrescu**
3. Dispossesed **Rincón**
4. Pass **Petrescu**
5. Pass **Popescu**
6. Pass **Munteanu**
7. Goal **Hagi**

KEY

Ball movement ———	Player with ball ··············
Shot ——●	Player without ball ················

PHILIPPE ALBERT – Belgium vs Germany

1. Goal kick (long ball) **Illgner**
2. Aeriel **Emmers**
3. Aeriel **Buchwald**
4. Head pass **Emmers**
5. Head pass **Boffin**
6. Pass **Albert**
7. Ball recovery **Albert**
8. Lay-off (chipped) **Weber**
9. Pass **Albert**
10. Challenge **Wagner**
11. Pass **Van der Elst**
12. Challenge **Kohler**
13. Take on **Albert**
14. Goal **Albert**

DANIEL AMOKACHI – Nigeria vs Greece

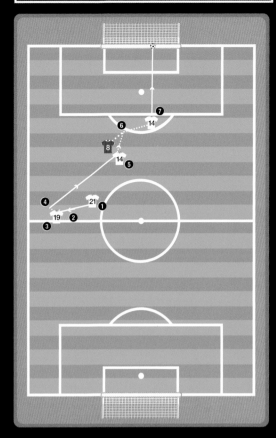

1. Pass **Amokachi**
2. Interception **Adepoju**
3. Ball recovery **Emenalo**
4. Pass **Emenalo**
5. Take on **Amokachi**
6. Challenge **Nioplias**
7. Goal **Amokachi**

YORDAN LETCHKOV – Bulgaria vs Germany

1. Throw in **Kiriakov**
2. Pass **Kostadinov**
3. Pass **Kiriakov**
4. Take on **Yankov**
5. Challenge **Berthold**
6. Pass (cross, chipped) **Yankov**
7. Goal (head) **Letchkov**

HRISTO STOICHKOV – Bulgaria vs Mexico

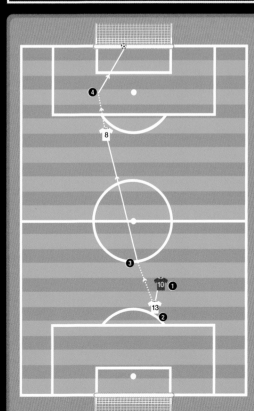

1. Pass **García**
2. Ball recovery **Yordanov**
3. Pass **Yordanov**
4. Goal **Stoichkov**

THE FLAIR LEAGUE

We all love a wow moment; those demonstrations of skill that are worth the ticket price alone. When it comes to individuals, EA Sports *FIFA 16* listed its best dribblers as Lionel Messi (Barcelona), Arjen Robben (Bayern München) and Eden Hazard (Chelsea), while Cristiano Ronaldo (Real Madrid), Paul Pogba (Juventus) and Hulk (Zenit St Petersburg) are the best shooters from distance. But which league tops the flair charts? Take a look at these comparison charts and see who are the mazy masters and who are the hot-shot kings.

Paul Pogba has a fierce long-range shot which he deploys playing for Juventus and France.

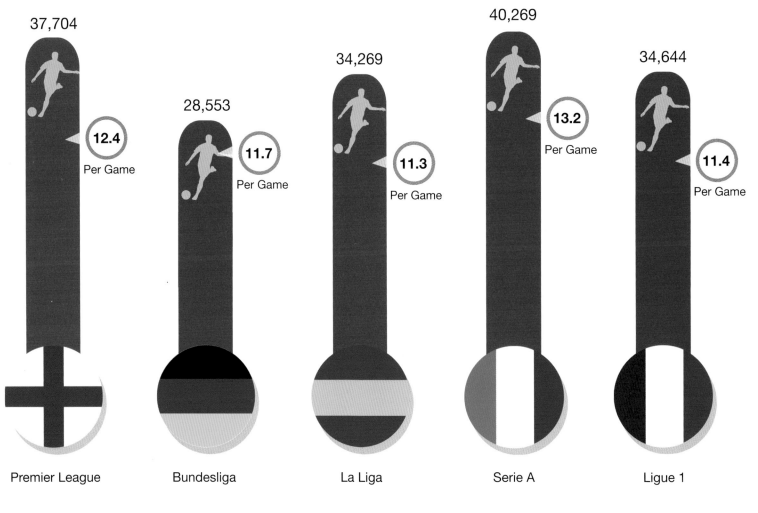

37,704	28,553	34,269	40,269	34,644
12.4 Per Game	11.7 Per Game	11.3 Per Game	13.2 Per Game	11.4 Per Game
Premier League	Bundesliga	La Liga	Serie A	Ligue 1

LONG SHOTS

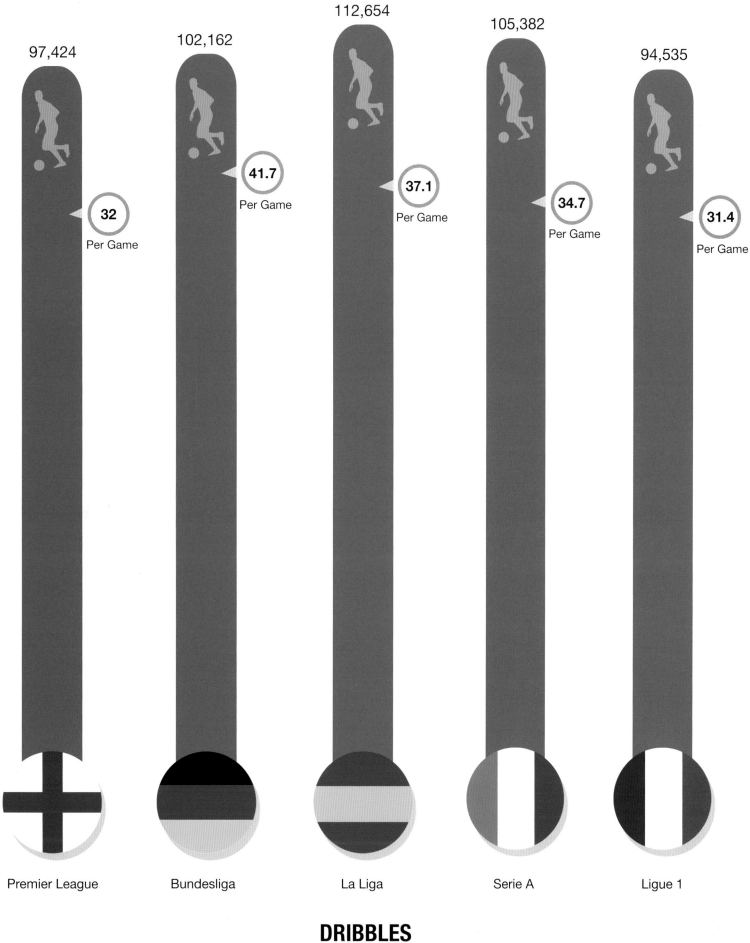

97,424

102,162

112,654

105,382

94,535

32
Per Game

41.7
Per Game

37.1
Per Game

34.7
Per Game

31.4
Per Game

Premier League

Bundesliga

La Liga

Serie A

Ligue 1

DRIBBLES

Source: Opta (August 2007–May 2015)

ITALIAN SERIE A SHIRT COLOURS

Many of the shirt colours of Italian clubs are reiterated in their nicknames:
Internazionale Milano are the *Nerazzurri* (black-blues); AC Milan, the *Rossoneri* (red-blacks); Lazio, the *Biancocelesti* (blue-whites) and Fiorentina, *La Viola*, the purple ones.
Teams such as Verona, Roma, Livorno sport kit reflecting the colours of their city,
but few are as recognized around the world as the black and white stripes of Juventus,
who long ago replaced their pink shirts with the colours of English team Notts County.

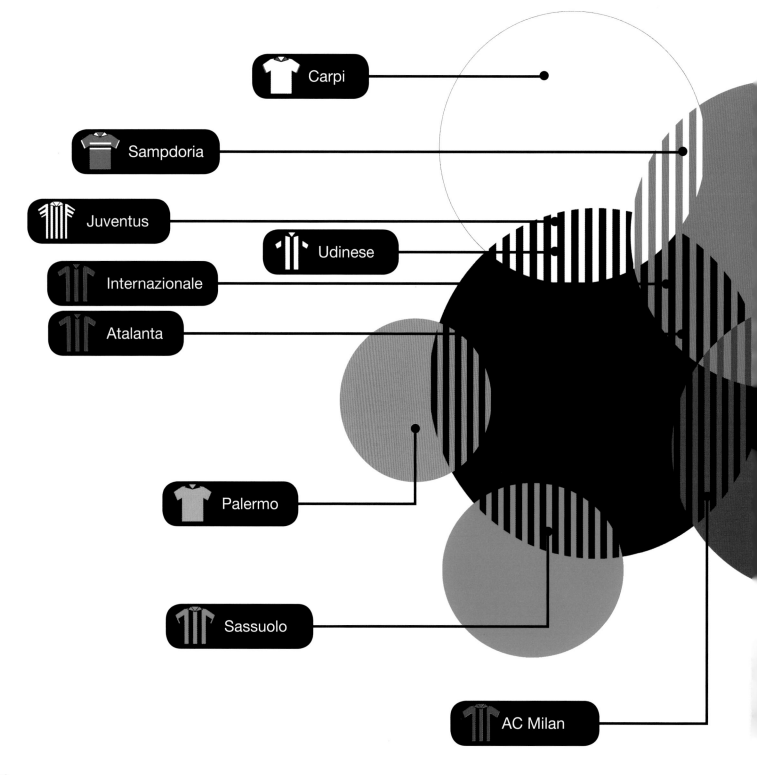

Carpi

Sampdoria

Juventus

Udinese

Internazionale

Atalanta

Palermo

Sassuolo

AC Milan

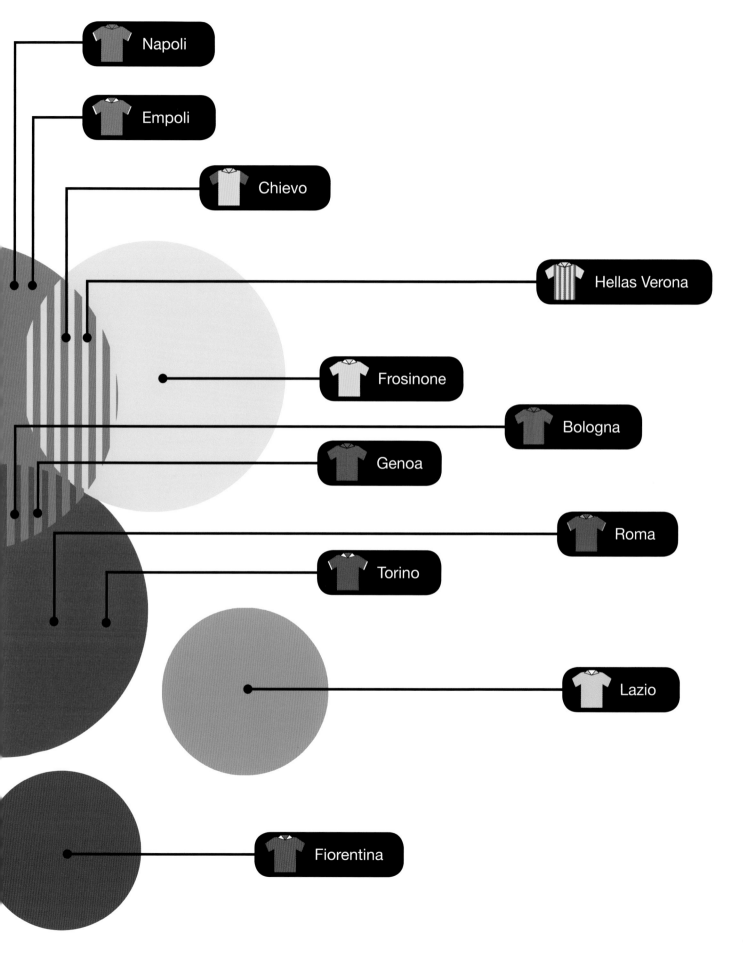

Napoli

Empoli

Chievo

Hellas Verona

Frosinone

Bologna

Genoa

Roma

Torino

Lazio

Fiorentina

PREMIER LEAGUE GOALS

There have been over 24,000 goals scored at a rate of 2.64 goals a game in the Premier League since 1992. In 13 of the 24 seasons Manchester United have finished as the top scorers with only Manchester City (102 in 2013–14) and Chelsea (103 in 2009–10) breaking the 100-goal barrier. On the striker front, it is Blackburn Rovers and Newcastle United goal-king, Alan Shearer, who dominates, while Manchester United's Ryan Giggs impressively hit the net in every season for two straight decades – from 1992–2013.

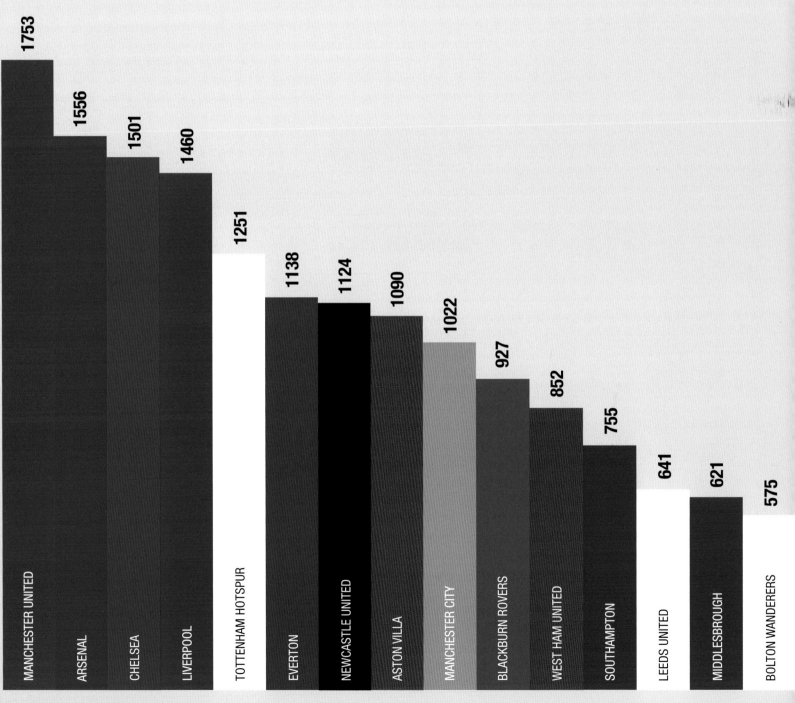

Team	Goals
MANCHESTER UNITED	1753
ARSENAL	1556
CHELSEA	1501
LIVERPOOL	1460
TOTTENHAM HOTSPUR	1251
EVERTON	1138
NEWCASTLE UNITED	1124
ASTON VILLA	1090
MANCHESTER CITY	1022
BLACKBURN ROVERS	927
WEST HAM UNITED	852
SOUTHAMPTON	755
LEEDS UNITED	641
MIDDLESBROUGH	621
BOLTON WANDERERS	575

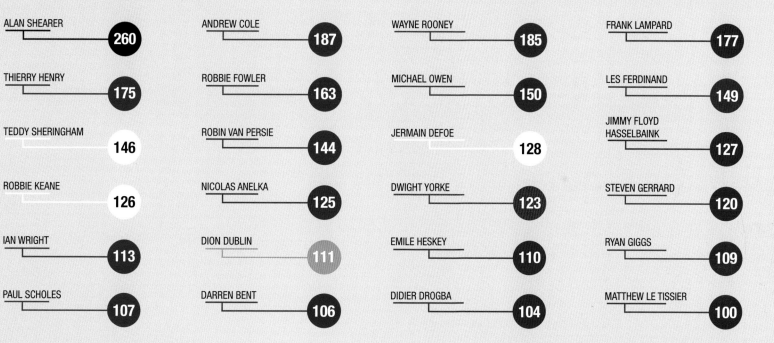

ALAN SHEARER **260**

THIERRY HENRY **175**

TEDDY SHERINGHAM **146**

ROBBIE KEANE **126**

IAN WRIGHT **113**

PAUL SCHOLES **107**

ANDREW COLE **187**

ROBBIE FOWLER **163**

ROBIN VAN PERSIE **144**

NICOLAS ANELKA **125**

DION DUBLIN **111**

DARREN BENT **106**

WAYNE ROONEY **185**

MICHAEL OWEN **150**

JERMAIN DEFOE **128**

DWIGHT YORKE **123**

EMILE HESKEY **110**

DIDIER DROGBA **104**

FRANK LAMPARD **177**

LES FERDINAND **149**

JIMMY FLOYD HASSELBAINK **127**

STEVEN GERRARD **120**

RYAN GIGGS **109**

MATTHEW LE TISSIER **100**

Source: Opta (August 2015)
Colour relates to the team the player scored the highest number of goals for.

FULHAM **570**

SUNDERLAND **535**

SHEFFIELD WEDNESDAY **409**

LEICESTER CITY **400**

COVENTRY CITY **387**

WIMBLEDON **384**

WEST BROMWICH ALBION **367**

CHARLTON ATHLETIC **342**

QUEENS PARK RANGERS **339**

NORWICH CITY **326**

WIGAN ATHLETIC **316**

PORTSMOUTH **292**

STOKE CITY **281**

BIRMINGHAM CITY **273**

DERBY COUNTY **271**

COPA AMÉRICA TROPHIES AND GOALS

The South American international tournament, Copa América is one of the most intensely fought competitions in world football. There have been 44 (often intermittent) tournaments in the Copa América's 100 years in which, apart from guest nations, all but Ecuador and Venezuela have been victors. Chile's one success came in 2015, while Bolivia's only win came on high-altitude home soil in 1963. Interestingly, both Pelé and Maradona – and their World Cup winning teams – failed to secure a Copa América triumph.

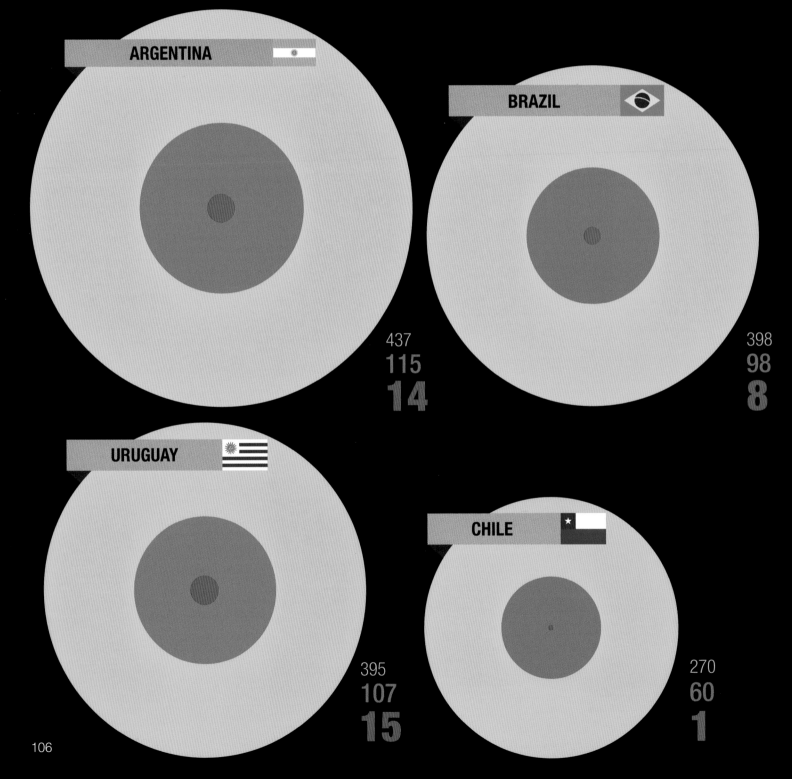

ARGENTINA

437
115
14

BRAZIL

398
98
8

URUGUAY

395
107
15

CHILE

270
60
1

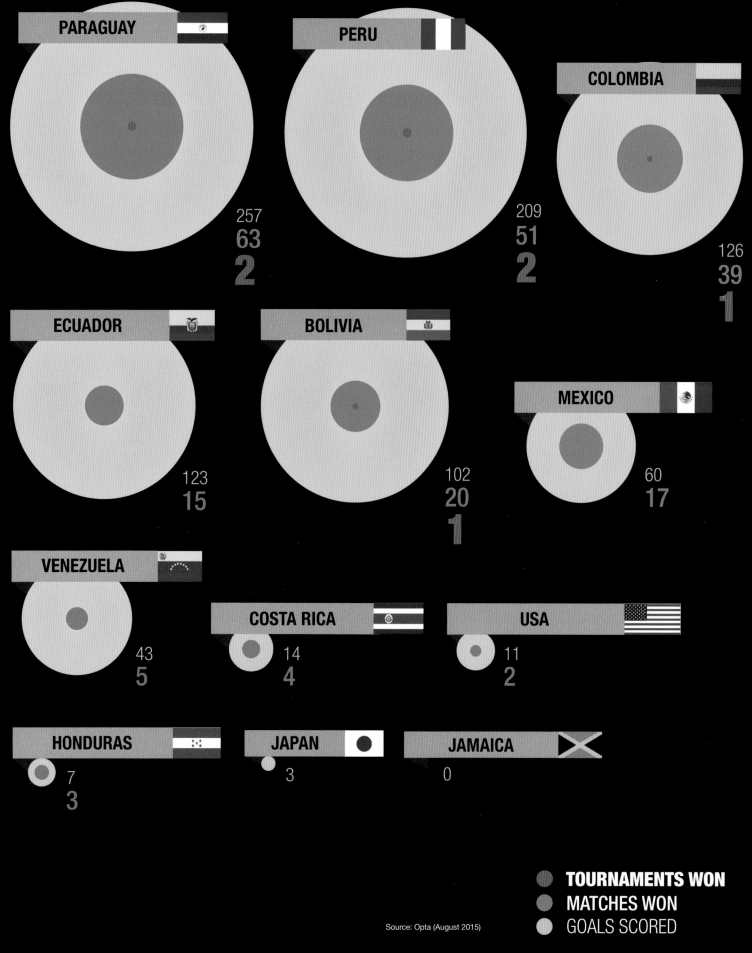

PARAGUAY

257
63
2

PERU

209
51
2

COLOMBIA

126
39
1

ECUADOR

123
15

BOLIVIA

102
20
1

MEXICO

60
17

VENEZUELA

43
5

COSTA RICA

14
4

USA

11
2

HONDURAS

7
3

JAPAN

3

JAMAICA

0

● **TOURNAMENTS WON**
● **MATCHES WON**
● GOALS SCORED

Source: Opta (August 2015)

WORLD CUP GOALKEEPERS

The Golden Glove Award, introduced in 1994 (named the Yashin Award until 2010), is awarded to the best goalkeeper of the World Cup finals. Gianluigi Buffon, Iker Casillas, and Manuel Neuer are recent winners in 2006, 2010 and 2014 respectively. At the 2002 FIFA World Cup, German keeper Oliver Kahn became the first and so far only goalkeeper in the tournament's history to win the Golden Ball, the award given to the player voted as the most outstanding at the FIFA World Cup finals.

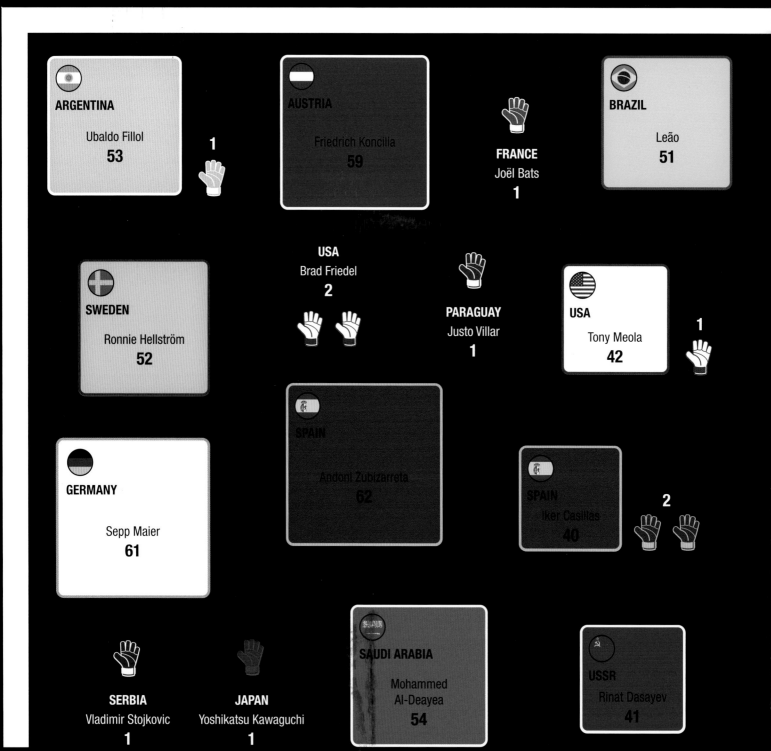

ARGENTINA
Ubaldo Fillol
53
1

AUSTRIA
Friedrich Koncilla
59

FRANCE
Joël Bats
1

BRAZIL
Leão
51

USA
Brad Friedel
2

PARAGUAY
Justo Villar
1

USA
Tony Meola
42
1

SWEDEN
Ronnie Hellström
52

SPAIN
Andoni Zubizarreta
62

SPAIN
Iker Casillas
40
2

GERMANY
Sepp Maier
61

SAUDI ARABIA
Mohammed Al-Deayea
54

USSR
Rinat Dasayev
41

SERBIA
Vladimir Stojkovic
1

JAPAN
Yoshikatsu Kawaguchi
1

SAVES

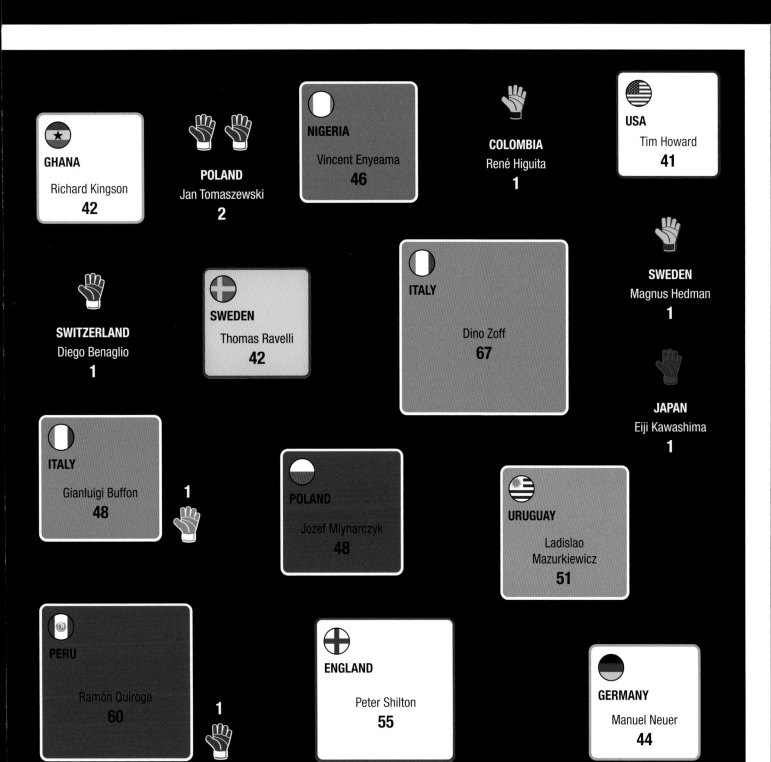

PENALTY SAVES

Source: Opta (October 2015)
All data from 1966–2014.

GHANA
Richard Kingson
42

POLAND
Jan Tomaszewski
2

NIGERIA
Vincent Enyeama
46

COLOMBIA
René Higuita
1

USA
Tim Howard
41

SWITZERLAND
Diego Benaglio
1

SWEDEN
Thomas Ravelli
42

ITALY
Dino Zoff
67

SWEDEN
Magnus Hedman
1

JAPAN
Eiji Kawashima
1

ITALY
Gianluigi Buffon
48

1

POLAND
Jozef Mlynarczyk
48

URUGUAY
Ladislao
Mazurkiewicz
51

PERU
Ramón Quiroga
60

1

ENGLAND
Peter Shilton
55

GERMANY
Manuel Neuer
44

BUNDESLIGA GAME WINS

Although there is no doubting the dominance of Bayern München over their Bundesliga rivals, this infographic clearly illustrates the competitive nature of the league. A total of 53 clubs have competed in the Bundesliga for more than three decades, with eight teams earning a win ratio of more than 40 per cent. Bayern München hold the record for the most wins in a season, reaching 29 in both 2012–13 and 2013–14, clocking up a run of 19 unbeaten games in a row.

Club	Wins
ROT-WEISS ESSEN	61
SV WALDHOF MANNHEIM	71
OFC KICKERS 1901	77
TSG 1899 HOFFENHEIM	78
1. FSV MAINZ 05	103
FC HANSA ROSTOCK	124
KFC UERDINGEN 05	138
DSC ARMINIA BIELEFELD	159
SC FREIBURG	166
TSV 1860 MÜNCHEN	238
VFL WOLFSBURG	239
KARLSRUHER SC	241
EINTRACHT BRAUNSCHWEIG	242
FORTUNA DÜSSELDORF	245
HANNOVER 96	286
MSV DUISBERG	296
1. FC NÜRNBERG	341
VFL BOCHUM 1848	356
HERTHA BSC	392
BAYER 04 LEVERKUSEN	521
EINTRACHT FRANKFURT	571
1. FC KAISERSLAUTERN	575

Source: Opta (August 2015)

Under 60 Wins

FC ST PAULI **58**	SG DYNAMO DRESDEN **33**	STUTTGARTER KICKERS **20**	SC PREUSSEN MÜNSTER **7**
FC ENERGIE COTTBUS **56**	1. FC SAARBRÜCKEN **32**	SV DARMSTADT 98 **12**	SPVGG GREUTHER FÜRTH **4**
FC AUGSBURG **46**	SC BORUSSIA NEUNKIRCHEN **25**	TENNIS BORUSSIA BERLIN **11**	BLAU-WEISS 1890 BERLIN **3**
ALEMANNIA AACHEN **43**	WUPPERTALER SV **25**	SSV ULM 1846 **9**	VFB LEIPZIG **3**
ROT-WEISS OBERHAUSEN **36**	FC 08 HOMBURG **21**	SC FORTUNA KÖLN **8**	TASMANIA 1900 BERLIN **2**
SG WATTENSCHEID 09 **34**	SPVGG UNTERHACHING **20**	SC PADERBORN 07 **7**	

1. FC KÖLN **602**

FC SCHALKE 04 **629**

BORUSSIA MÖNCHENGLADBACH **643**

BORUSSIA DORTMUND **704**

VFB STUTTGART **709**

HAMBURGER SV **717**

SV WERDER BREMEN **737**

BAYERN MÜNCHEN **991**

1998 WORLD CUP GOALS

Host nation France lit up their own World Cup in 1998, and finished the tournament with the greatest triumph of all – defeating Ronaldo's Brazil in the final. England met Argentina in Saint-Étienne, unarguably the match of the tournament, while five goals secured the Golden Boot for Davor Šuker of Croatia. Rivaldo hit the winner as Brazil and Denmark shared five goals in a riveting quarter-final, while goals such as Michael Owen's run-and-shoot, and Dennis Bergkamp's control-and-finish for the Netherlands – both against Argentina – highlighted that world-class football at its best can transcend any country's border.

DENNIS BERGKAMP – **Netherlands** vs Argentina

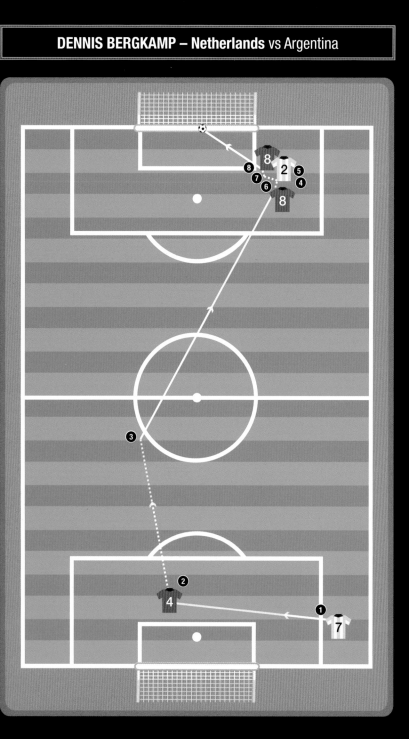

Dennis Bergkamp clips it beautifully past Argentinian goalkeeper Carlos Roa, 4 July 1998.

1. Pass (cross, long ball, chipped) **López**
2. Ball recovery **de Boer**
3. Pass (long ball, chipped) **de Boer**
4. Take on **Bergkamp**
5. Challenge **Ayala**
6. Good skill **Bergkamp**
7. Good skill **Bergkamp**
8. Goal **Bergkamp**

KEY

Ball movement

Shot

Player with ball

Player without ball

MICHAEL OWEN – England vs Argentina

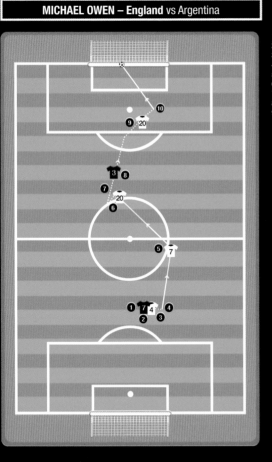

1. Take on **López**
2. Tackle **Ince**
3. Ball recovery **Ince**
4. Pass **Ince**
5. Pass **Beckham**
6. Good skill **Owen**
7. Take on **Owen**
8. Challenge **Chamot**
9. Take on **Owen**
10. Goal **Owen**

EMMANUEL PETIT – France vs Brazil

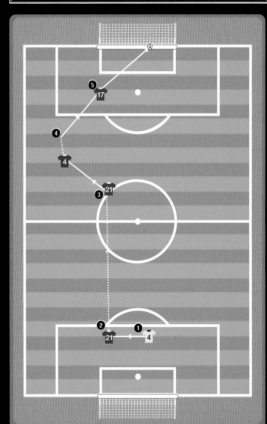

1. Ball recovery **Dugarry**
2. Head pass **Júnior Baiano**
3. Pass **Dugarry**
4. Through ball **Vieira**
5. Goal **Petit**

RONALDO – Brazil vs Morocco

1. Pass (chipped) **Bassir**
2. Head pass **Cafu**
3. Ball recovery **Sampaio**
4. Pass **Sampaio**
5. Launch **Aldair**
6. Head pass **Rossi**
7. Pass **Dunga**
8. Lay-off **Rivaldo**
9. Pass **Dunga**
10. Pass **Bebeto**
11. Through ball (chipped) **Rivaldo**
12. Goal **Ronaldo**

BOUDEWIJN ZENDEN – Netherlands vs Croatia

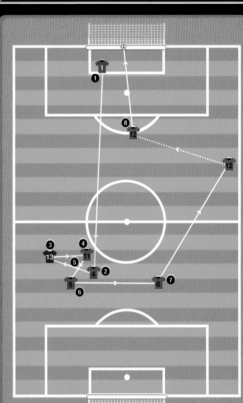

1. Goal kick (long ball) **Ladić**
2. Head pass **de Boer**
3. Pass **Stanić**
4. Interception **Cocu**
5. Pass **Cocu**
6. Pass **Numan**
7. Pass (long ball) **Jonk**
8. Goal **Zenden**

LONGEST UNBEATEN RUNS

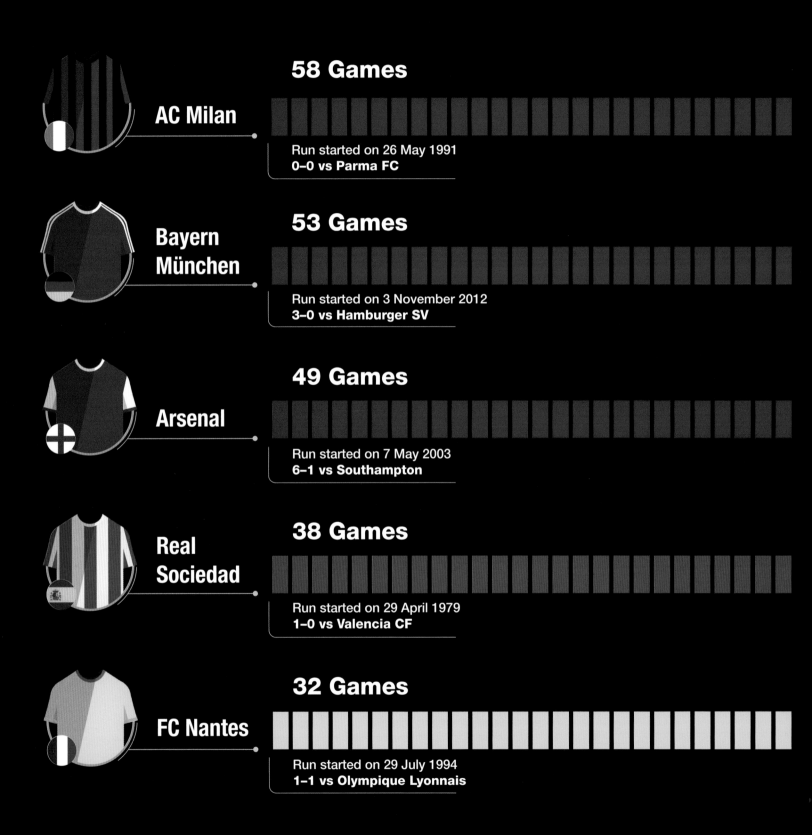

AC Milan

58 Games

Run started on 26 May 1991
0–0 vs Parma FC

Bayern München

53 Games

Run started on 3 November 2012
3–0 vs Hamburger SV

Arsenal

49 Games

Run started on 7 May 2003
6–1 vs Southampton

Real Sociedad

38 Games

Run started on 29 April 1979
1–0 vs Valencia CF

FC Nantes

32 Games

Run started on 29 July 1994
1–1 vs Olympique Lyonnais

"The Invincibles" was a nickname first given to the 1880s Preston North End team when they won the first "Double", completing the season unbeaten with just four draws. Arsenal would inherit the title in their unbeaten (12-draw) Premier League-winning season of 2003–04. In Europe, Juventus, AC Milan, S.L. Benfica, FC Porto, AFC Ajax and others have all completed an unbeaten campaign, but no Ligue 1, Bundesliga or modern-era La Liga club have yet managed the feat.

Run ended on 14 March 1993
0–1 vs Parma FC

Run ended on 29 March 2014
0–1 vs FC Augsburg

Run ended on 16 October 2004
0–2 vs Manchester United

Run ended on 4 May 1980
1–2 vs Sevilla FC

Run ended on 8 April 1995
0–2 vs RC Strasbourg Alsace

Source: Opta (August 2015)

ASIAN CUP RECORDS BY NATION

The Asian Cup is contested by the nations of the Asian Football Confederation, which stretches from Iraq to Japan to Australia (who joined the AFC in 2006). It was held every four years from the inaugural 1956 tournament until 2004, then from 2007 (switching to avoid conflicting with the Olympics and European Championship). The number of nations competing in the finals increased from an original four to 12 in 1996, to 16 in 2004 and will increase to 24 in 2019.

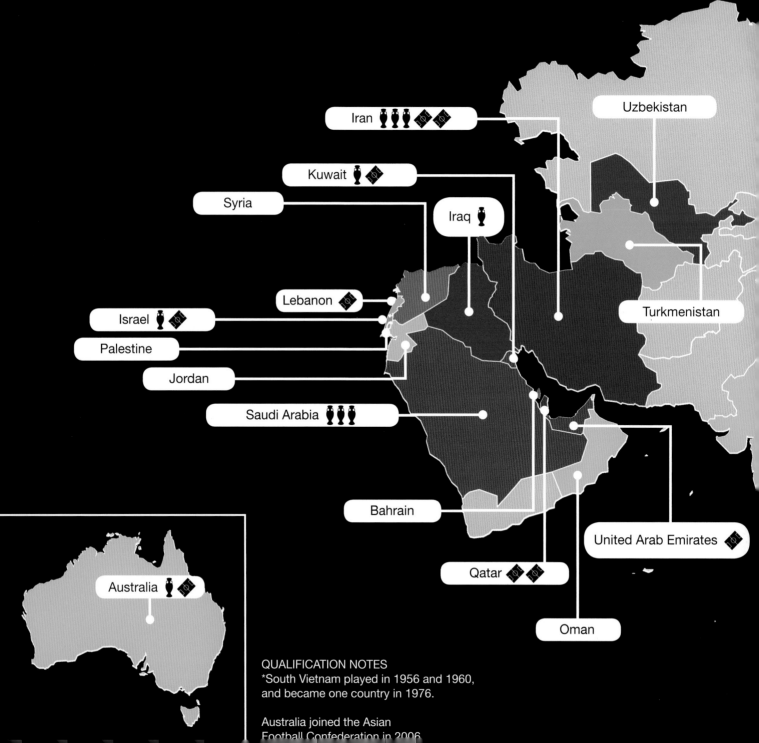

QUALIFICATION NOTES
*South Vietnam played in 1956 and 1960, and became one country in 1976.

Australia joined the Asian
Football Confederation in 2006.

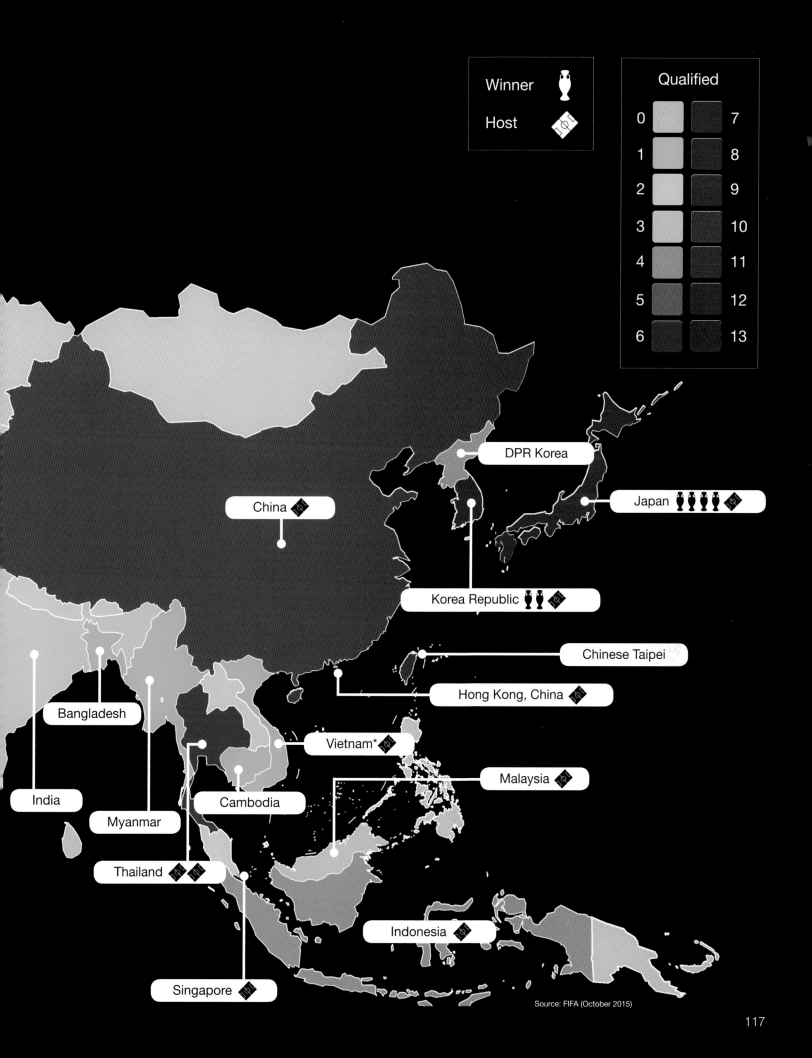

Winner 🏆
Host ⚽

Qualified

0		7
1		8
2		9
3		10
4		11
5		12
6		13

China ⚽

DPR Korea

Japan 🏆🏆🏆🏆⚽

Korea Republic 🏆🏆⚽

Chinese Taipei

Hong Kong, China ⚽

Vietnam* ⚽

Malaysia ⚽

Bangladesh

India

Myanmar

Cambodia

Thailand ⚽⚽

Indonesia ⚽

Singapore ⚽

Source: FIFA (October 2015)

117

LA LIGA TOP GOALSCORERS 1998–2015

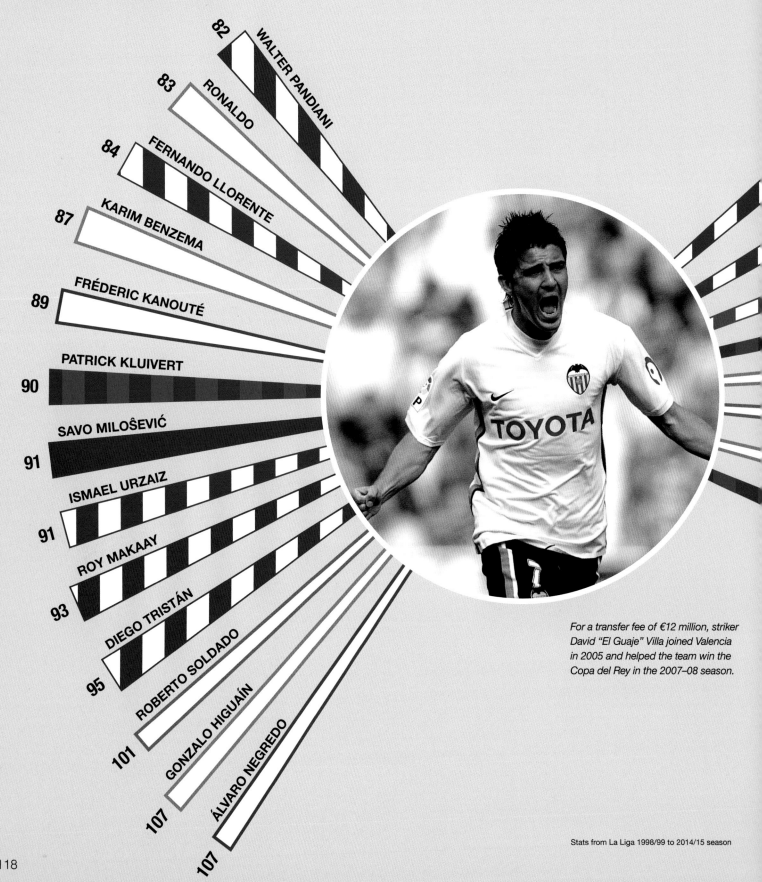

82 WALTER PANDIANI

83 RONALDO

84 FERNANDO LLORENTE

87 KARIM BENZEMA

89 FRÉDERIC KANOUTÉ

PATRICK KLUIVERT **90**

SAVO MILOŜEVIĆ **91**

ISMAEL URZAIZ **91**

ROY MAKAAY **93**

DIEGO TRISTÁN **95**

ROBERTO SOLDADO **101**

GONZALO HIGUAÍN **107**

ÁLVARO NEGREDO **107**

For a transfer fee of €12 million, striker David "El Guaje" Villa joined Valencia in 2005 and helped the team win the Copa del Rey in the 2007–08 season.

Stats from La Liga 1998/99 to 2014/15 season

Lionel Messi and Cristiano Ronaldo dominate La Liga goalscoring records. The world's best players are instantly recognizable but outside of Spain, few might know of Telmo Zarra, whose record stands the equal of these modern superstars. Zarra played at Athletic Bilbao for 15 seasons, scoring a goal almost every game in taking Bilbao to league title winners in 1943. His name now lives on in the Zarra trophy, awarded to La Liga's top goalscorer each season.

ADURIZ 110

DIEGO FORLÁN 128

RAÚL TAMUDO 144

SAMUEL ETO'O 161

RAÚL 169

DAVID VILLA 186

CRISTIANO RONALDO 225

LIONEL MESSI 286

EUROPEAN CUP WINS BY NATION

The recent Champions League successes of Barcelona and Real Madrid have secured Spain's claim to be most successful European nation. Real Madrid's consecutive triumphs in the European Cup's first five competitions help Spain top the list, although England have had more successful clubs and Italy have had more finalists.

In later years, the concentration of financial might in Europe's major leagues has increased the dominance of those nations. The era of the Champions League (beginning in 1992) has seen Spain register eight wins, followed by Italy (five), England (four) and Germany (three).

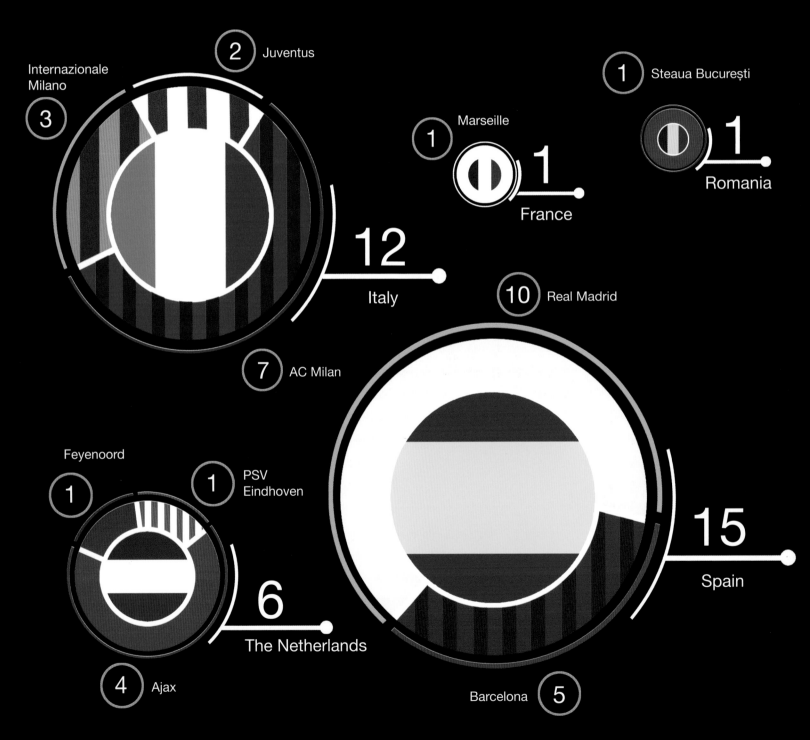

Internazionale Milano **3**

2 Juventus

1 Steaua București

Marseille **1**

1 France

1 Romania

12 Italy

10 Real Madrid

7 AC Milan

15 Spain

Feyenoord **1**

1 PSV Eindhoven

6 The Netherlands

4 Ajax

Barcelona **5**

1 Chelsea

1 Aston Viilla

Nottingham Forest

2

3

Manchester United

12 England

5 Liverpool

1 Borussia Dortmund

Hamburger SV

1

1 Celtic

1 Scotland

7 Germany

5 Bayern München

Porto 2

1 Red Star Belgrade

4 Portugal

2 Benfica

1 Yugoslavia

Source: Opta (October 2015)

FOOTBALL RIVALRIES, PART 3

Football fans know that it's the tough and tense matches between fierce rivals that really heighten their emotions during a season. AFC Ajax vs Feyenoord, for example, has become the most ferocious game in the Netherlands as the capital's city slickers do battle with the working-class port labourers. In Turkey's capital Istanbul, neighbours Fenerbahçe S.K. and Galatasaray S.K. continue a rivalry more than 100 years old. Across the Atlantic Ocean, it is New York City FC and the New York Red Bulls that have developed a more recent mutual antagonism after just a handful of matches.

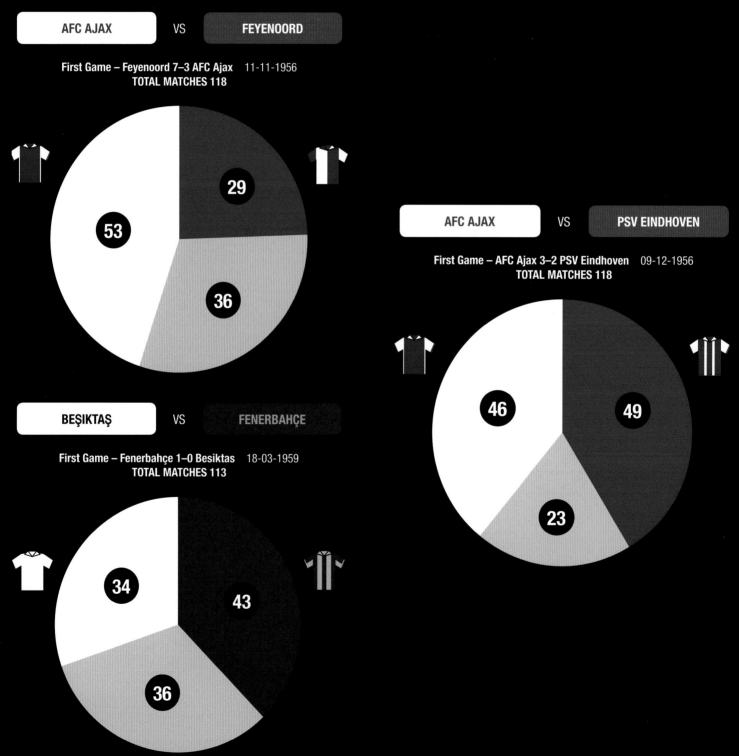

AFC AJAX VS **FEYENOORD**

First Game – Feyenoord 7–3 AFC Ajax   11-11-1956
TOTAL MATCHES 118

53

29

36

AFC AJAX VS **PSV EINDHOVEN**

First Game – AFC Ajax 3–2 PSV Eindhoven   09-12-1956
TOTAL MATCHES 118

46

49

23

BEŞIKTAŞ VS **FENERBAHÇE**

First Game – Fenerbahçe 1–0 Besiktas   18-03-1959
TOTAL MATCHES 113

34

43

36

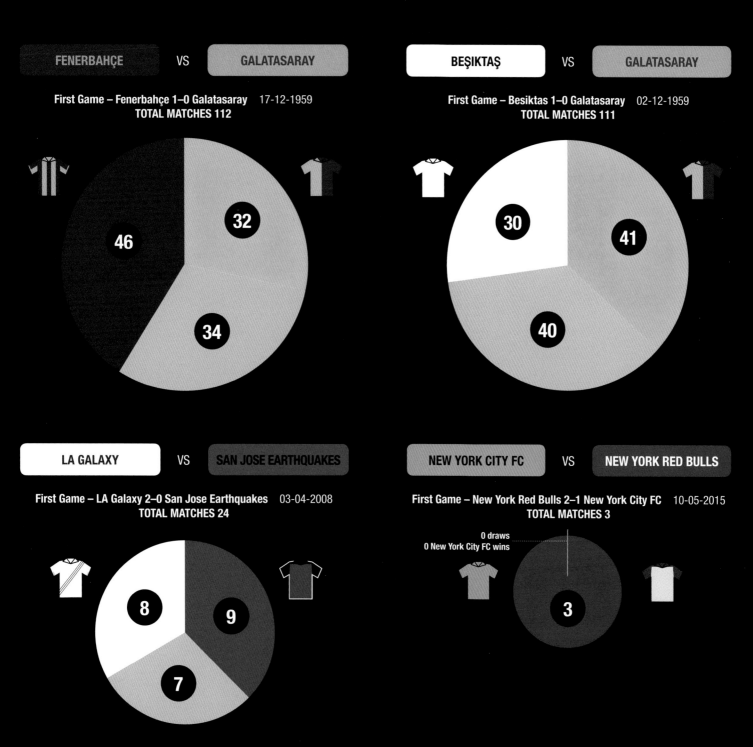

FENERBAHÇE VS **GALATASARAY**

First Game – Fenerbahçe 1–0 Galatasaray   17-12-1959
TOTAL MATCHES 112

46   32   34

BEŞIKTAŞ VS **GALATASARAY**

First Game – Besiktas 1–0 Galatasaray   02-12-1959
TOTAL MATCHES 111

30   41   40

LA GALAXY VS **SAN JOSE EARTHQUAKES**

First Game – LA Galaxy 2–0 San Jose Earthquakes   03-04-2008
TOTAL MATCHES 24

8   9   7

NEW YORK CITY FC VS **NEW YORK RED BULLS**

First Game – New York Red Bulls 2–1 New York City FC   10-05-2015
TOTAL MATCHES 3

0 draws
0 New York City FC wins

3

Source: Opta (October 2015)

SERIE A GAME WINS

Sixty-five teams have taken part in the 84 Serie A Championships with only Inter having competed in every season. Apart from the largely pre-war success of Torino and Bologna, Serie A has been dominated by *Le Sette Sorelle* ("The Seven Sisters"): Juventus, Roma, AC Milan, Internazionale Milano, Fiorentina, Lazio, and Parma, who more recently have been replaced by Napoli. The league is usually won by a team amassing around 25 game wins, although Juventus won 33 of the 38 in their 2013–14 title-winning season.

COMO 109
ASCOLI 110
LECCE 114
PRO PATRIA 118
PERUGIA 126
MODENA 130
NOVARA 133
ALESSANDRIA 136
CHIEVO 149
SPAL 151
CATANIA 162
LIVORNO 171
PADOVA 182
BRESCIA 188
VERONA 222
TRIESTINA 253
BARI 258
PALERMO 291
VICENZA 296
PARMA 327
CAGLIARI 357
UDINESE 476
GENOA 521
ATALANTA 522
SAMPDORIA 728
BOLOGNA 818
TORINO 859

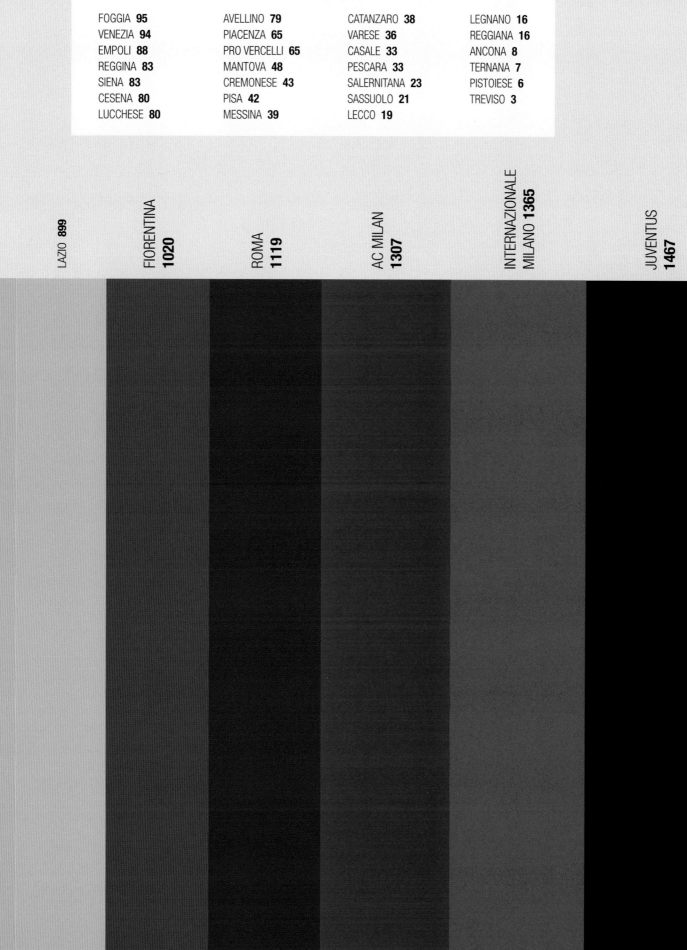

Source: Opta (August 2015)

Under 100 Wins

FOGGIA **95**	AVELLINO **79**	CATANZARO **38**	LEGNANO **16**
VENEZIA **94**	PIACENZA **65**	VARESE **36**	REGGIANA **16**
EMPOLI **88**	PRO VERCELLI **65**	CASALE **33**	ANCONA **8**
REGGINA **83**	MANTOVA **48**	PESCARA **33**	TERNANA **7**
SIENA **83**	CREMONESE **43**	SALERNITANA **23**	PISTOIESE **6**
CESENA **80**	PISA **42**	SASSUOLO **21**	TREVISO **3**
LUCCHESE **80**	MESSINA **39**	LECCO **19**	

NAPOLI **860**

LAZIO **899**

FIORENTINA **1020**

ROMA **1119**

AC MILAN **1307**

INTERNAZIONALE MILANO **1365**

JUVENTUS **1467**

2002 WORLD CUP GOALS

Japan and South Korea co-hosted Asia's first World Cup in 2002 and it is a tournament remembered for being full of surprises. Reigning champions France and fancied favourites Argentina went home after the group stage and South Korea beat Spain, Italy and Portugal on their way to the semi-finals. Few fans were shocked, however, by Brazil's clear run to victory, powered by a player at the top of his game – Ronaldo. Uruguay's Diego Forlán's chest and volley, Matt Holland's superstrike for Ireland and Brazil's Edmílson's overhead kick are goals also still regularly voted in World Cup Greatest Goals lists, along with these ones too...

JARED BORGETTI – Mexico vs Italy

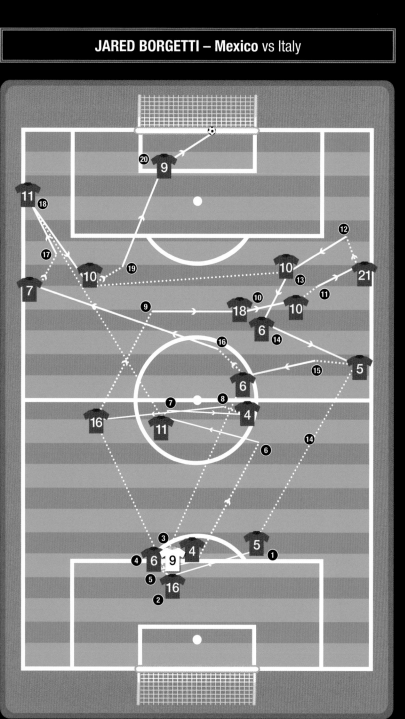

Mexico's Jared Borgetti scored the first goal against Italy with a knockout strike past goalkeeper Gianluigi Buffon, 13 June 2002.

1. Clearance **Vidrio**
2. Tackle **Carmona**
3. Take on **Inzaghi**
4. Ball recovery **Torrado**
5. Pass **Torrado**
6. Pass **Márquez**
7. Pass **Luna**
8. Pass **Márquez**
9. Pass **Carmona**
10. Pass **Rodríguez**
11. Pass **Blanco**
12. Pass **Arellano**
13. Pass **Blanco**
14. Pass **Torrado**
15. Pass **Vidrio**
16. Pass (long ball) **Torrado**
17. Pass **Morales**
18. Pass **Luna**
19. Pass (chipped) **Blanco**
20. Goal **Borgetti**

KEY

Ball movement	Player with ball
Shot	Player without ball

SALIF DIAO – Senegal vs Denmark

1. Take on **Jørgenson**
2. Tackle **Camara**
3. Ball recovery **Camara**
4. Pass **Camara**
5. Pass **Diouf**
6. Pass (long ball) **Diao**
7. Through ball **Fadiga**
8. Goal **Diao**

EDMÍLSON – Brazil vs Costa Rica

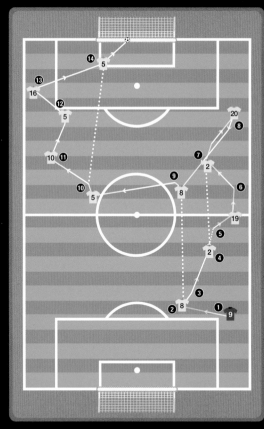

1. Pass **Wanchope**
2. Interception **Silva**
3. Pass **Cafu**
4. Ball recovery **Cafu**
5. Pass **Cafu**
6. Pass **Juninho**
7. Pass **Cafu**
8. Pass **Edmílson**
9. Pass **Silva**
10. Pass **Edmilson**
11. Pass **Rivaldo**
12. Pass **Edmílson**
13. Pass (cross, chipped) **Júnior**
14. Goal **Edmílson**

RONALDINHO – Brazil vs England

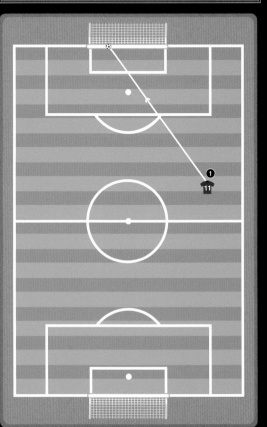

1. Goal (free kick) **Ronaldinho**

CHRISTIAN VIERI – Italy vs Ecuador

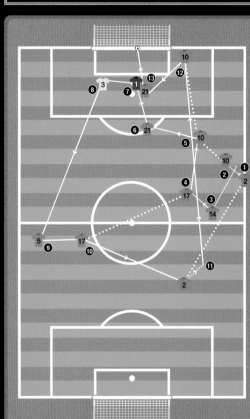

1. Throw in **Panucci**
2. Pass **Totti**
3. Head pass **Di Biagio**
4. Pass **Tommasi**
5. Through ball **Totti**
6. Attempt saved **Vieri**
7. Save (parried danger) **Cevallos**
8. Clearance **Hurtado**
9. Head pass **Cannavaro**
10. Pass (long ball, chipped) **Tommasi**
11. Pass (long ball, chipped) **Panucci**
12. Pull back **Totti**
13. Goal **Vieri**

MLS TROPHY WINS PER CLUB

Major League Soccer (MLS), the top-tier football league in the USA and Canada, was formed as a result of the success of the 1994 FIFA World Cup, hosted by the United States. Formed in 1993, the MLS originally consisted of ten teams. In the following two decades the number of teams has doubled – 17 teams for the US, three for Canada. Organized into an Eastern and Western conference, clubs compete for a place in national play-offs to represent their conference in a final to win the MLS Cup, also known as the Philip F. Anschutz Trophy.

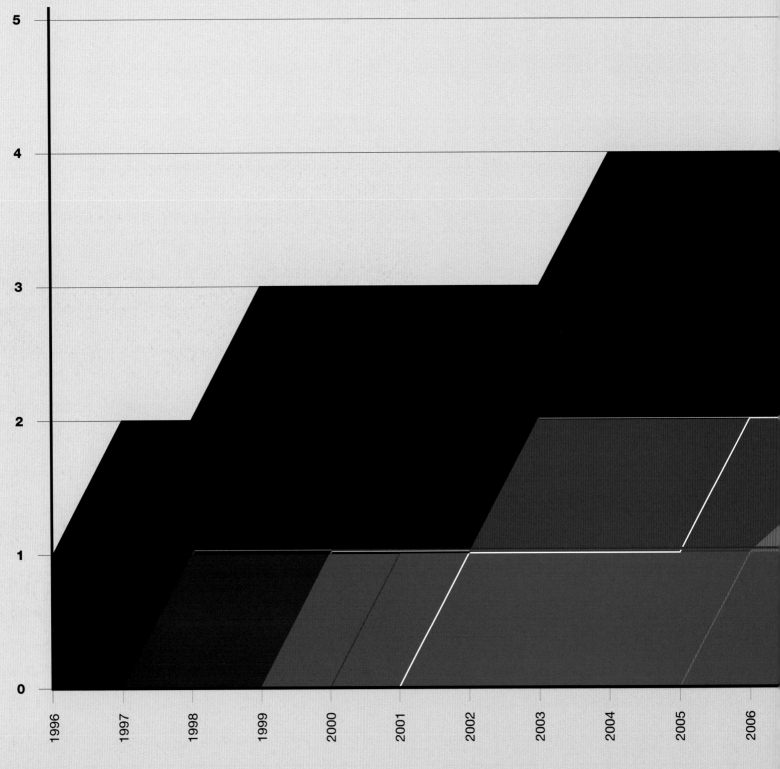

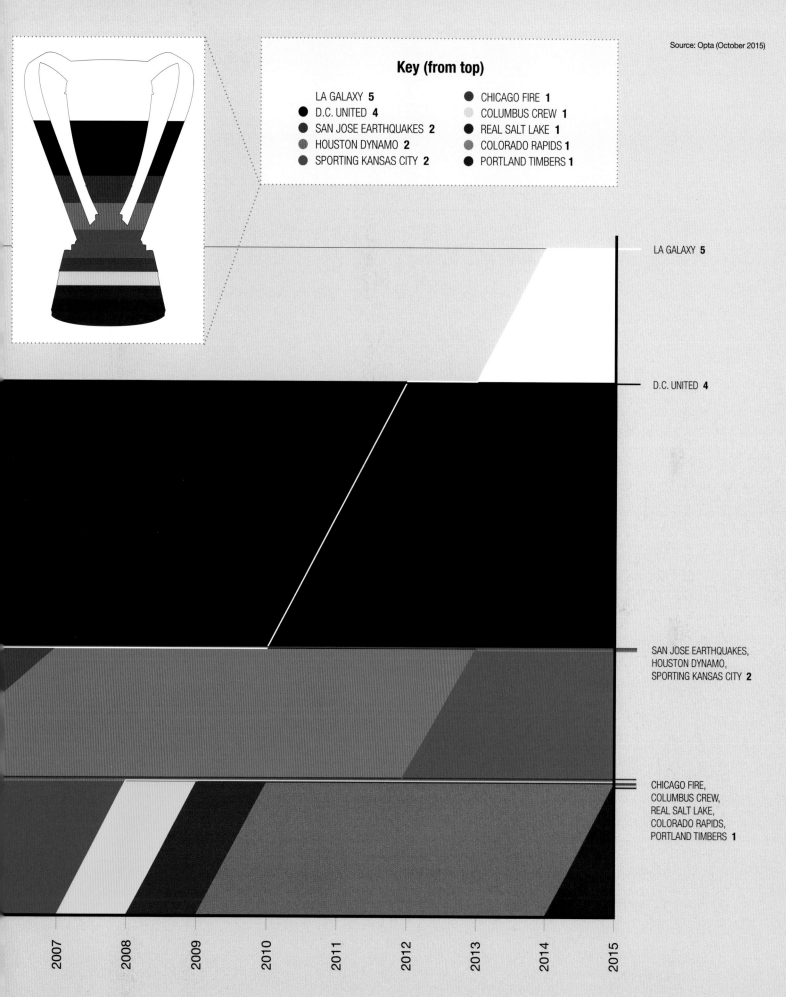

Source: Opta (October 2015)

Key (from top)

LA GALAXY **5**

● D.C. UNITED **4**

● SAN JOSE EARTHQUAKES **2**

● HOUSTON DYNAMO **2**

● SPORTING KANSAS CITY **2**

● CHICAGO FIRE **1**

○ COLUMBUS CREW **1**

● REAL SALT LAKE **1**

● COLORADO RAPIDS **1**

● PORTLAND TIMBERS **1**

LA GALAXY **5**

D.C. UNITED **4**

SAN JOSE EARTHQUAKES, HOUSTON DYNAMO, SPORTING KANSAS CITY **2**

CHICAGO FIRE, COLUMBUS CREW, REAL SALT LAKE, COLORADO RAPIDS, PORTLAND TIMBERS **1**

2007 2008 2009 2010 2011 2012 2013 2014 2015

WORLD CUP GOALSCORERS BY COUNTRY

It was Lucien Laurent, for France, who scored the first World Cup finals goal at the 1930 competition. Since then over 2,300 goals have been scored by 80 different countries in 20 finals tournaments. Germany and Brazil have both been tournament top scorers on four occasions,

GERMANY

Miroslav Klose **16**

Jürgen Klinsmann **11**

Thomas Müller **10**

Helmut Rahn **10**

Uwe Seeler **9**

Rudi Völler **8**

Max Morlock **6**

Helmut Haller **6**

Gerd Müller **14**

Karl-Heinz Rummenigge **9**

Hans Schäfer **7**

Lothar Matthäus **6**

Lukas Podolski **5**

Franz Beckenbauer **5**

ITALY

Roberto Baggio **9**

Paolo Rossi **9**

Salvatore Schillaci **6**

Christian Vieri **9**

Alessandro Altobelli **5**

Silvio Piola **5**

ARGENTINA

Gabriel Batistuta **10**

Diego Maradona **8**

Mario Alberto Kempes **6**

G. Stábile **8**

Lionel Messi **5**

Gonzalo Higuaín **5**

BRAZIL

Ronaldo **15**

Vavá **9**

Rivaldo **8**

Ademir **8**

Jairzinho **9**

Careca **7**

Bebeto **6**

Garrincha **5**

Pelé **12**

Leônidas da Silva **8**

Rivellino **6**

Zico **5**

Romário **5**

NETHERLANDS

Johnny Rep **7**

Wesley Sneijder **6**

Robin van Persie **6**

Dennis Bergkamp **6**

Arjen Robben **6**

Rob Rensenbrink **6**

Johan Neeskens **5**

Hungary have the highest strike rate at 2.72 goals scored per match (helped by their record 27 goals in 1954), while Canada, China, Dutch East Indies, Trinidad & Tobago and Zaire all have reached the finals but failed to register a single goal – a notable achievement in itself.

Source: Opta (August 2015)

SPAIN

David Villa **9**

Fernando Morientes **5**

Fernando Hierro **5**

Basora **5**

E. Butragueño **5**

Raúl **5**

FRANCE

Just Fontaine **13**

Thierry Henry **6**

Michel Platini **5**

Zinedine Zidane **5**

HUNGARY

Sándor Kocsis **11**

Lajos Tichy **7**

György Sárosi **6**

G. Zsengellér **5**

URUGUAY

Óscar Míguez **8**

Diego Forlán **6**

Juan Alberto Schiaffino **5**

Luis Suárez **5**

Pedro Cea **5**

ENGLAND

Gary Lineker **10**

Geoff Hurst **5**

CZECHOSLOVAKIA

Oldřich Nejedlý **7**

Tomáš Skuhravý **5**

AUSTRIA

Erich Probst **6**

Hans Krankl **5**

PERU

Teófilo Cubillas **10**

BULGARIA

Hristo Stoichkov **6**

COLOMBIA

James Rodríguez **6**

CROATIA

Davor Šuker **6**

GHANA

Asamoah Gyan **6**

AUSTRALIA

Tim Cahill **5**

BELGIUM

Marc Wilmots **5**

CAMEROON

Roger Milla **5**

RUSSIA

Oleg Salenko **6**

POLAND

Grzegorz Lato **10**

Andrzej Szarmach **7**

SWEDEN

Henrik Larsson **5**

Kennet Andersson **5**

DENMARK

Jon Dahl Tomasson **5**

USA

Landon Donovan **5**

PORTUGAL

Zbigniew Boniek **6**

Eusébio **9**

SWITZERLAND

Josef Hügi **6**

NORTHERN IRELAND

Peter McParland **5**

USSR

Valentin Ivanov **5**

GOALS PER GAME PER DECADE

Watch any major European match this year and you can expect to see around 2.5 goals. The goals-per-game ratio had declined steadily from four per match in the late 1950s to the 2000s, but since 2010 has shown signs of rising again, due to prolific goalscorers such as Neymar, Ibrahimović and Ronaldo. You'll need to travel to Puerto Rico, Taiwan or Bermuda to have a good chance of a four-goal, top-flight match, while it's worth noting that top-level games in Tanzania, Lesotho and Jordan struggle to register two.

*German Bundesliga not formed until 1965.

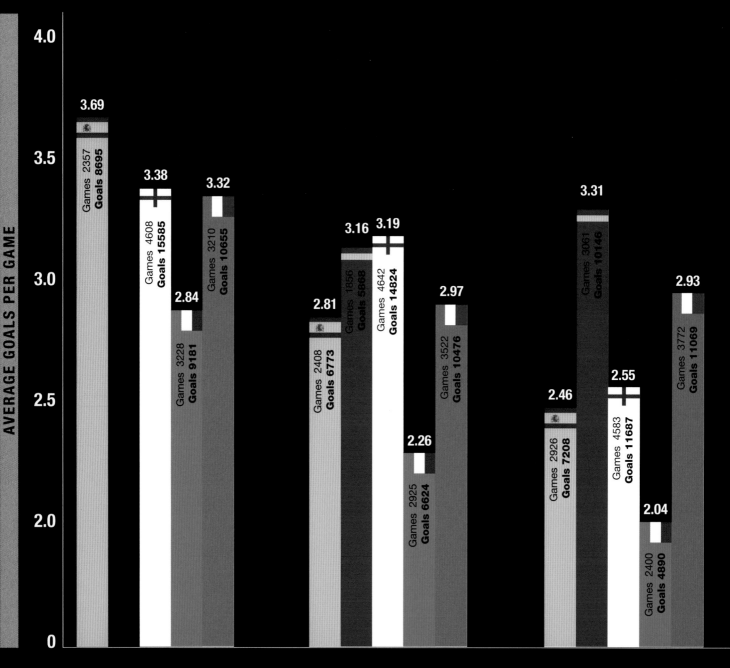

AVERAGE GOALS PER GAME

4.0

3.5

3.0

2.5

2.0

0

1950s

3.69 — Games 2357 Goals 8695
3.38 — Games 4608 Goals 15585
2.84 — Games 3228 Goals 9181
3.32 — Games 3210 Goals 10655

1960s

2.81 — Games 2408 Goals 6773
3.16 — Games 1856 Goals 5868
3.19 — Games 4642 Goals 14824
2.26 — Games 2925 Goals 6624
2.97 — Games 3522 Goals 10476

1970s

2.46 — Games 2926 Goals 7208
3.31 — Games 3061 Goals 10146
2.55 — Games 4583 Goals 11687
2.04 — Games 2400 Goals 4890
2.93 — Games 3772 Goals 11069

Gerd Müller scores goal number two in the European Cup Final replay, Bayern München vs Atlético Madrid, 15 May 1974.

Source: Opta (August 2015)

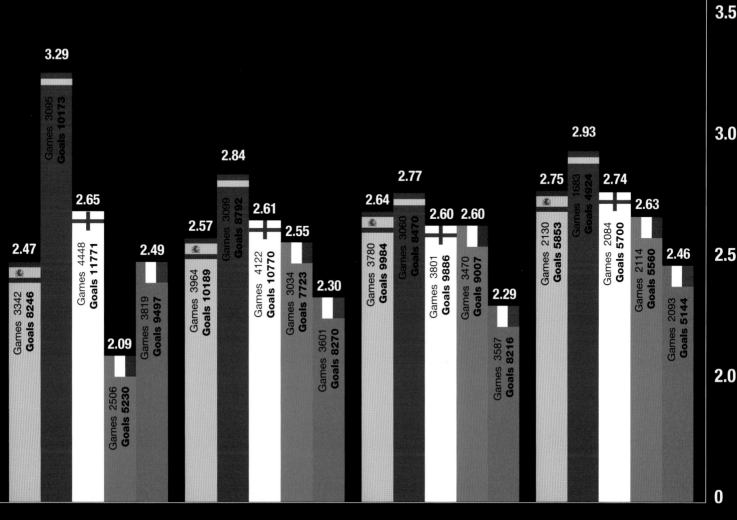

1980s

3.29 — Games 3095 **Goals 10173**
2.47 — Games 3342 **Goals 8246**
2.65 — Games 4448 **Goals 11771**
2.09 — Games 2506 **Goals 5230**
2.49 — Games 3819 **Goals 9497**

1990s

2.84 — Games 3099 **Goals 8792**
2.57 — Games 3964 **Goals 10189**
2.61 — Games 4122 **Goals 10770**
2.55 — Games 3034 **Goals 7723**
2.30 — Games 3601 **Goals 8270**

2000s

2.77 — Games 3060 **Goals 8470**
2.64 — Games 3780 **Goals 9984**
2.60 — Games 3801 **Goals 9886**
2.60 — Games 3470 **Goals 9007**
2.29 — Games 3587 **Goals 8216**

2010s

2.93 — Games 1683 **Goals 4924**
2.75 — Games 2130 **Goals 5853**
2.74 — Games 2084 **Goals 5700**
2.63 — Games 2114 **Goals 5560**
2.46 — Games 2093 **Goals 5144**

4.0
3.5
3.0
2.5
2.0
0

LA LIGA GAME WINS PER CLUB

The teams that founded La Liga in 1929 still feature in this top flight division and have now played more than 2500 games. It is astonishing to observe not only the near identical records of Real Madrid and Barcelona, but also the parity of the "bridesmaid clubs" Athletic Bilbao, Atlético Madrid and Sevilla. Even Real Madrid's 2011–12 record of 32 wins in a season was matched by Barcelona the following season, although Barcelona's 16 consecutive wins in 2010–11 has never been equalled.

ELCHE **20**
LAS PALMAS **22**
TENERIFE **26**
REAL OVIEDO **33**
NUMANCIA **37**
GRANADA CF **42**
RECREATIVO **42**
SPORTING DE GIJÓN **44**
ALMERÍA **62**
ALAVÉS **76**
LEVANTE **87**
RAYO VALLECANO **102**
REAL VALLADOLID **120**
GETAFE **138**
RACING DE SANTANDER **141**
REAL ZARAGOZA **156**
REAL BETIS **157**
CELTA DE VIGO **157**
OSASUNA **168**
MÁLAGA **180**
REAL SOCIEDAD **185**
MALLORCA **210**
ESPANYOL **215**

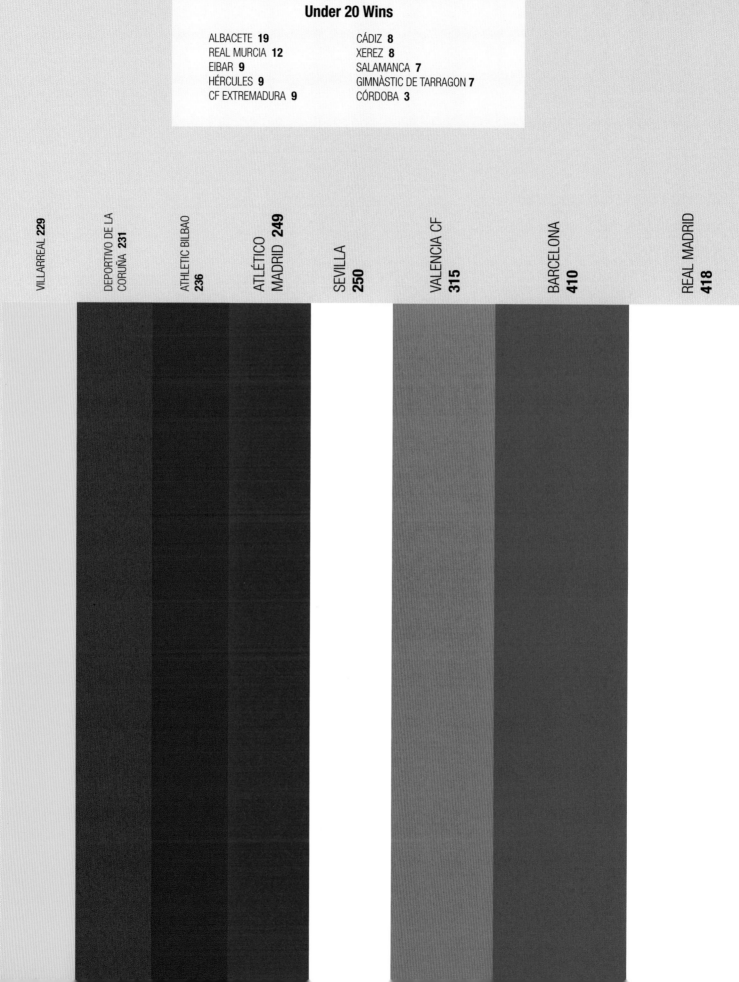

Source: Opta (October 2015)

Under 20 Wins

ALBACETE **19**	CÁDIZ **8**
REAL MURCIA **12**	XEREZ **8**
EIBAR **9**	SALAMANCA **7**
HÉRCULES **9**	GIMNÀSTIC DE TARRAGON **7**
CF EXTREMADURA **9**	CÓRDOBA **3**

VILLARREAL **229**

DEPORTIVO DE LA CORUÑA **231**

ATHLETIC BILBAO **236**

ATLÉTICO MADRID **249**

SEVILLA **250**

VALENCIA CF **315**

BARCELONA **410**

REAL MADRID **418**

FOOTBALL STADIUMS BY SIZE

Even in a world facing severe financial troubles new football stadiums continue to emerge. The footballing world may still mourn the loss of iconic turf such as Arsenal's stadium at Highbury, Benfica's Estádio da Luz and Athletic Bilbao's La Catedral at San Mamés, but the grounds that replaced them, and other new stadiums such as Manchester City's Etihad, the Allianz Arena, Munich, and Juventus' stadium in Turin, look set to join Camp Nou, Old Trafford and La Bombonera on the list of the world's most hallowed grounds.

Source: Google (October 2015)

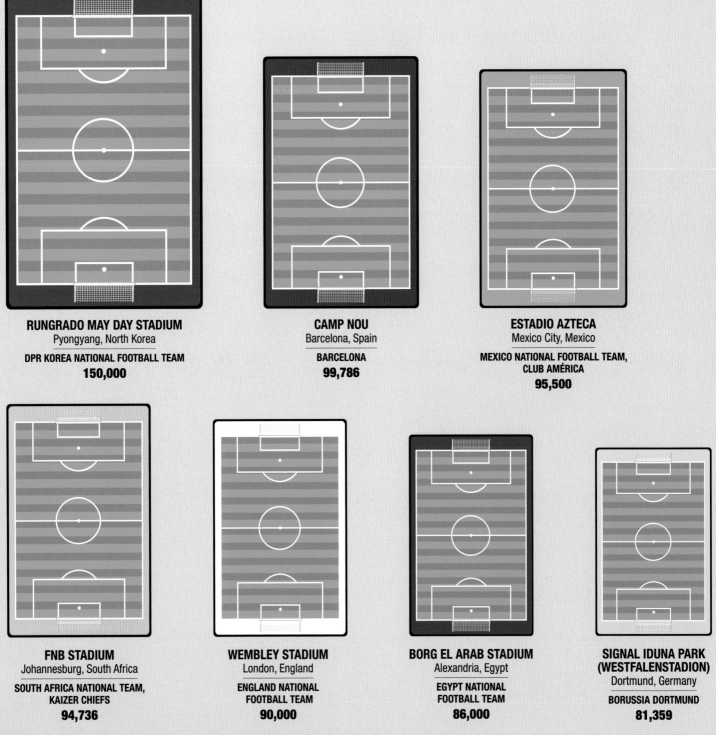

RUNGRADO MAY DAY STADIUM
Pyongyang, North Korea

DPR KOREA NATIONAL FOOTBALL TEAM
150,000

CAMP NOU
Barcelona, Spain

BARCELONA
99,786

ESTADIO AZTECA
Mexico City, Mexico

MEXICO NATIONAL FOOTBALL TEAM, CLUB AMÉRICA
95,500

FNB STADIUM
Johannesburg, South Africa

SOUTH AFRICA NATIONAL TEAM, KAIZER CHIEFS
94,736

WEMBLEY STADIUM
London, England

ENGLAND NATIONAL FOOTBALL TEAM
90,000

BORG EL ARAB STADIUM
Alexandria, Egypt

EGYPT NATIONAL FOOTBALL TEAM
86,000

SIGNAL IDUNA PARK (WESTFALENSTADION)
Dortmund, Germany

BORUSSIA DORTMUND
81,359

STADE DE FRANCE
Saint-Denis, France
FRANCE NATIONAL FOOTBALL TEAM
81,338

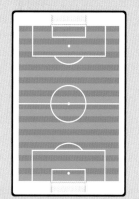

SANTIAGO BERNABÉU STADIUM
Madrid, Spain
REAL MADRID
81,044

**STADIO GIUSEPPE MEAZZA
(SAN SIRO)**
Milan, Italy
INTERNAZIONALE MILANO, AC MILAN
80,018

**GUANGDONG OLYMPIC
STADIUM**
Guangzhou, China
**GUANGZHOU EVERGRANDE
(SOME GAMES)**
80,012

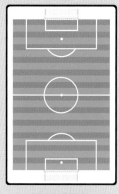

AT&T STADIUM
Arlington, United States
**2009, 2011 AND 2013
CONCACAF GOLD CUP**
80,000

MARACANÃ STADIUM
Rio De Janeiro, Brazil
**BRAZIL NATIONAL TEAM,
CR FLAMENGO, FLUMINENSE FC,
BOTAFOGO FR**
78,383

OLD TRAFFORD
Manchester, England
MANCHESTER UNITED
75,731

ALLIANZ ARENA
Munich, Germany
**BAYERN MÜNCHEN,
TSV 1860 MUNICH**
75,024

**INTERNATIONAL STADIUM
YOKOHAMA**
Yokohama, Japan
YOKOHAMA F. MARINOS
72,327

**OLYMPIC STADIUM ATHENS
SPIROS LOUIS**
Athens, Greece
**GREECE NATIONAL FOOTBALL TEAM,
AEK ATHENS, PANATHINAIKOS FC**
70,030

SHAH ALAM STADIUM
Shah Alam, Malaysia
SELANGOR FA
69,372

ESTÁDIO DA LUZ
Lisbon, Portugal
S.L. BENFICA
65,647

CELTIC PARK
Glasgow, Scotland
CELTIC FC
60,355

EMIRATES STADIUM
London, England
ARSENAL
60,338

FRIENDS ARENA
Solna, Sweden
**SWEDEN NATIONAL FOOTBALL TEAM,
AIK**
60,000

AVIVA STADIUM
Dublin, Republic of Ireland
**REPUBLIC OF IRELAND
NATIONAL FOOTBALL TEAM**
51,700

TÓRSVØLLUR
Tórshavn, Faroe Islands
FAROE ISLANDS NATIONAL TEAM
2,000

**ESTADI COMUNAL
D'ANDORRA LA VELLA**
La Vella, Andorra
ANDORRA NATIONAL TEAM
1,300

2006 WORLD CUP GOALS

The 2006 World Cup, hosted by Germany, will forever be dominated by one image: the world's greatest footballer, Zinedine Zidane, playing his last game ever, headbutting Italy's Marco Materazzi in the chest. In a low-scoring tournament, five goals were enough to reward Germany's Miroslav Klose the Golden Boot, while Philipp Lahm's wonderstrike in the opening game, Bakari Koné's solo effort for the Ivory Coast and Argentina's Cambiasso's finishing an exquisite 24-pass movement stood out as the tournament's best goals.

ESTEBAN CAMBIASSO – **Argentina** vs Serbia & Montenegro

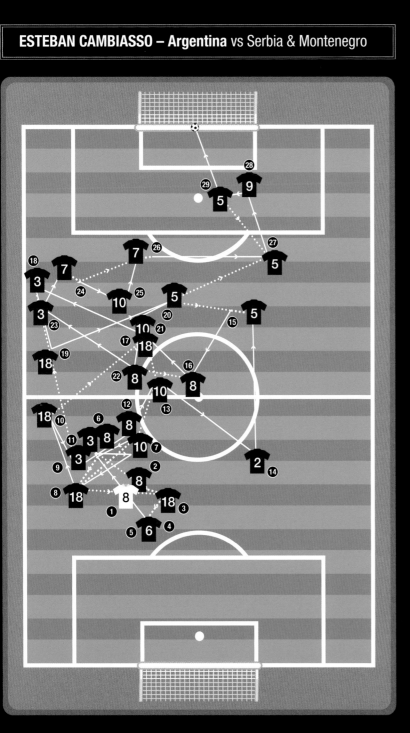

Esteban Cambiasso celebrates in style after scoring the second goal against Serbia & Montenegro, 16 June 2006.

1. Dispossesed **Kežman**
2. Challenge **Mascherano**
3. Tackle **Rodríguez**
4. Ball recovery **Heinze**
5. Pass **Heinze**
6. Pass **Mascherano**
7. Pass **Riquelme**
8. Pass **Rodríguez**
9. Pass **Sorín**
10. Pass **Rodríguez**
11. Pass **Sorín**
12. Pass **Mascherano**
13. Pass **Riquelme**
14. Pass **Ayala**
15. Pass **Cambiasso**
16. Pass **Mascherano**
17. Pass **Rodríguez**
18. Pass **Sorín**
19. Pass **Rodríguez**
20. Pass **Cambiasso**
21. Pass **Riquelme**
22. Pass **Mascherano**
23. Pass **Mascherano**
24. Pass **Saviola**
25. Pass **Riquelme**
26. Pass **Saviola**
27. Pass **Cambiasso**
28. Pass **Crespo**
29. Goal **Cambiasso**

KEY

Ball movement ——— Player with ball ···········

Shot ———⚽ Player without ball ···········

JOE COLE – England vs Sweden

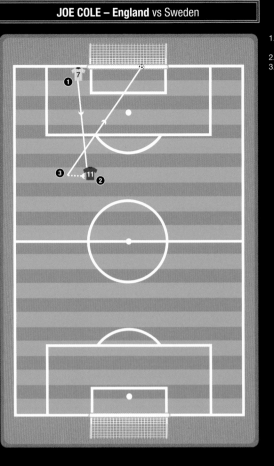

1. Clearance **Alexandersson**
2. Good skill **Cole**
3. Goal **Cole**

DECO – Portugal vs Iran

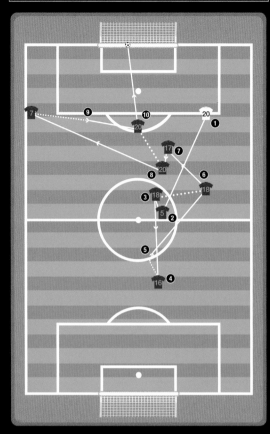

1. Launch **Nosrati**
2. Head pass **Meira**
3. Head pass **Maniche**
4. Ball recovery **Carvalho**
5. Pass **Carvalho**
6. Pass **Maniche**
7. Pass **Ronaldo**
8. Pass (long ball) **Deco**
9. Pass **Figo**
10. Goal **Deco**

MAXI RODRÍGUEZ – Argentina vs Mexico

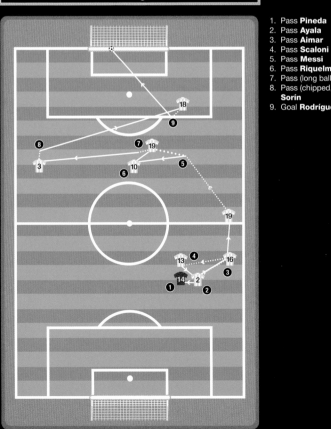

1. Pass **Pineda**
2. Pass **Ayala**
3. Pass **Aimar**
4. Pass **Scaloni**
5. Pass **Messi**
6. Pass **Riquelme**
7. Pass (long ball) **Messi**
8. Pass (chipped, long ball) **Sorín**
9. Goal **Rodríguez**

FERNANDO TORRES – Spain vs Ukraine

1. Pass **Shelayev**
2. Interception **Puyol**
3. Take on **Puyol**
4. Pass **Puyol**
5. Challenge **Tymoshchuk**
6. Pass **Torres**
7. Pass **Fàbregas**
8. Flick-on **Puyol**
9. Goal **Torres**

GERMAN BUNDESLIGA SHIRT COLOURS

The teams of the Bundesliga have embraced all the tricks and fads of modern shirt design, playing with sashes, single stripes, trims and complex patterns. The current fashion seems to see clubs returning to their 1970s colours. Many will recognize the all-red kit of Champions League winners Bayern München, while some will be familiar with the yellow and black of Borussia Dortmund, the green of Werder Bremen and the blue and white stripes of Hertha BSC.

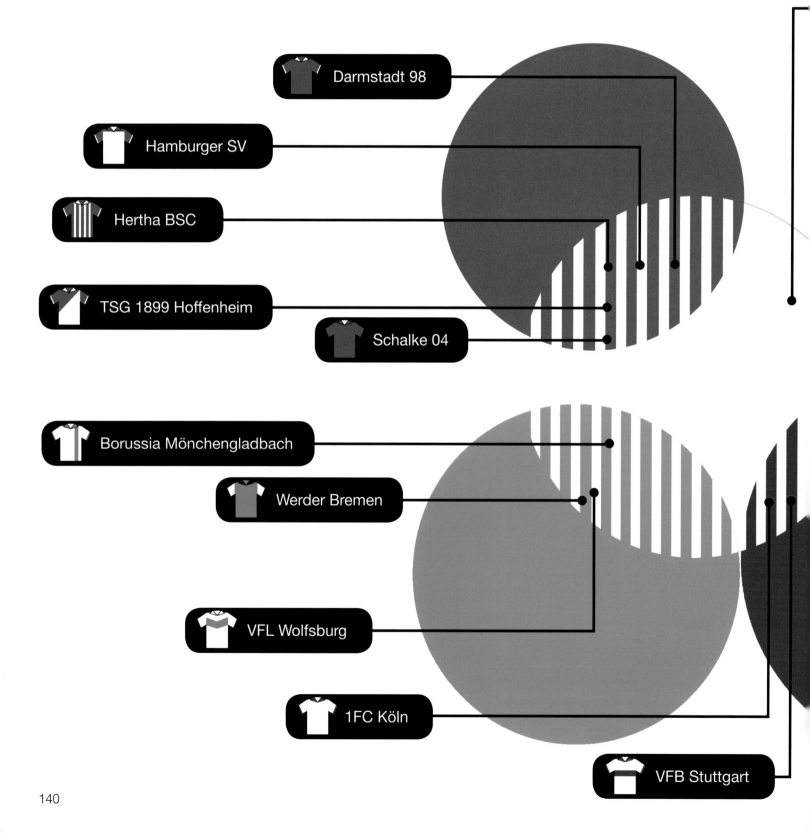

Darmstadt 98

Hamburger SV

Hertha BSC

TSG 1899 Hoffenheim

Schalke 04

Borussia Mönchengladbach

Werder Bremen

VFL Wolfsburg

1FC Köln

VFB Stuttgart

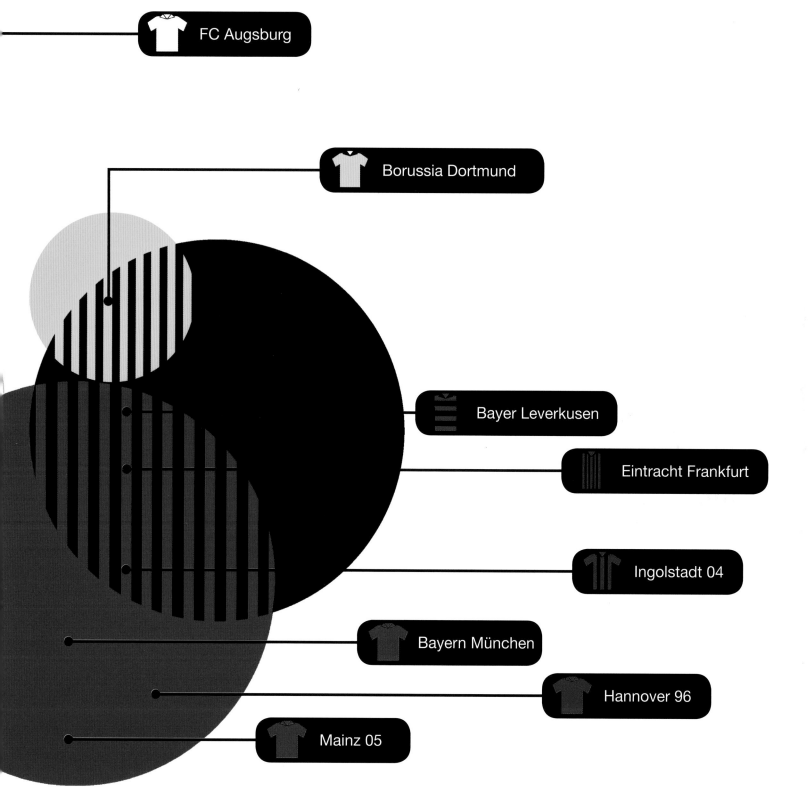

FC Augsburg

Borussia Dortmund

Bayer Leverkusen

Eintracht Frankfurt

Ingolstadt 04

Bayern München

Hannover 96

Mainz 05

COPA LIBERTADORES WINS BY NATION

Copa Libertadores de América is the most prestigious club tournament in South America. It is broadcast in over 130 countries and watched by more than a billion TV viewers. Played annually every February the tournament is now contested by 38 teams from 11 countries (including Mexican teams since 2000). At least three clubs from each country compete, with Argentina and Brazil both entitled to enter five teams, in the hope of making the *Sueño Libertador* (dream of winning) come true... and winning the US$2,300,000 top prize money.

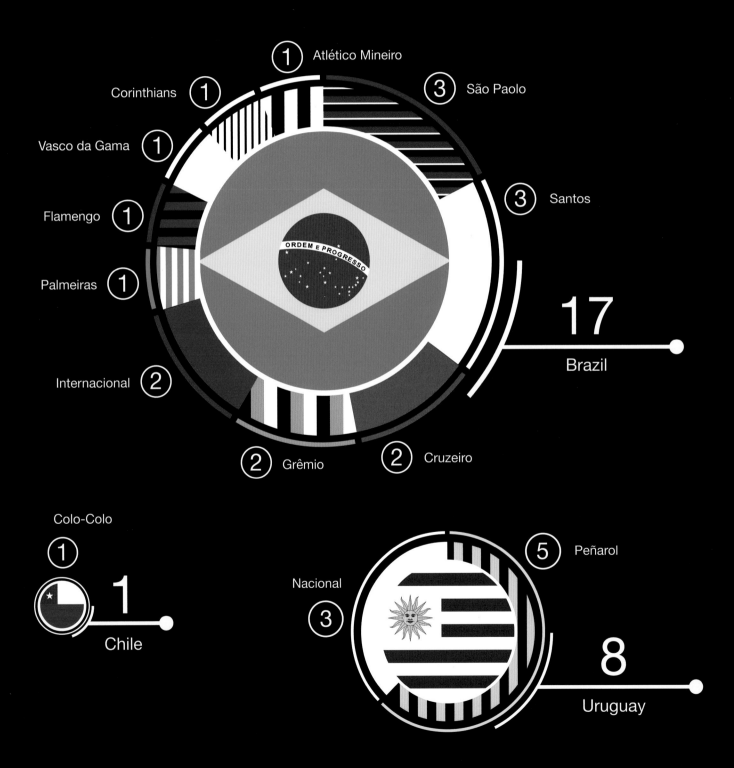

Atlético Mineiro ①

Corinthians ①

São Paolo ③

Vasco da Gama ①

Santos ③

Flamengo ①

Palmeiras ①

17
Brazil

Internacional ②

Grêmio ②

Cruzeiro ②

Colo-Colo

①

1
Chile

Nacional ③

Peñarol ⑤

8
Uruguay

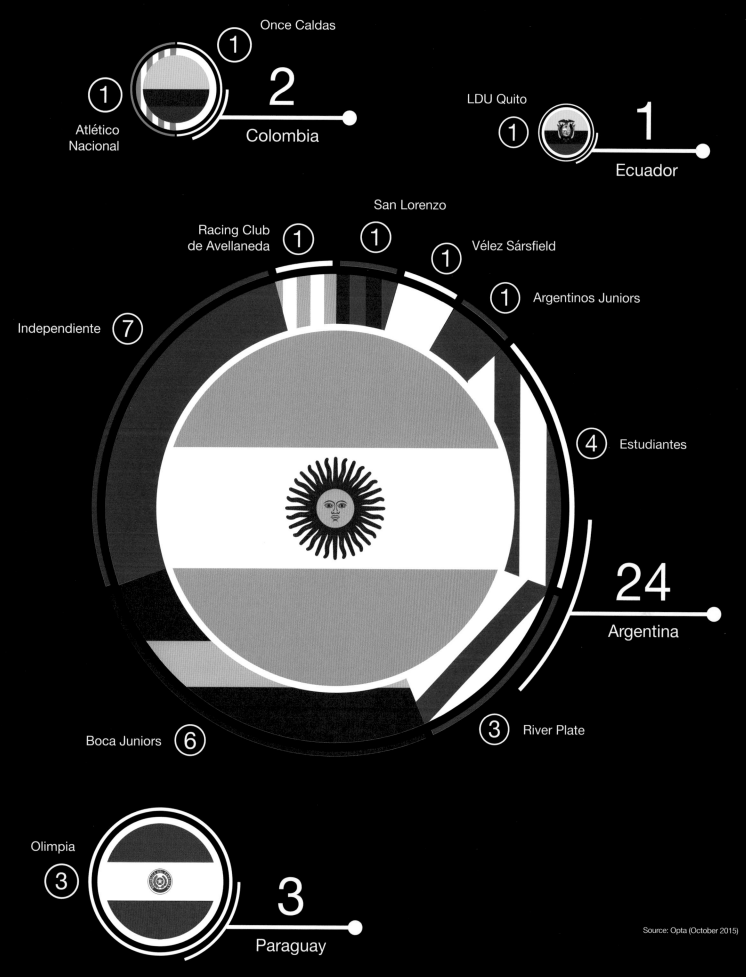

Once Caldas ①

① Atlético
Nacional

2
Colombia

LDU Quito
①

1
Ecuador

Racing Club
de Avellaneda ①

San Lorenzo ①

Vélez Sársfield ①

Argentinos Juniors ①

Independiente ⑦

④ Estudiantes

24
Argentina

③ River Plate

Boca Juniors ⑥

Olimpia
③

3
Paraguay

Source: Opta (October 2015)

LIGUE 1 TITLE WINNERS

Ligue 1 began in 1932, switching to its current name in 2002. Although many view it as one of the weaker of the major European leagues, Ligue 1 is one of the most evenly contested. Paris Saint-Germain currently hold sway, but more recently Saint-Étienne (Ligue 1's most successful club), Olympique Lyonnais (winners of a record seven consecutive titles between 2002 and 2008) and Olympique de Marseille (most seasons and wins in the top flight) have all thrown their respective hats in the ring in the hope of being crowned top dog in the league.

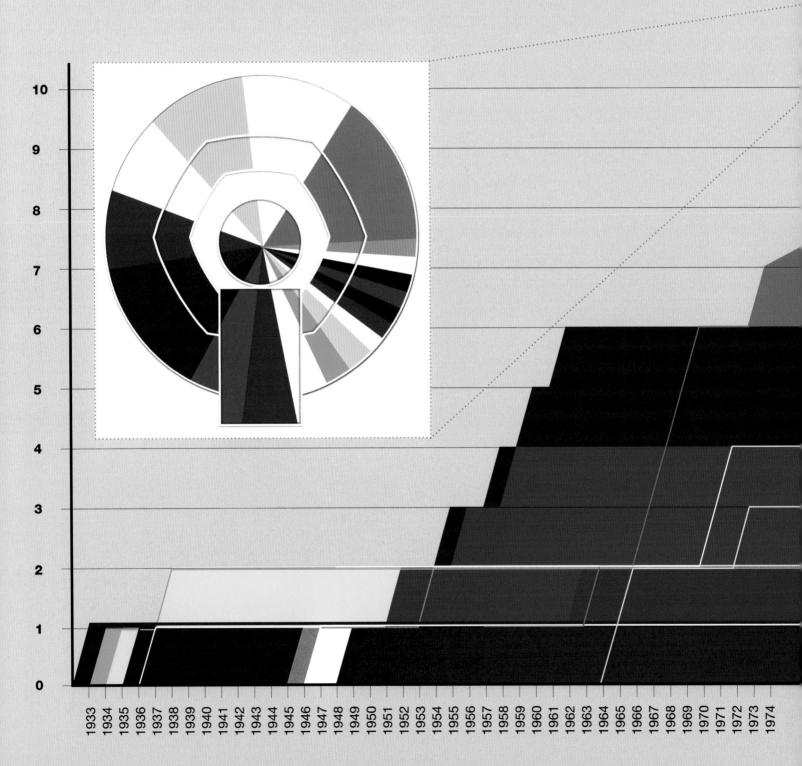

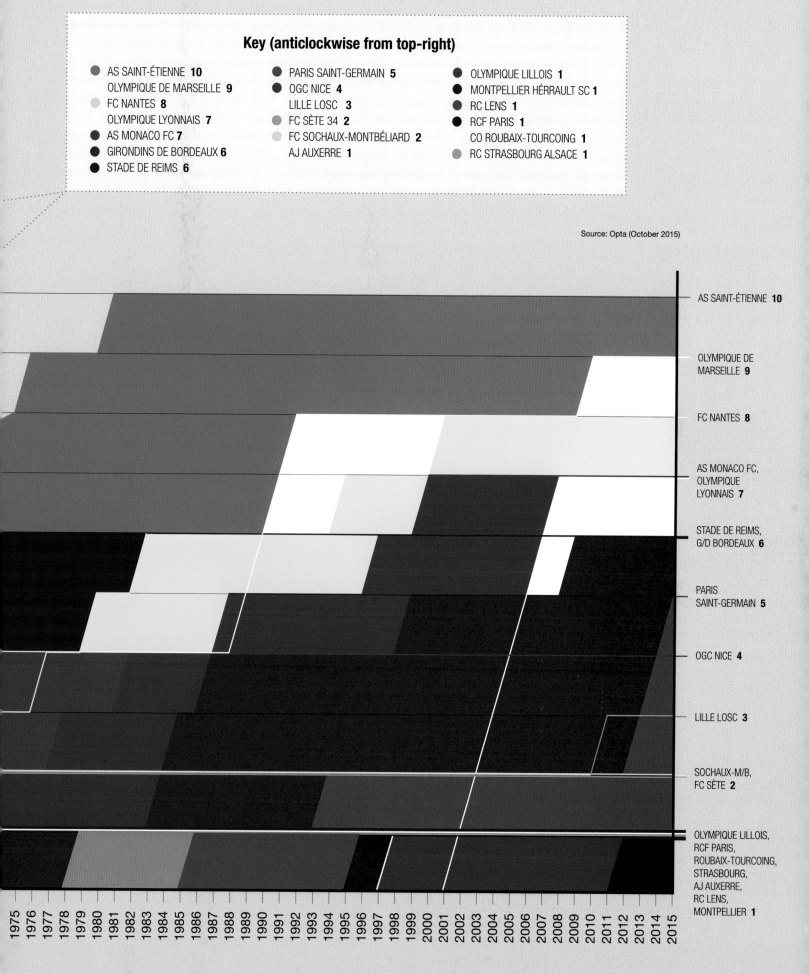

Key (anticlockwise from top-right)

- AS SAINT-ÉTIENNE **10**
  OLYMPIQUE DE MARSEILLE **9**
- FC NANTES **8**
  OLYMPIQUE LYONNAIS **7**
- AS MONACO FC **7**
- GIRONDINS DE BORDEAUX **6**
- STADE DE REIMS **6**

- PARIS SAINT-GERMAIN **5**
- OGC NICE **4**
  LILLE LOSC **3**
- FC SÈTE 34 **2**
- FC SOCHAUX-MONTBÉLIARD **2**
  AJ AUXERRE **1**

- OLYMPIQUE LILLOIS **1**
- MONTPELLIER HÉRRAULT SC **1**
- RC LENS **1**
- RCF PARIS **1**
  CO ROUBAIX-TOURCOING **1**
- RC STRASBOURG ALSACE **1**

Source: Opta (October 2015)

AS SAINT-ÉTIENNE **10**

OLYMPIQUE DE MARSEILLE **9**

FC NANTES **8**

AS MONACO FC, OLYMPIQUE LYONNAIS **7**

STADE DE REIMS, G/D BORDEAUX **6**

PARIS SAINT-GERMAIN **5**

OGC NICE **4**

LILLE LOSC **3**

SOCHAUX-M/B, FC SÈTE **2**

OLYMPIQUE LILLOIS, RCF PARIS, ROUBAIX-TOURCOING, STRASBOURG, AJ AUXERRE, RC LENS, MONTPELLIER **1**

1975 1976 1977 1978 1979 1980 1981 1982 1983 1984 1985 1986 1987 1988 1989 1990 1991 1992 1993 1994 1995 1996 1997 1998 1999 2000 2001 2002 2003 2004 2005 2006 2007 2008 2009 2010 2011 2012 2013 2014 2015

AFC ASIAN CUP TROPHIES, WINS & GOALS

The most recent AFC Asian Cup in 2015 crowned host nation Australia the "Champions of Asia" after defeating the Republic of Korea 2–1 after extra time. The next tournament in 2019, which is to be hosted by the United Arab Emirates, will see the possible number of national teams expand from 16 to 24. The Asian Cup is the world's second oldest continental football championship, after Copa América, and the cup's most consistent side to date is Japan, who have triumphantly held the trophy aloft in four out of seven tournaments since 1992.

IRAN

119
37
3

KOREA REPUBLIC

100
32
2

CHINA PR

86
21

JAPAN

80
24
4

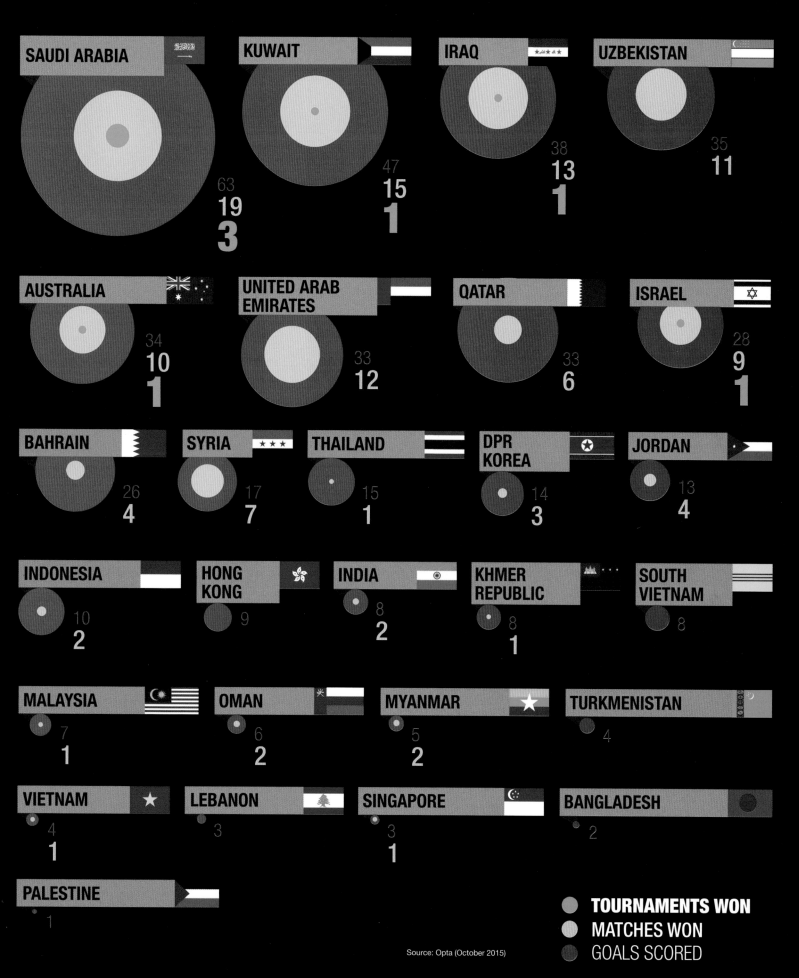

SAUDI ARABIA 63 19 3

KUWAIT 47 15 1

IRAQ 38 13 1

UZBEKISTAN 35 11

AUSTRALIA 34 10 1

UNITED ARAB EMIRATES 33 12

QATAR 33 6

ISRAEL 28 9 1

BAHRAIN 26 4

SYRIA 17 7

THAILAND 15 1

DPR KOREA 14 3

JORDAN 13 4

INDONESIA 10 2

HONG KONG 9

INDIA 8 2

KHMER REPUBLIC 8 1

SOUTH VIETNAM 8

MALAYSIA 7 1

OMAN 6 2

MYANMAR 5 2

TURKMENISTAN 4

VIETNAM 4 1

LEBANON 3

SINGAPORE 3 1

BANGLADESH 2

PALESTINE 1

● **TOURNAMENTS WON**
● **MATCHES WON**
● GOALS SCORED

Source: Opta (October 2015)

147

100 INTERNATIONAL CAPS

At Wembley Stadium, on 11 April 1959, England captain Billy Wright became the first footballer to make 100 appearances for his country, but since then this feat has been repeated by many players around the world. The modern game's proliferation of matches (major nations play more games a year than their pre-1990s counterparts) and multiple substitution rules give today's players a better chance of becoming "Centurions" and also accounts for the absence in the list of such greats as Pelé (92 appearances), Diego Maradona (91), Eusébio (64) and Johan Cruyff (48).

Ahmed Hassan — Egypt — 184	Mohamed Al-Deayea — Saudi Arabia — 178	Claudio Suárez — Mexico — 177	Hossam Hassan — Egypt — 169	Iván Hurtado — Ecuador — 168	Vitalijs Astafjevs — Latvia — 165	Iker Casillas — Spain — 165	Cobi Jones — United States — 164	Mohammed Al-Khilaiwi — Saudi Arabia — 163
Adnan Al-Talyani — United Arab Emirates — 161	Bader Al-Mutawa — Kuwait — 158	Landon Donovan — United States — 157	Sami Al-Jaber — Saudi Arabia — 156	Martin Reim — Estonia — 156	Gianlulgi Buffon — Italy — 154	Yasuhito Endo — Japan — 152	Lothar Matthäus — West Germany / Germany — 150	Salman Isa — Bahrain — 149
Ali Daei — Iran — 149	Javad Nekounam — Iran — 148	Mohammed Husain — Bahrain — 145	Pável Pardo — Mexico — 145	Javier Zanetti — Argentina — 143	Gerado Torrado — Mexico — 143	Fawzi Doorbeen — Oman — 143	Robbie Keane — Republic of Ireland — 143	Thomas Ravelli — Sweden — 143
Anders Svensson — Sweden — 143	Cafu — Brazil — 142	Marko Kristal — Estonia — 142	Lilan Thuram — France — 142	Essam El-Hadary — Egypt — 141	Abdullah Zubromawi — Saudi Arabia — 141	Anatoliy Tymoshchuk — Ukraine — 141	Giorgos Karagounis — Greece — 139	Rigobert Song — Cameroon — 137
Jari Litmanen — Finland — 137	Miroslav Klose — Germany — 137	Amado Guevara — Honduras — 137	Younis Mahmoud — Iraq — 137	Hussein Saeed — Iraq — 137	Fabio Cannavaro — Italy — 136	Hong Myung-Bo — South Korea — 136	Walter Centeno — Costa Rica — 135	Waleed Ali Jumah — Kuwait — 135
Dorinel Munteanu — Romania — 134	Hussein Sulaimani — Saudi Arabia — 134	Jeff Agoos — United States — 134	Andres Oper — Estonia — 133	Noel Valladares — Honduras — 133	Bashar Abdullah — Kuwait — 133	Saud Kariri — Saudi Arabia — 133	Xavi — Spain — 133	Paulo da Silva — Paraguay — 131
Shay Given — Republic of Ireland — 131	Shahril Bin Ishak — Singapore — 131	Lee Woon-Jae — South Korea — 131	Kiatisuk Senamuang — Thailand — 131	Sargis Hovseyan — Armenia — 130	Edwin van der Sar — Netherlands — 130	Jorge Campos — Mexico — 129	Rafael Márquez — Mexico — 129	Sergio Ramos — Spain — 129
Roberto Palacios — Peru — 128	Daniel Bennett — Singapore — 128	Juan Arango — Venezuela — 128	Dennis Rommedahl — Denmark — 127	Ali Karimi — Iran — 127	Luís Figo — Portugal — 127	Lee Young-Pyo — South Korea — 127	Andreas Isaksson — Sweden — 127	Marcelo Balboa — United States — 127
Luis Marin — Costa Rica — 126	Darijo Srna — Croatia — 126	Paolo Maldini — Italy — 126	Andoni Zubizarreta — Spain — 126	Roberto Carlos — Brazil — 125	Ibrahim Hassan — Egypt — 125	Peter Shilton — England — 125	Carlos Ruiz — Guatemala — 125	Musaed Neda — Kuwait — 125
Mario Fick — Liechtenstein — 125	Kim Källström — Sweden — 125	Hany Ramzy — Egypt — 124	Lukas Podolski — Germany — 124	Ian Goodison — Jamaica — 124	Gheorghe Hagi — Romania — 124	Thierry Henry — France — 124	Maynor Figueroa — Honduras — 123	Didier Zokora — Ivory Coast — 123
Cristiano Ronaldo — Portugal — 123	DaMarcus Beasley — United States — 123	Javier Mascherano — Argentina — 122	Masami Ihara — Japan — 122	Carlos Salcido — Mexico — 122	Andrés Guardado — Mexico — 122	Amad Al-Hosni — Oman — 122	Ali Al-Habsi — Oman — 122	Baihakki Bin Khaizan — Singapore — 122
Peter Schmeichel — Denmark — 121	Wesley Sneijder — Netherlands — 121	Mohamed Abd Al-Jawad — Saudi Arabia — 121	Aide Iskandar — Singapore — 121	Mart Poom — Estonia — 120	Yoo Sang-Chul — South Korea — 120	Rüstü Reçber — Turkey — 120	Subait Khater Al-Junaibi — United Arab Emirates — 120	Theodoros Zagorakis — Greece — 119
Amer Shafi — Jordan — 119	David Carabott — Malta — 119	Gilbert Agius — Malta — 119	Ramón Ramirez — Mexico — 119	Cuauhtémoc Blanco — Mexico — 119	Pat Jennings — Northern Ireland — 119	Cha-Bum-Kun — South Korea — 119	Clint Dempsey — United States — 119	Timur Kapadze — Uzbekistan — 119
Heinz Hermann — Switzerland — 118	Geremi — Cameroon — 118	Samuel Eto'o — Cameroon — 118	Karel Poborský — Czech Republic — 118	Petr Cech — Czech Republic — 118	Kolo Touré — Ivory Coast — 118	Enar Jääger — Estonia — 118	Mohammed Al-Shalhoub — Saudi Arabia — 117	Olof Mellberg — Sweden — 117
Marcel Desailly — France — 116	Kostas Katsouranis — Greece — 116	Andrea Pirlo — Italy — 116	Theodore Whitmore — Jamaica — 116	Yoshikatsu Kawaguchi — Japan — 116	Peter Jehle — Liechtenstein — 116	Majed Abdullah — Saudi Arabia — 116	Ahmed Madani — Saudi Arabia — 116	Roland Nilsson — Sweden — 116
Roberto Ayala — Argentina — 115	David Beckham — England — 115	Noureddine Naybet — Morocco — 115	Gabriel Gómez — Panama — 115	Gheorghe Popescu — Romania — 115	Shunmugham Subramani — Singapore — 115	Abdulraheem Jumaa — United Arab Emirates — 115	Ismail Matar — United Arab Emirates — 115	Stipe Pletikosa — Croatia — 114
Steven Gerrard — England — 114	Kristen Viikmäe — Estonia — 114	Raio Piiroja — Estonia — 114	Nawaf Al-Khaldi — Kuwait — 114	Khaled Al-Muwallid — Saudi Arabia — 114	Indra Sahdan Daud — Singapore — 114	Björn Nordqvist — Sweden — 114	Abdulla Al-Mazooqi — Bahrain — 113	Viktor Onopko — CIS/Russia — 113

Source: Opta (December 2015)

Player	Country	Caps
Philipp Lahm	Germany	113
Bastian Schweinsteiger	Germany	113
Amer Khalil	Jordan	113
Andrejs Rubins	Latvia	113
Martin Stocklasa	Liechtenstein	113
Ahmad Al-Dossari	Saudi Arabia	113
Xabi Alonso	Spain	113
Angus Eve	Trinidad & Tobago	113
Alain Geiger	Switzerland	112
Li Weifeng	PR China	112
Yénier Márquez	Cuba	112
Jon Dahl Tomasson	Denmark	112
Édison Méndez	Ecuador	112
Abdel-Zaher El-Saqua	Egypt	112
Dino Zoff	Italy	112
Juris Laizans	Latvia	112
Michael Mifsud	Malta	112
Frank de Boer	Netherlands	112
Justo Villar	Paraguay	112
Wesam Abdulmajid	Qatar	112
Yasser Al-Qahtani	Saudi Arabia	112
Osama Al-Hawsawi	Saudi Arabia	112
Hakan Sükür	Turkey	112
Zuhair Bakheet	United Arab Emirates	112
Diego Forlán	Uruguay	112
Server Djeparov	Uzbekistan	112
Carlos Valderrama	Colombia	112
Rolando Fonseca	Costa Rica	111
Odelin Molina	Cuba	111
Wael Gomaa	Egypt	111
Nashat Akram	Iraq	111
Jarah Al-Ataiqi	Kuwait	111
Sergei Ignashevich	Russia	111
Zlatan Ibrahimovic	Sweden	111
Andriy Shevchenko	Ukraine	111
Abdulsalam Jumaa	United Arab Emirates	111
Claudio Reyna	United States	111
Mehdi Mahdavikia	Iran	110
Yuli Nakazawa	Japan	110
Carmel Busuttil	Malta	110
John Arne Riise	Norway	110
Carlos Gamarra	Paraguay	110
Roque Santa Cruz	Paraguay	110
Fernando Couto	Portugal	110
Kevin Kilbane	Republic of Ireland	110
Fernando Torres	Spain	110
Paul Caligiuri	United States	110
Mark Schwarzer	Australia	109
Mauricio Solis	Costa Rica	109
Walter Ayovi	Ecuador	109
Wayne Rooney	England	109
Hawar Mulla Mohammed	Iraq	109
Rafael van der Vaart	Netherlands	109
Niclas Alexandersson	Sweden	109
Totchtawan Sripan	Thailand	109
Maxi Pereira	Uruguay	109
José Rey	Venezuala	109
Thomas Helveg	Denmark	108
Álex Aguinaga	Ecuador	108
Zinedine Zidane	France	108
Nohayr Al-Mutairi	Kuwait	108
Alberto García Aspe	Mexico	108
Jaime Penedo	Panama	108
Bilal Mohammed	Qatar	108
Răzvan Raţ	Romania	108
Stern John	Trinidad & Tobago	108
Carlos Bocanegra	United States	108
Michael Bradley	United States	108
Jürgen Klinsmann	West Germany/Germany	108
Ahmed El-Kass	Egypt	108
Bobby Moore	England	107
Ashley Cole	England	107
Patrick Vieira	France	107
Jamal Mubarak	Kuwait	107
Miroslav Karhan	Slovakia	107
Aaron Mokoena	South Africa	107
Andrés Iniesta	Spain	107
Henrik Larsson	Sweden	107
Diego Simeone	Argentina	107
Fan Zhiyi	PR China	106
Hao Haidong	PR China	106
Ahmed Fathi	Egypt	106
Frank Lampard	England	106
Guillermo Ramirez	Guatemala	106
Boniek García	Honduras	106
Francisco Javier Rodríguez	Mexico	106
Giovanni van Bronckhorst	Netherlands	106
John O'Shea	Republic of Ireland	106
Taisir Al-Jassim	Saudi Arabia	106
Muhsin Musabah	United Arab Emirates	106
Eric Wynalda	United States	106
Joseph Musonda	Zambia	106
Óscar Sonejee	Andorra	105
Lionel Messi	Argentina	105
Lúcio	Brazil	105
Stiliyan Petrov	Bulgaria	105
Bobby Charlton	England	105
Ragnar Klavan	Estonia	105
Jonatan Johansson	Finland	105
Sami Hyypiä	Finland	105
Ali Hussein Rehema	Iraq	105
Imants Bleidelis	Latvia	105
Khamis Al-Dosari	Saudi Arabia	105
Radhi Jaïdi	Tunisia	105
Tim Howard	United States	105
Jürgen Kohler	West Germany / Germany	105
Ismail Abdul-Latif	Bahrain	105
Josip Šimunic	Croatia	104
Nader El-Sayed	Egypt	104
Billy Wright	England	104
Per Mertesacker	Germany	104
Gustavo Cabrera	Guatemala	104
Didier Drogba	Ivory Coast	104
Mihails Zemļinskis	Latvia	104
Dirk Kuyt	Netherlands	104
Héctor Chumpitaz	Peru	104
Khairul Amri	Singapore	104
Kim Tae-Young	South Korea	104
Stéphane Chapuisat	Switzerland	103
Andreas Herzog	Austria	103
Ioannis Okkas	Cyprus	103
Michael Laudrup	Denmark	103
Indrek Zelinski	Estonia	103
Didier Deschamps	France	103
Mahdi Kareem	Iraq	103
Máris Verpakovskis	Latvia	103
Andrès Quintana	Qatar	103
Mohammed Al-Jahani	Saudi Arabia	103
Hwang Sun-Hong	South Korea	103
Lee Dong-Gook	South Korea	103
Franz Beckenbauer	West Germany	103
Hussain Ali Baba	Bahrain	103
Mario Yepes	Colombia	102
Ivica Olic	Croatia	102
Martin Jørgensen	Denmark	102
Hani Al-Dhabit	Oman	102
Michał Żewłakow	Poland	102
Steve Staunton	Republic of Ireland	102
Kenny Dalglish	Scotland	102
Raúl	Spain	102
Bülent Korkmaz	Turkey	102
Mohamed Omar	United Arab Emirates	102
Kennedy Mweene	Zambia	102
Savo Milošević	Fr Yugoslavia/Serbia & Montenegro/Serbia	102
Dejan Stankovic	Fr Yugoslavia/Serbia & Montenegro/Serbia	102
Rashad Sadygov	Azerbaijan	101
Husain Ahmed	Bahrain	101
Alyaksandr Kulchy	Belarus	101
Taffarel	Brazil	101
Leonel Álvarez	Colombia	101
Álvaro Saborío	Costa Rica	101
Thomas Häßler	West Germany / Germany	101
Ulises De La Cruz	Ecuador	101
Ahmed Shobair	Egypt	101
József Bozsik	Hungary	101
Gábor Király	Hungary	101
Daniele De Rossi	Italy	101
Joe Brincat	Malta	101
Phillip Cocu	Netherlands	101
Robin van Persie	Netherlands	101
Vincent Enyeama	Nigeria	101
Thorbjørn Svensson	Norway	101
László Bölöni	Romania	101
Oleg Blokhin	Soviet Union	101
Cesc Fàbregas	Spain	101
Kasey Keller	United States	101
Thomas Sørenson	Denmark	101
Elijah Tana	Zambia	101
Dario Šimic	Croatia	100
Tomáš Rosický	Czech Republic	100
Ulf Kirsten	East Germany / Germany	100
Luis Capurro	Ecuador	100
Levan Kobiashvili	Georgia	100
Angelos Basinas	Greece	100
Carlos Pavón	Honduras	100
Rúnar Kristinsson	Iceland	100
Emad Mohammed	Iraq	100
Siaka Tiéné	Ivory Coast	100
Igors Stepanovs	Latvia	100
Joseph Yobo	Nigeria	100
Henning Berg	Norway	100
Denis Caniza	Paraguay	100
Jorge Soto	Peru	100
Nazri Bin Nasir	Singapore	100
Park Ji-Sung	South Korea	100
Carles Puyol	Spain	100
Joe-Max Moore	United States	100
Earnie Stewart	United States	100
Tony Meola	United States	100

LIGUE 1 GAME WINS

Ligue 1 has been graced by 73 teams in its history with a third of them making a serious impression on league records. The sixth-ranked league in Europe, it has seen one of the most evident shifts between traditional clubs and those benefitting from wealthy benefactors and investors. Those familiar with the current success of PSG might find it surprising to view their win record lagging behind clubs with long histories such as Sochaux, Metz and Stade Rennais.

Club	Wins
SO MONTPELLIER	104
GUINGAMP	108
LORIENT	125
CO ROUBAIX	130
AJACCIO	131
TOULON	134
BREST	140
STADE FRANÇAIS	143
TROYES	148
LAVAL	157
CAEN	157
RED STAR	168
FC NANCY	181
SÈTE	198
ROUEN	233
CANNES	246
LE HAVRE	257
TOULOUSE FC	269
ANGERS	284
SEDAN	291
MONTPELLIER	291
TOULOUSE	326
NANCY	366
VALENCIENNES	375
BASTIA	412
RC PARIS	426
NIMES	482
AUXERRE	483
REIMS	513
STRASBOURG	690
PARIS SAINT-GERMAIN	690
METZ	698

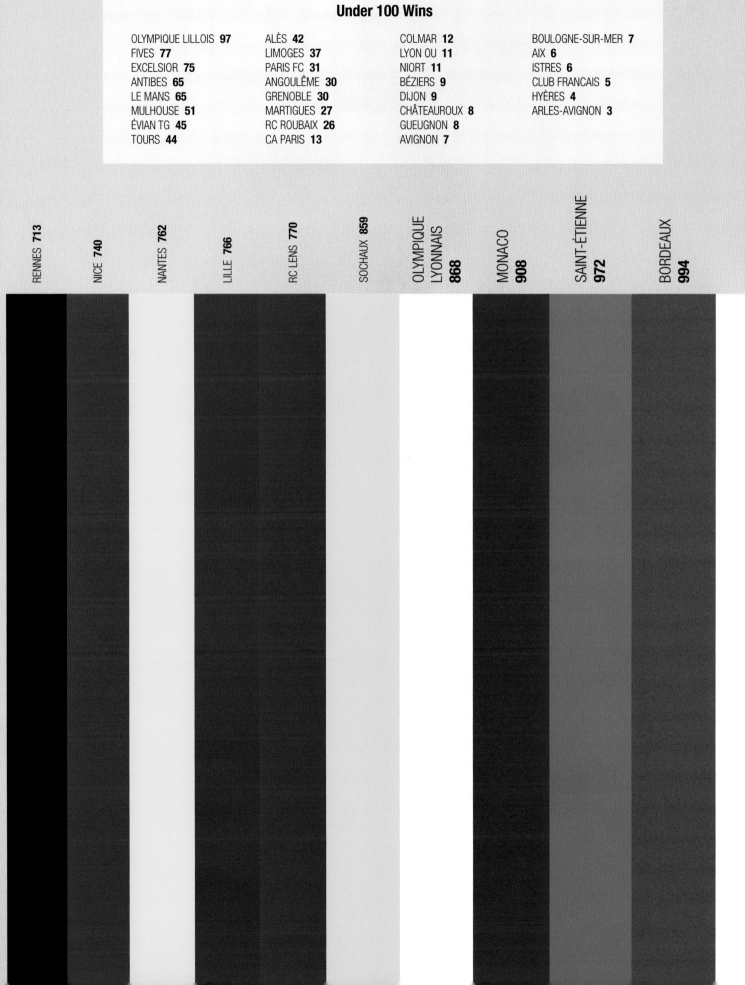

Under 100 Wins

OLYMPIQUE LILLOIS **97**	ALÈS **42**	COLMAR **12**	BOULOGNE-SUR-MER **7**
FIVES **77**	LIMOGES **37**	LYON OU **11**	AIX **6**
EXCELSIOR **75**	PARIS FC **31**	NIORT **11**	ISTRES **6**
ANTIBES **65**	ANGOULÊME **30**	BÉZIERS **9**	CLUB FRANCAIS **5**
LE MANS **65**	GRENOBLE **30**	DIJON **9**	HYÈRES **4**
MULHOUSE **51**	MARTIGUES **27**	CHÂTEAUROUX **8**	ARLES-AVIGNON **3**
ÉVIAN TG **45**	RC ROUBAIX **26**	GUEUGNON **8**	
TOURS **44**	CA PARIS **13**	AVIGNON **7**	

RENNES **713**

NICE **740**

NANTES **762**

LILLE **766**

RC LENS **770**

SOCHAUX **859**

OLYMPIQUE LYONNAIS **868**

MONACO **908**

SAINT-ÉTIENNE **972**

BORDEAUX **994**

MARSEILLE **1031**

2010 WORLD CUP GOALS

The 2010 World Cup in South Africa was the first to be hosted on African soil. To the background blast of thousands of vuvuzelas, it was Ghana and Uruguay who were the surprise packages – separated only by penalties in the quarter-final, after Luis Suárez's villainous last-minute handball save. Spain would triumph over Netherlands in the final of a tournament illuminated by goals such as Brazil's Maicon's incredible effort from an impossible angle, a precision chip from Italy's Fabio Quagliarella and, most memorable of all, South Africa's Siphiwe Tshabalala's powerful left-foot punt...

SIPHIWE TSHABALALA – South Africa vs Mexico

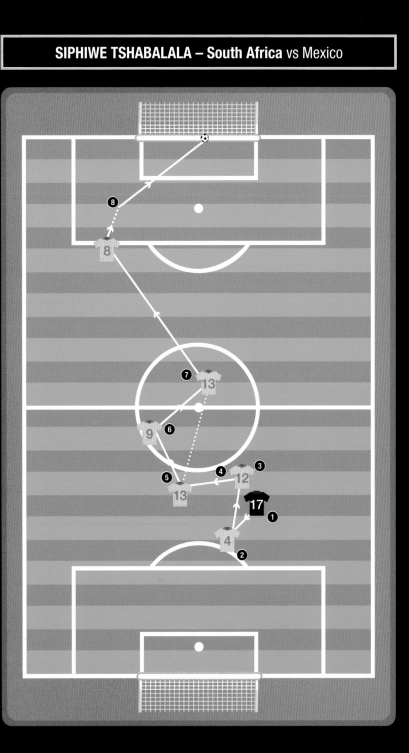

Siphiwe Tshabalala belts the ball hard from the 18-yard box to take South Africa into the lead against Mexico, 11 June 2010.

1. Flick-on **dos Santos**
2. Interception **Mokoena**
3. Ball recovery **Letsholonyane**
4. Pass **Letsholonyane**
5. Pass **Dikgacoi**
6. Pass **Mphela**
7. Through ball **Dikgacoi**
8. Goal **Tshabalala**

KEY

Ball movement ▬▬▬▬ Player with ball ··········

Shot ▬▬▬⚽ Player without ball ··········

MAICON – **Brazil** vs DPR Korea

1. Throw in **Silva**
2. Pass (long ball, chipped) **Melo**
3. Pass **Elano**
4. Goal **Maicon**

MESUT ÖZIL – **Germany** vs Ghana

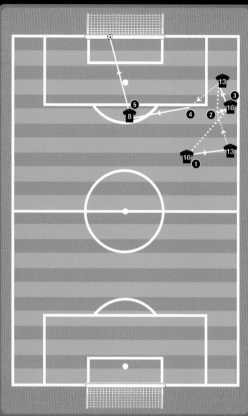

1. Pass **Lahm**
2. Pass **Müller**
3. Pass **Lahm**
4. Pass **Müller**
5. Goal **Özil**

FABIO QUAGLIARELLA – **Italy** vs Slovakia

1. Launch (long ball) **Škrtel**
2. Ball recovery **Chiellini**
3. Pass **Chiellini**
4. Pass **Marchetti**
5. Lay-off **Cannavaro**
6. Pass **Chiellini**
7. Pass **Pirlo**
8. Lay-off **Quagliarella**
9. Pass (chipped, long ball) **Pirlo**
10. Pass **Maggio**
11. Clearance **Zabavnik**
12. Pass **Pirlo**
13. Blocked **De Rossi**
14. Block **Kopúnek**
15. Pass **De Rossi**
16. Goal **Quagliarella**

GIOVANNI VAN BRONCKHORST – **Netherlands** vs Uruguay

1. Pass (long ball) **Kuyt**
2. Pass **de Zeeuw**
3. Pass **Sneijder**
4. Pass **de Zeeuw**
5. Goal **Van Bronckhorst**

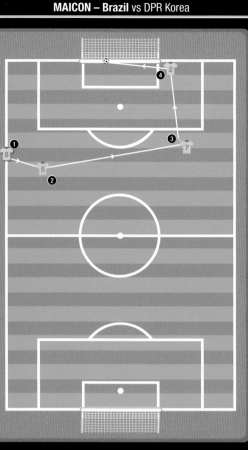

MOST SUCCESSFUL EUROPEAN MANAGERS

1 Bob Paisley

2 Carlo Ancelotti

3 Alex Ferguson

4 Helenio Herrera

5 Nereo Rocco

6 José Mourinho

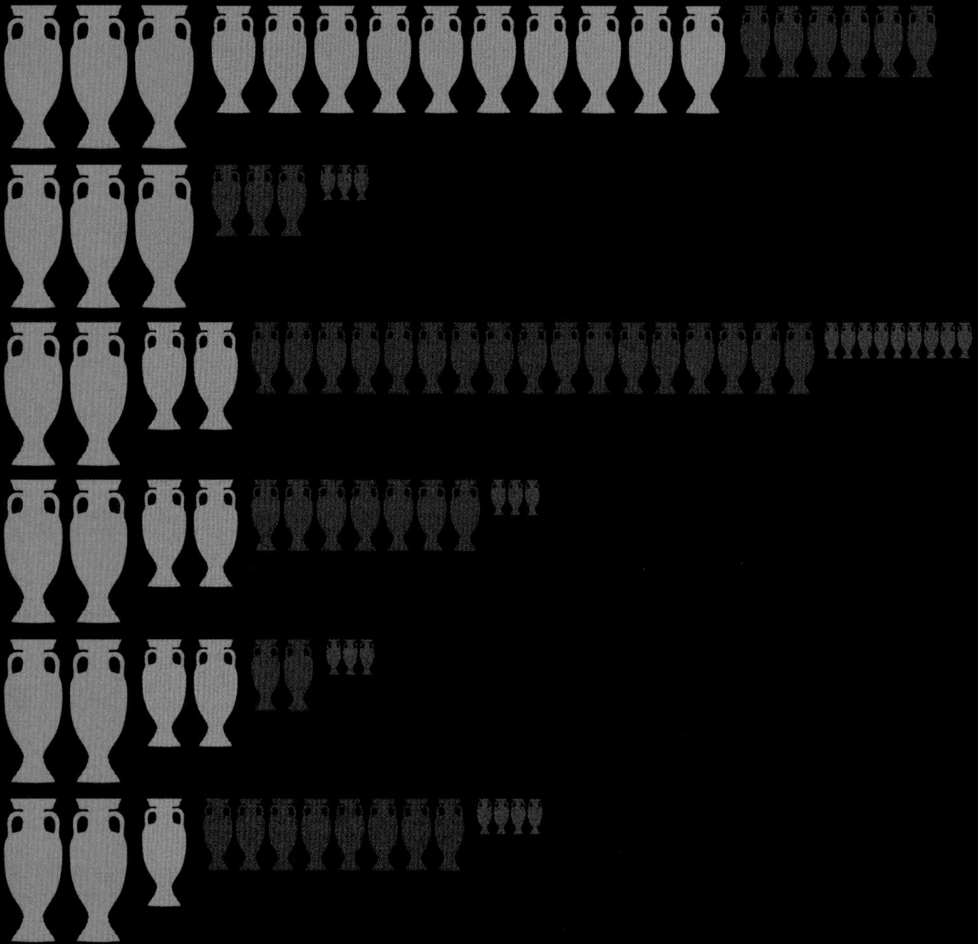

No matter how wealthy the club, it is still a magnificent feat to guide a team to a major league title. It is something else entirely to take them to European success. Repeating this achievement takes a coach to legendary status. Separating the greatest from the great, however, is a tougher call. How do we rank Bob Paisley's European and League titles against Helenio Herrera's record? And how greater an accomplishment are the against-the-odds European triumphs of José Mourinho's Porto or Jock Stein's Celtic? We may never be able to settle that argument objectively, but the data tells its own story...

11 Ernst Happel

12 Josep Guardiola

13 Béla Guttmann

14 Ștefan Kovács

15 Vicente del Bosque

16 Brian Clough

17 Arrigo Sacchi

18 Dettmar Cramer

19 Giovanni Trapattoni

20 Johan Cruyff

21 Raymond Goethals

22 Rafael Benítez

23 Udo Lattek

24 Rinus Michels

25 Louis van Gaal

26 Jock Stein

27 Fabio Capello

28 Guus Hiddink

29 Emerich Jenei

30 Matt Busby

31 Marcello Lippi

32 Ljupko Petrović

33 Artur Jorge

34 Frank Rijkaard

35 Joe Fagan

36 Roberto Di Matteo

37 Tony Barton

KEY

Champions League / European Cup

Domestic League Titles

Other European (UEFA Cup, UEFA League, Intertoto Cup, Fairs Cup, Cup-Winners Cup)

Domestic Cups (premier tournament in nation only e.g. FA Cup, Copa Del Rey, DFB Pokal)

155

LIGUE 1 GOALS

Seen by many of the world's richest clubs as a nursery for emerging young players, Ligue 1 has given renowned strikers such as Thierry Henry, Didier Drogba, Karim Benzema and Eden Hazard their first-team breaks. Zlatan Ibrahimović, a rare star import to the league, has hit 75 goals in just 91 Ligue 1 games, but is still a long way from catching record holder Delio Onnis (an Argentinian nicknamed "The Italian"!) who netted an unbelievable 299 goals in 449 appearances between 1972 and 1986.

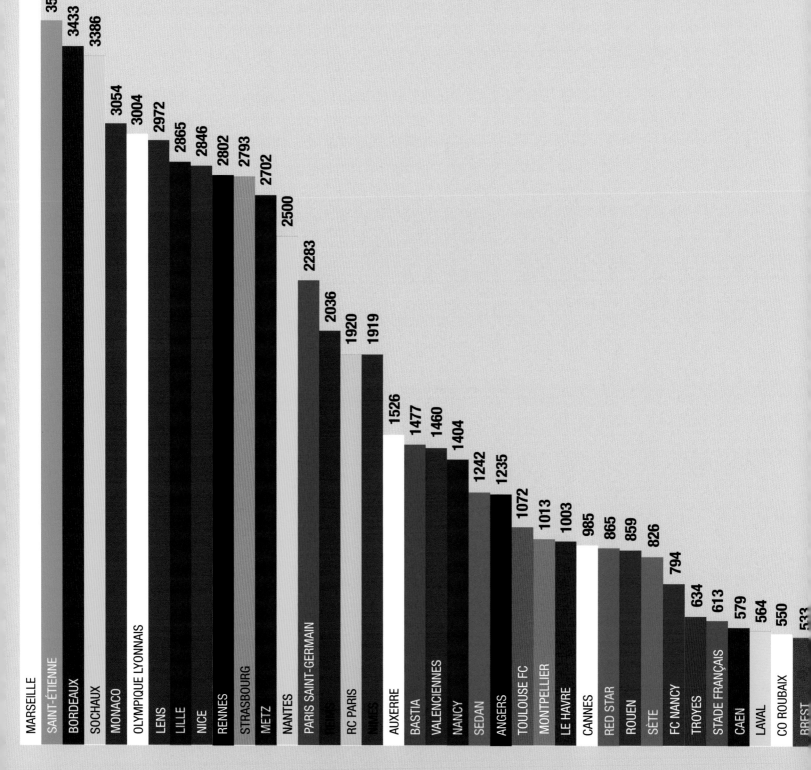

Club	Goals
MARSEILLE	3740
SAINT-ÉTIENNE	3558
BORDEAUX	3433
SOCHAUX	3386
MONACO	3054
OLYMPIQUE LYONNAIS	3004
LENS	2972
LILLE	2865
NICE	2846
RENNES	2802
STRASBOURG	2793
METZ	2702
NANTES	2500
PARIS SAINT-GERMAIN	2283
REIMS	2036
RC PARIS	1920
NIMES	1919
AUXERRE	1526
BASTIA	1477
VALENCIENNES	1460
NANCY	1404
SEDAN	1242
ANGERS	1235
TOULOUSE FC	1072
MONTPELLIER	1013
LE HAVRE	1003
CANNES	985
RED STAR	865
ROUEN	859
SETE	826
FC NANCY	794
TROYES	634
STADE FRANÇAIS	613
CAEN	579
LAVAL	564
CO ROUBAIX	550
BREST	533

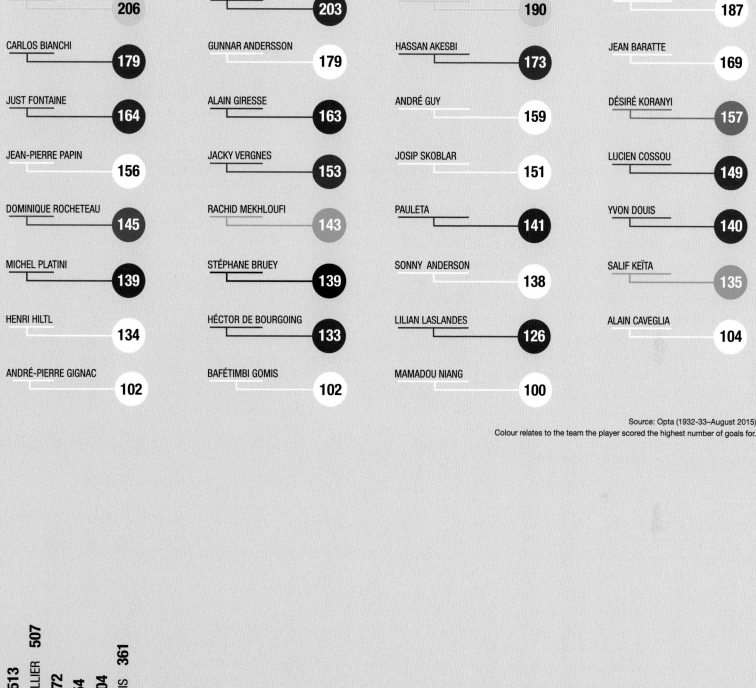

DELIO ONNIS **299**

THADÉE CISOWSKI **206**

CARLOS BIANCHI **179**

JUST FONTAINE **164**

JEAN-PIERRE PAPIN **156**

DOMINIQUE ROCHETEAU **145**

MICHEL PLATINI **139**

HENRI HILTL **134**

ANDRÉ-PIERRE GIGNAC **102**

BERNARD LACOMBE **255**

ROGER PIANTONI **203**

GUNNAR ANDERSSON **179**

ALAIN GIRESSE **163**

JACKY VERGNES **153**

RACHID MEKHLOUFI **143**

STÉPHANE BRUEY **139**

HÉCTOR DE BOURGOING **133**

BAFÉTIMBI GOMIS **102**

HERVÉ REVELLI **216**

JOSEPH UJLAKI **190**

HASSAN AKESBI **173**

ANDRÉ GUY **159**

JOSIP SKOBLAR **151**

PAULETA **141**

SONNY ANDERSON **138**

LILIAN LASLANDES **126**

MAMADOU NIANG **100**

ROGER COURTOIS **210**

FLEURY DI NALLO **187**

JEAN BARATTE **169**

DÉSIRÉ KORANYI **157**

LUCIEN COSSOU **149**

YVON DOUIS **140**

SALIF KEÏTA **135**

ALAIN CAVEGLIA **104**

Source: Opta (1932-33–August 2015)
Colour relates to the team the player scored the highest number of goals for.

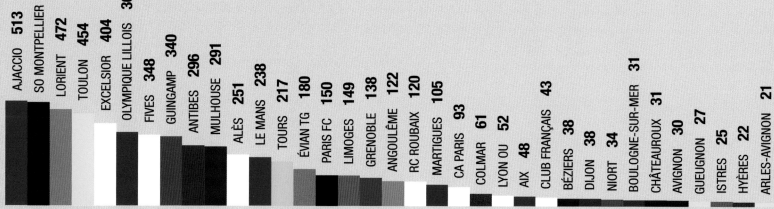

AJACCIO **513**
SO MONTPELLIER **507**
LORIENT **472**
TOULON **454**
EXCELSIOR **404**
OLYMPIQUE LILLOIS **361**
FIVES **348**
GUINGAMP **340**
ANTIBES **296**
MULHOUSE **291**
ALÈS **251**
LE MANS **238**
TOURS **217**
ÉVIAN TG **180**
PARIS FC **150**
LIMOGES **149**
GRENOBLE **138**
ANGOULÊME **122**
RC ROUBAIX **120**
MARTIGUES **105**
CA PARIS **93**
COLMAR **61**
LYON OU **52**
AIX **48**
CLUB FRANÇAIS **43**
BÉZIERS **38**
DIJON **38**
NIORT **34**
BOULOGNE-SUR-MER **31**
CHÂTEAUROUX **31**
AVIGNON **30**
GUEUGNON **27**
ISTRES **25**
HYÈRES **22**
ARLES-AVIGNON **21**

WORLD CUP FOULS AND CARDS

Behind these figures lie some of the most controversial and downright disgraceful moments in World Cup history. They include the South Africa vs Denmark tie in 1998, which resulted in seven yellow and three red cards, plus the three yellows in one match collected by Josip Šimunić for Croatia against Australia in 2006. If you thought that was bad, let's not forget the final itself, which saw two Argentinians sent off in 1990 and Zinedine Zidane seeing red after a confrontation with Marco Materazzi in 2006.

ARGENTINA 112	GERMANY 110	BRAZIL 95	ITALY 89	NETHERLANDS 89	MEXICO 67
SPAIN 65	URUGUAY 61	KOREA REPUBLIC 60	FRANCE 56	ENGLAND 50	USA 48
CAMEROON 45	CHILE 43	POLAND 40	PORTUGAL 40	PARAGUAY 39	SWEDEN 38
BELGIUM 37	GHANA 33	CROATIA 33	BULGARIA 33	ROMANIA 32	DENMARK 31
JAPAN 31	SWITZERLAND 31	COSTA RICA 30	TUNISIA 28	YUGOSLAVIA 27	NIGERIA 27
AUSTRIA 24	ECUADOR 23	AUSTRALIA 23	COLOMBIA 22	SAUDI ARABIA 22	USSR 21
SOUTH AFRICA 20	GREECE 19	SLOVENIA 19	MOROCCO 19	IVORY COAST 19	RUSSIA 19
IRAN 18	SERBIA 18	TURKEY 17	SCOTLAND 17	CZECHOSLOVAKIA 17	REPUBLIC OF IRELAND 16
ALGERIA 14	SENEGAL 14	HONDURAS 13	NORWAY 13	UKRAINE 12	SLOVAKIA 11
PERU 10	EAST GERMANY 10	ANGOLA 9	NORTHERN IRELAND 9	EL SALVADOR 9	TOGO 8
IRAQ 8	TRINIDAD & TOBAGO 8	UNITED ARAB EMIRATES 6	BOLIVIA 6	NEW ZEALAND 6	CHINA PR 5
CZECH REPUBLIC 5	JAMAICA 4	EGYPT 4	HUNGARY 4	ISRAEL 4	HAITI 3
KUWAIT 3	BOSNIA & HERZEGOVINA 3	DPR KOREA 2	ZAIRE 2	CANADA 1	

ARGENTINA 10 CAMEROON 8 URUGUAY 8 NETHERLANDS 7 ITALY 6 PORTUGAL 6

BRAZIL 6 MEXICO 6 FRANCE 6 GERMANY 5 CROATIA 4 USA 4

AUSTRALIA 4 ENGLAND 3 DENMARK 3 BELGIUM 3 BULGARIA 3 SWEDEN 3

SERBIA 3 ALGERIA 2 CHILE 2 TURKEY 2 KOREA REPUBLIC 2 BOLIVIA 2

PARAGUAY 2 HUNGARY 2 USSR 2 HONDURAS 2 CZECHOSLOVAKIA 2 SOUTH AFRICA 2

CZECH REPUBLIC 2 TUNISIA 1 CANADA 1 POLAND 1 JAMAICA 1 GREECE 1

SLOVENIA 1 TOGO 1 ANGOLA 1 UNITED ARAB EMIRATES 1 COSTA RICA 1 UKRAINE 1

IVORY COAST 1 SENEGAL 1 GHANA 1 IRAQ 1 YUGOSLAVIA 1 TRINIDAD & TOBAGO 1

ZAIRE 1 SAUDI ARABIA 1 RUSSIA 1 ECUADOR 1 SCOTLAND 1 ROMANIA 1

SWITZERLAND 1 NORTHERN IRELAND 1 CHINA PR 1 AUSTRIA 1 NIGERIA 1 SPAIN 1

Total Fouls 1966–2014

GERMANY 1339	SWEDEN 467	SWITZERLAND 291	ALGERIA 205	TURKEY 117	TOGO 56
BRAZIL 1212	CAMEROON 438	COLOMBIA 284	MOROCCO 202	EL SALVADOR 109	EGYPT 52
ARGENTINA 1153	USSR 421	AUSTRIA 277	CZECHOSLOVAKIA 197	UKRAINE 108	CZECH REPUBLIC 52
ITALY 1147	PORTUGAL 399	ROMANIA 270	SAUDI ARABIA 184	SLOVENIA 103	ZAIRE 51
NETHERLANDS 996	USA 396	DENMARK 269	ECUADOR 184	SENEGAL 100	TRINIDAD AND TOBAGO 50
FRANCE 781	BULGARIA 383	COSTA RICA 252	SOUTH AFRICA 157	SERBIA 89	UNITED ARAB EMIRATES 48
ENGLAND 773	CHILE 357	AUSTRALIA 249	IVORY COAST 151	NEW ZEALAND 88	CANADA 45
SPAIN 735	PARAGUAY 348	IRAN 246	GREECE 150	DPR KOREA 86	BOSNIA AND HERZEGOVINA 41
MEXICO 683	YUGOSLAVIA 343	REPUBLIC OF IRELAND 238	NORTHERN IRELAND 150	ANGOLA 73	BOLIVIA 40
URUGUAY 652	JAPAN 319	TUNISIA 237	RUSSIA 141	SLOVAKIA 69	CHINA PR 40
BELGIUM 592	SCOTLAND 312	GHANA 233	HONDURAS 135	ISRAEL 68	HAITI 34
POLAND 574	NIGERIA 296	PERU 215	NORWAY 126	IRAQ 61	KUWAIT 32
KOREA REPUBLIC 516	CROATIA 291	HUNGARY 206	EAST GERMANY 119	JAMAICA 56	

Source: Opta (August 2015)

BUNDESLIGA GOALS

The German Bundesliga is the go-to league for goals, with the highest goals-per-game ratio in Europe – 2.75 a game. As in all Bundesliga records, it's hard to ignore Bayern München. They are the only team to net 100 goals in a season (101 in 1971–72) and in Gerd Müller, seven-time leading goalscorer, they have arguably the game's greatest ever goal poacher. Only Robert Lewandowski, also now a Bayern München player, steals some headlines with his incredible five goals in nine minutes against Wolfsburg in September 2015.

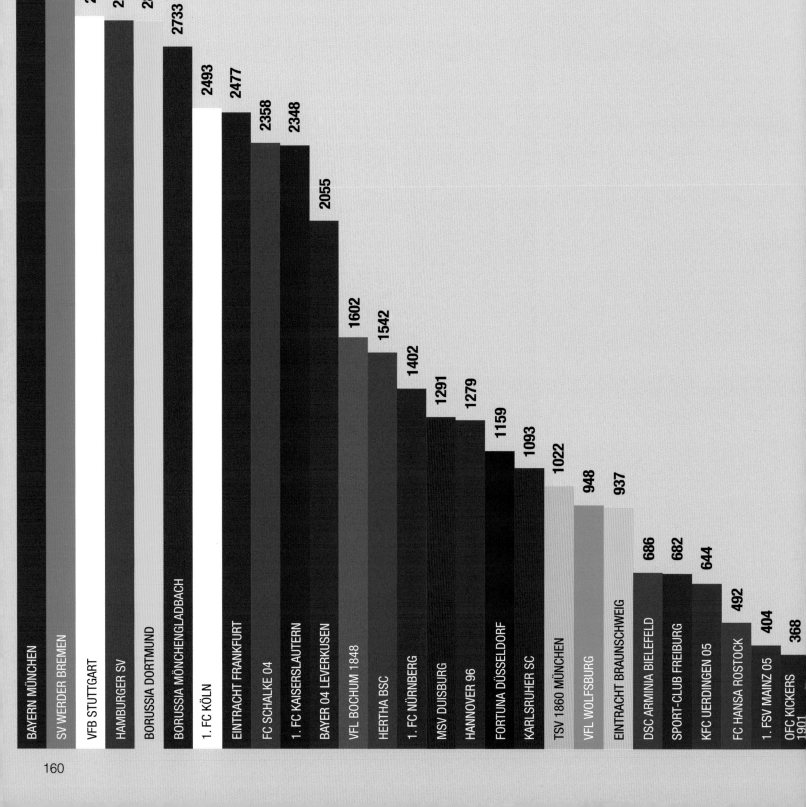

Club	Goals
BAYERN MÜNCHEN	3689
SV WERDER BREMEN	2925
VFB STUTTGART	2851
HAMBURGER SV	2835
BORUSSIA DORTMUND	2833
BORUSSIA MÖNCHENGLADBACH	2733
1. FC KÖLN	2493
EINTRACHT FRANKFURT	2477
FC SCHALKE 04	2358
1. FC KAISERSLAUTERN	2348
BAYER 04 LEVERKUSEN	2055
VFL BOCHUM 1848	1602
HERTHA BSC	1542
1. FC NÜRNBERG	1402
MSV DUISBURG	1291
HANNOVER 96	1279
FORTUNA DÜSSELDORF	1159
KARLSRUHER SC	1093
TSV 1860 MÜNCHEN	1022
VFL WOLFSBURG	948
EINTRACHT BRAUNSCHWEIG	937
DSC ARMINIA BIELEFELD	686
SPORT-CLUB FREIBURG	682
KFC UERDINGEN 05	644
FC HANSA ROSTOCK	492
1. FSV MAINZ 05	404
OFC KICKERS 1901	368

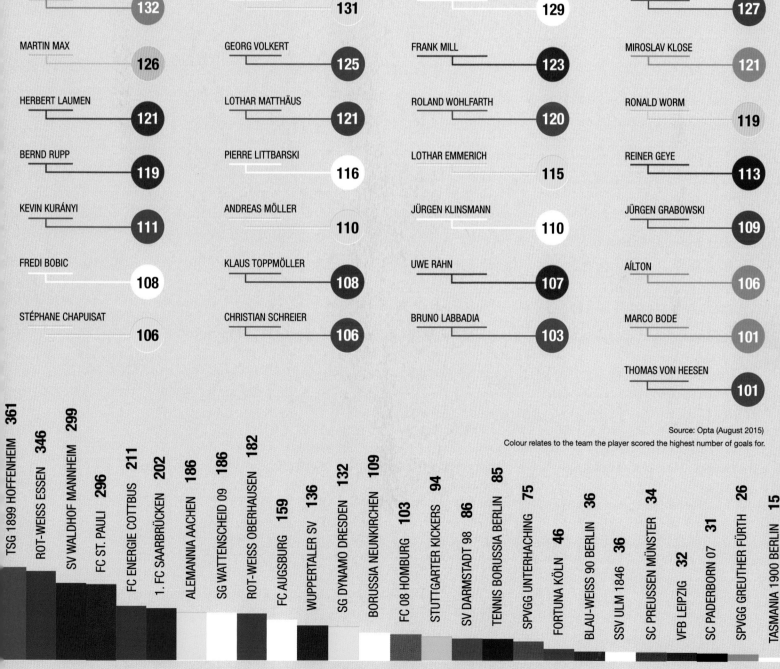

GERD MÜLLER **365**	KLAUS FISCHER **268**	JUPP HEYNCKES **220**	MANFRED BURGSMÜLLER **213**
ULF KIRSTEN **182**	STEFAN KUNTZ **179**	KLAUS ALLOFS **177**	DIETER MÜLLER **177**
CLAUDIO PIZARRO **176**	JOHANNES LÖHR **166**	KARL-HEINZ RUMMENIGGE **162**	BERND HÖLZENBEIN **160**
FRITZ WALTER **157**	THOMAS ALLOFS **148**	BERND NICKEL **141**	MARIO GÓMEZ **138**
UWE SEELER **137**	HORST HRUBESCH **136**	STEFAN KIESSLING **135**	GIOVANE ÉLBER **133**
RUDI VÖLLER **132**	MICHAEL ZORC **131**	KARL ALLGÖWER **129**	DIETER HOENESS **127**
MARTIN MAX **126**	GEORG VOLKERT **125**	FRANK MILL **123**	MIROSLAV KLOSE **121**
HERBERT LAUMEN **121**	LOTHAR MATTHÄUS **121**	ROLAND WOHLFARTH **120**	RONALD WORM **119**
BERND RUPP **119**	PIERRE LITTBARSKI **116**	LOTHAR EMMERICH **115**	REINER GEYE **113**
KEVIN KURÁNYI **111**	ANDREAS MÖLLER **110**	JÜRGEN KLINSMANN **110**	JÜRGEN GRABOWSKI **109**
FREDI BOBIC **108**	KLAUS TOPPMÖLLER **108**	UWE RAHN **107**	AÍLTON **106**
STÉPHANE CHAPUISAT **106**	CHRISTIAN SCHREIER **106**	BRUNO LABBADIA **103**	MARCO BODE **101**
			THOMAS VON HEESEN **101**

Source: Opta (August 2015)

Colour relates to the team the player scored the highest number of goals for.

TSG 1899 HOFFENHEIM **361**
ROT-WEISS ESSEN **346**
SV WALDHOF MANNHEIM **299**
FC ST. PAULI **296**
FC ENERGIE COTTBUS **211**
1. FC SAARBRÜCKEN **202**
ALEMANNIA AACHEN **186**
SG WATTENSCHEID 09 **186**
ROT-WEISS OBERHAUSEN **182**
FC AUGSBURG **159**
WUPPERTALER SV **136**
SG DYNAMO DRESDEN **132**
BORUSSIA NEUNKIRCHEN **109**
FC 08 HOMBURG **103**
STUTTGARTER KICKERS **94**
SV DARMSTADT 98 **86**
TENNIS BORUSSIA BERLIN **85**
SPVGG UNTERHACHING **75**
FORTUNA KÖLN **46**
BLAU-WEISS 90 BERLIN **36**
SSV ULM 1846 **36**
SC PREUSSEN MÜNSTER **34**
VFB LEIPZIG **32**
SC PADERBORN 07 **31**
SPVGG GREUTHER FÜRTH **26**
TASMANIA 1900 BERLIN **15**

WOMEN'S WORLD CUP GOALSCORERS

Since Chinese defender Ma Li scored the first goal in Women's World Cup history, 770 goals have been scored in the finals. Among these are memorable strikes such as Germany's Birgit Prinz's stunning volley in 2003 and Brazilian Marta's unstoppable flick and finish in 2007. The 2015 World Cup competition was graced by fabulous long-range shots from England's Lucy

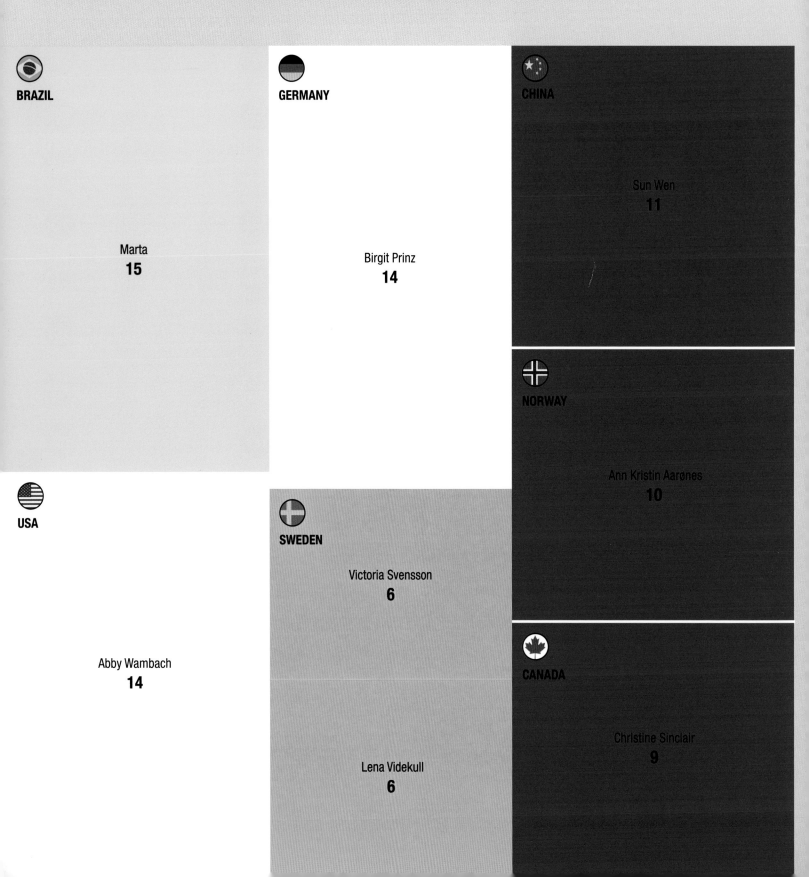

BRAZIL

Marta
15

GERMANY

Birgit Prinz
14

CHINA

Sun Wen
11

NORWAY

Ann Kristin Aarønes
10

USA

Abby Wambach
14

SWEDEN

Victoria Svensson
6

Lena Videkull
6

CANADA

Christine Sinclair
9

Bronze and France's Amandine Henry, but will surely be remembered most for the USA's Carli Lloyd's hat-trick in the final, capped by a sensational right foot strike (and lob) from the halfway line. The goal was was awarded Goal of the Tournament.

Source: Opta (August 2015)

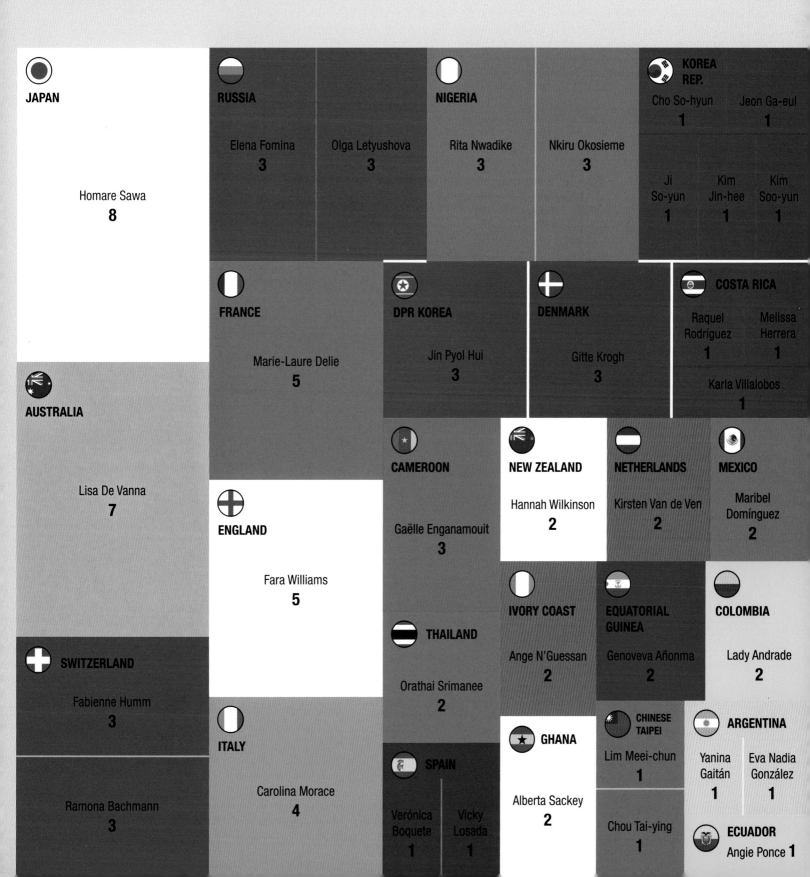

JAPAN

Homare Sawa
8

RUSSIA

Elena Fomina
3

Olga Letyushova
3

NIGERIA

Rita Nwadike
3

Nkiru Okosieme
3

KOREA REP.

Cho So-hyun
1

Jeon Ga-eul
1

Ji So-yun
1

Kim Jin-hee
1

Kim Soo-yun
1

FRANCE

Marie-Laure Delie
5

DPR KOREA

Jin Pyol Hui
3

DENMARK

Gitte Krogh
3

COSTA RICA

Raquel Rodríguez
1

Melissa Herrera
1

Karla Villalobos
1

AUSTRALIA

Lisa De Vanna
7

ENGLAND

Fara Williams
5

CAMEROON

Gaëlle Enganamouit
3

NEW ZEALAND

Hannah Wilkinson
2

NETHERLANDS

Kirsten Van de Ven
2

MEXICO

Maribel Domínguez
2

THAILAND

Orathai Srimanee
2

IVORY COAST

Ange N'Guessan
2

EQUATORIAL GUINEA

Genoveva Añonma
2

COLOMBIA

Lady Andrade
2

SWITZERLAND

Fabienne Humm
3

ITALY

Carolina Morace
4

Ramona Bachmann
3

SPAIN

Verónica Boquete
1

Vicky Losada
1

GHANA

Alberta Sackey
2

CHINESE TAIPEI

Lim Meei-chun
1

Chou Tai-ying
1

ARGENTINA

Yanina Gaitán
1

Eva Nadia González
1

ECUADOR

Angie Ponce **1**

MLS GAME WINS PER CLUB

The forerunner to the MLS was the ill-fated North American Soccer League (NASL), a division that relied too heavily on imported celebrity players such as Pelé and Franz Beckenbauer to have home success. The MLS too once enlisted the assistance of foreign stars to boost its appeal, including David Beckham, Cuauhtémoc Blanco, Andrea Pirlo and David Villa, but in recent years it has established itself as a sustainable league attracting an average of 18,600 fans a game, global TV interest and is dedicated to nurturing home-grown talent. Today, the MLS is the world's fastest growing sport.

NEW YORK CITY FC **10**
ORLANDO CITY SC **12**
MIAMI FUSION **49**
MONTREAL IMPACT **49**
VANCOUVER WHITECAPS **58**
PHILADELPHIA UNION **61**
PORTLAND TIMBERS **65**
TAMPA BAY MUTINY **75**
TORONTO FC **77**
SPORTING KANSAS CITY **81**
CHIVAS USA **93**
SEATTLE SOUNDERS **116**
HOUSTON DYNAMO **137**
REAL SALT LAKE **138**
KANSAS CITY WIZARDS **175**
SAN JOSE EARTHQUAKES **215**
COLORADO RAPIDS **234**

NEW ENGLAND REVOLUTION **239**

CHICAGO FIRE **244**

NEW YORK RED BULLS **253**

FC DALLAS **257**

COLUMBUS CREW SC **265**

D.C. UNITED **270**

LA GALAXY **324**

AFRICAN CUP OF NATIONS RECORDS BY NATION

The biennial African Cup of Nations tournament, contested by the nations of the Confederation of African Football, has been played since 1957. Just Egypt, Sudan and Ethiopia played the first two tournaments before it was enlarged to include four (1962), six (1963), eight (1968), 12 (1992) and then 16 teams (1996). Because of its apartheid policy South Africa was excluded from the competition until 1996. The tournament moved to odd-numbered years from 2013 to avoid conflict with the World Cup; this meant there were tournaments in consecutive years.

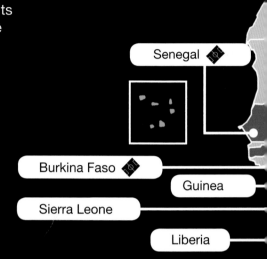

Senegal

Burkina Faso

Guinea

Sierra Leone

Liberia

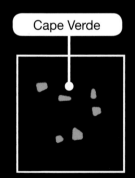

Cape Verde

Ivory Coast celebrate winning the African Cup of Nations in 2015. They overcame Ghana on penalties to secure their second continent tournament win.

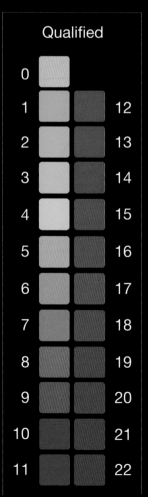

Qualified

0			
1			12
2			13
3			14
4			15
5			16
6			17
7			18
8			19
9			20
10			21
11			22

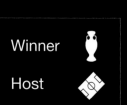

Winner

Host

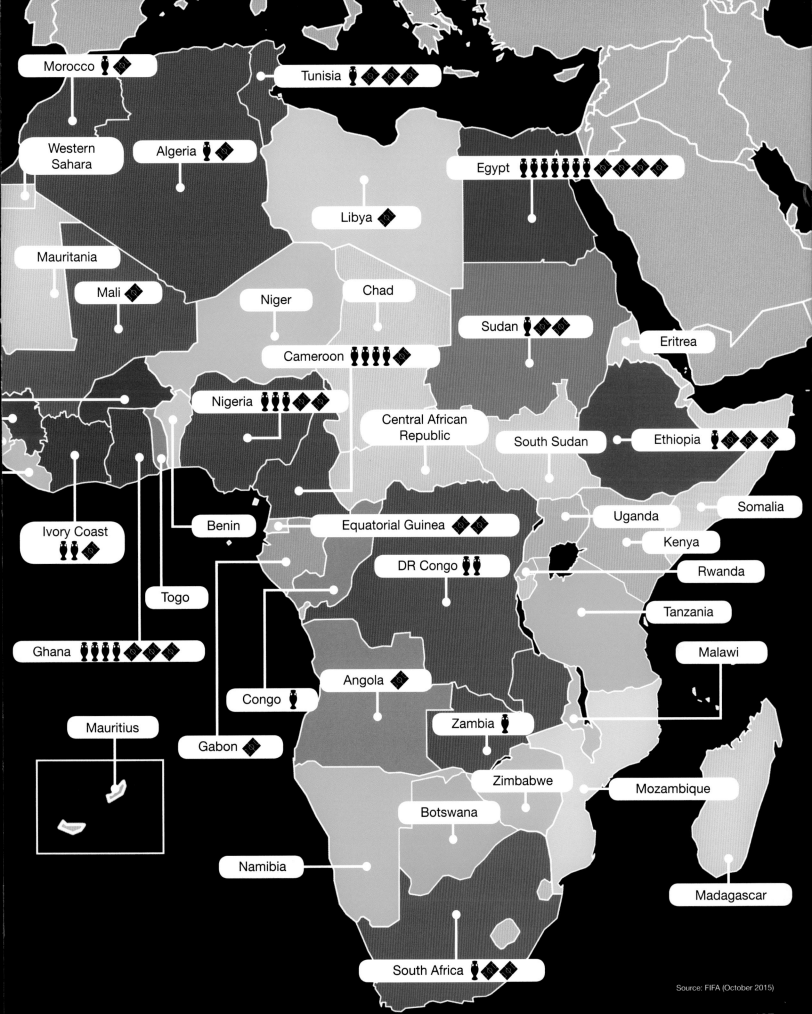

167

2014 WORLD CUP GOALS

There were too many unforgettable stories in Brazil's 2014 World Cup: reigning champions Spain crashing out in the group stage; the attacking zest displayed by Mexico, Costa Rica, USA and Colombia; Brazil's semi-final capitulation; and the superb football played by worthy winners, Germany. Miroslav Klose was crowned the competition's top scorer, Colombia's James Rodríguez scored from a top-class chest, swivel and volley smash, Robin van Persie perfected a diving header and Mario Götze hit a volley worthy of winning a World Cup final.

ROBIN VAN PERSIE – Netherlands vs Spain

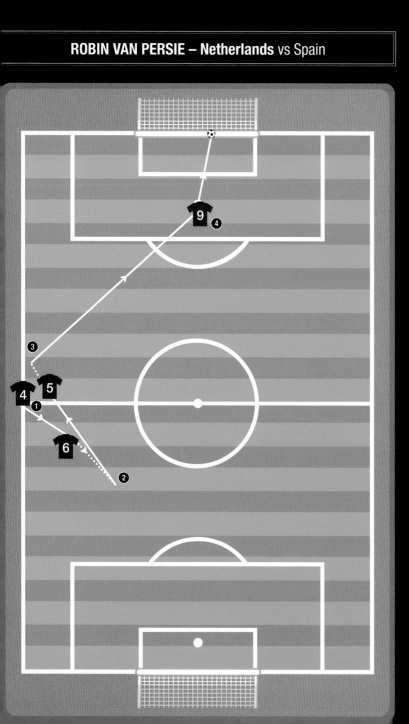

The Netherlands' Robin van Persie scores with his head to equalize in the match against Spain, 13 June 2014.

1. Throw in **Martins Indi**
2. Pass **De Jong**
3. Through ball (chipped, long ball) **Blind**
4. Goal (head) **Van Persie**

KEY

Ball movement	————	Player with ball ·············
Shot	——⚽	Player without ball ··········

MARIO GÖTZE – Germany vs Argentina

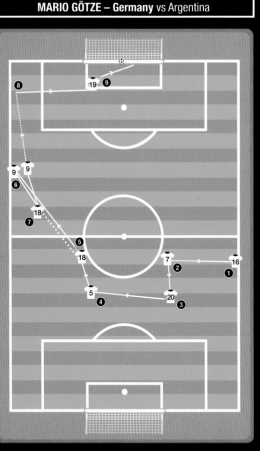

1. Free kick taken **Lahm**
2. Pass **Schweinsteiger**
3. Pass **Boateng**
4. Pass **Hummels**
5. Pass **Kroos**
6. Pass **Schürrle**
7. Pass **Kroos**
8. Pass (cross, chipped) **Schürrle**
9. Goal **Götze**

LIONEL MESSI – Argentina vs Bosnia

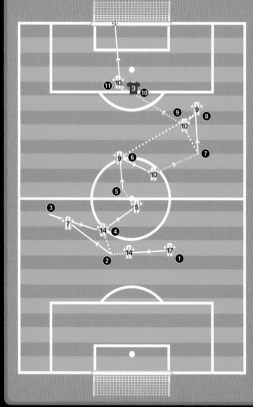

1. Free kick taken **Fernández**
2. Pass **Mascherano**
3. Pass **Di María**
4. Pass **Mascherano**
5. Pass **Gago**
6. Lay-off **Higuaín**
7. Pass **Messi**
8. Lay-off **Higuaín**
9. Take on **Messi**
10. Challenge **Bičakčić**
11. Goal **Messi**

JAMES RODRÍGUEZ – Colombia vs Uruguay

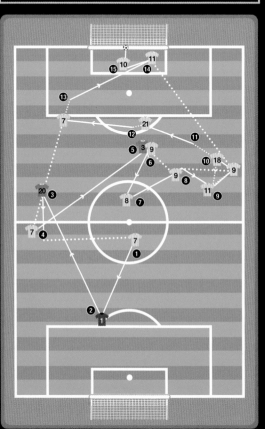

1. Pass **Armero**
2. Launch (long ball) **Ospina**
3. Head pass **González**
4. Pass (chipped, long ball) **Armero**
5. Head pass **Godín**
6. Pass (chipped) **Gutiérrez**
7. Pass **Aguilar**
8. Pass **Gutiérrez**
9. Pass **Cuadrado**
10. Pass **Zúñiga**
11. Pass **Gutiérrez**
12. Pass **Martínez**
13. Pass (cross, chipped) **Armero**
14. Head pass **Cuadrado**
15. Goal **Rodríguez**

DAVID VILLA – Spain vs Australia

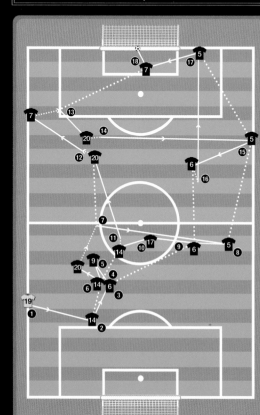

1. Throw In (long ball) **McGowan**
2. Interception **Alonso**
3. Ball recovery **Iniesta**
4. Pass **Iniesta**
5. Pass **Torres**
6. Pass **Alonso**
7. Pass (long ball) **Cazorla**
8. Pass **Juanfran**
9. Pass **Iniesta**
10. Pass **Koke**
11. Pass **Alonso**
12. Pass **Cazorla**
13. Pass **Villa**
14. Pass (chipped, long ball) **Cazorla**
15. Pass **Juanfran**
16. Pass **Iniesta**
17. Pass **Juanfran**
18. Goal **Villa**

Infographic Contents

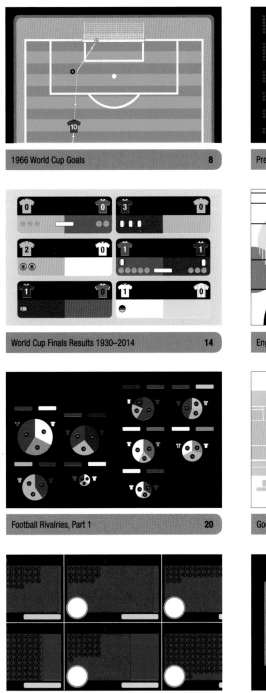
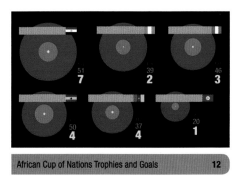
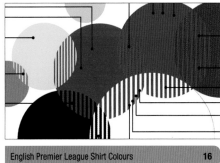

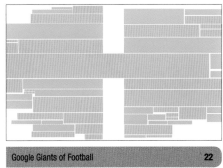
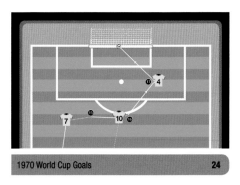
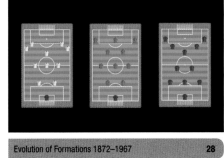
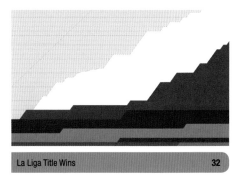
170

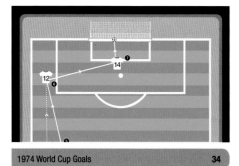

Serie A Title Winners 36

European Cup & Champions League Record Goalscorers 38

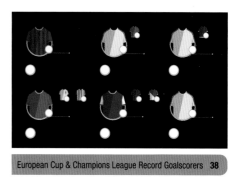

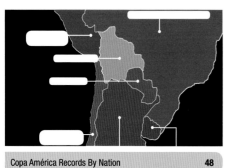

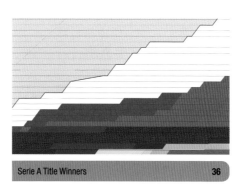

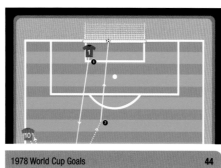

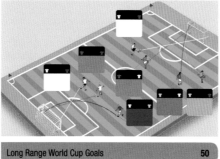

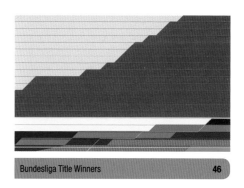

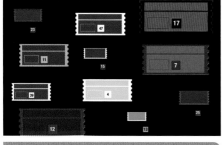

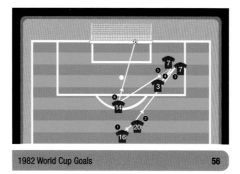

World Cup Goals By Body Part 60

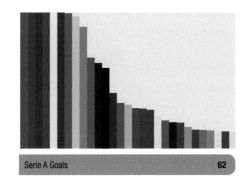

Serie A Goals 62

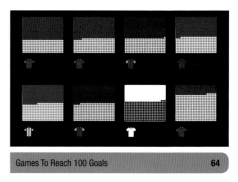

Games To Reach 100 Goals 64

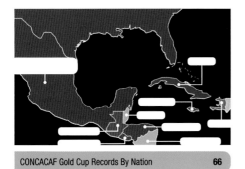

CONCACAF Gold Cup Records By Nation 66

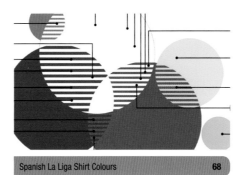

Spanish La Liga Shirt Colours 68

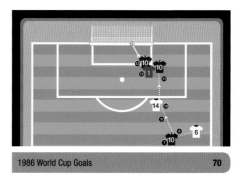

1986 World Cup Goals 70

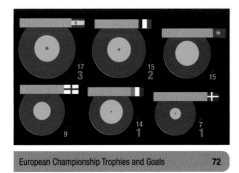

European Championship Trophies and Goals 72

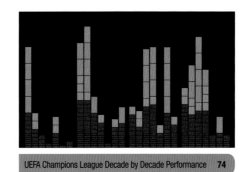

UEFA Champions League Decade by Decade Performance 74

FIFA World Cup Wins By Country 76

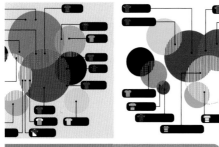

French Ligue 1 / Scottish Premier League Shirt Colours 78

Premier League Game Wins 80

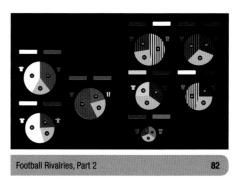

Football Rivalries, Part 2 82

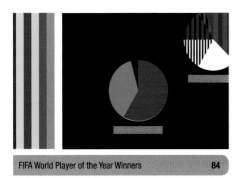

FIFA World Player of the Year Winners 84

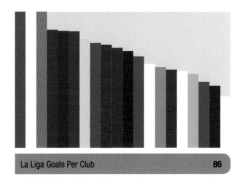

La Liga Goals Per Club 86

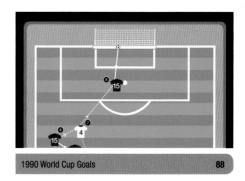

1990 World Cup Goals 88

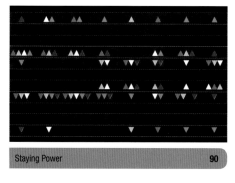

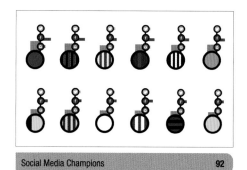

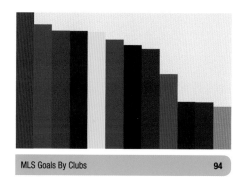

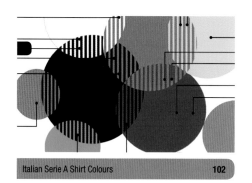

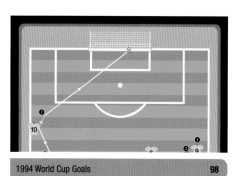

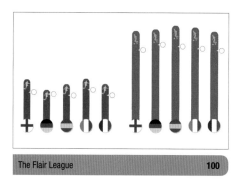

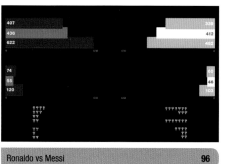

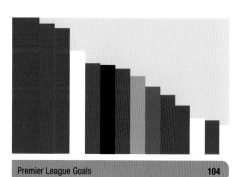

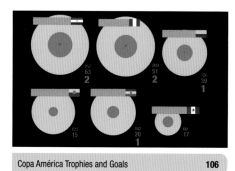

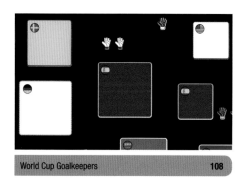

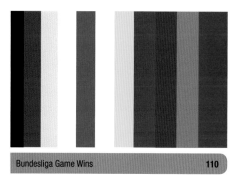

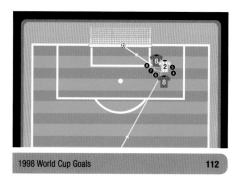

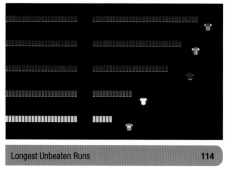

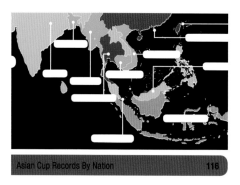

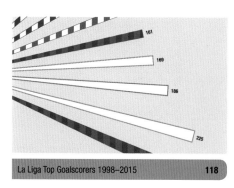

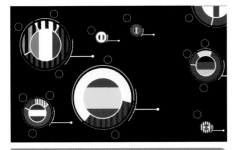

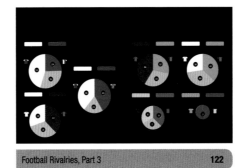

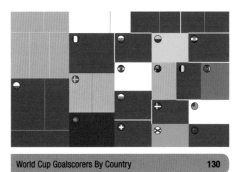

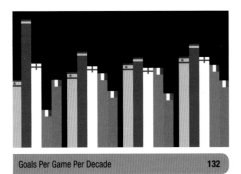

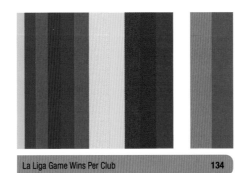

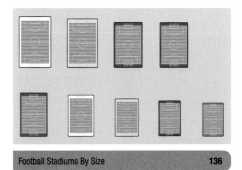

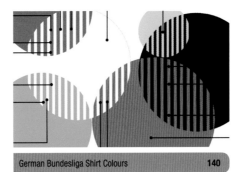

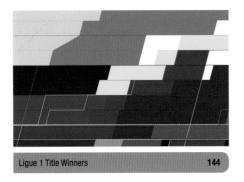

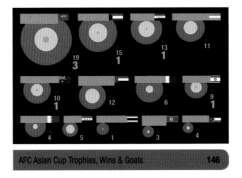

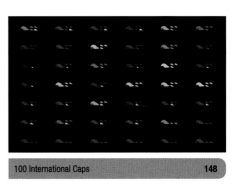

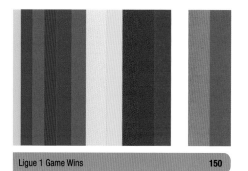

Ligue 1 Game Wins | 150

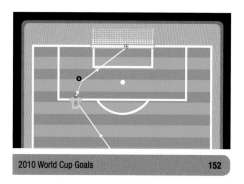

2010 World Cup Goals | 152

Most Successful European Managers | 154

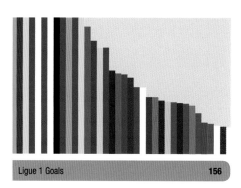

Ligue 1 Goals | 156

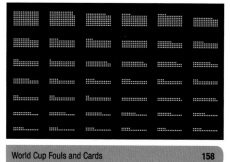

World Cup Fouls and Cards | 158

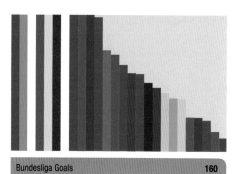

Bundesliga Goals | 160

Women's World Cup Goalscorers | 162

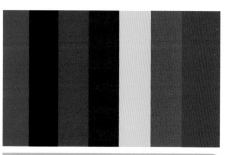

MLS Game Wins Per Club | 164

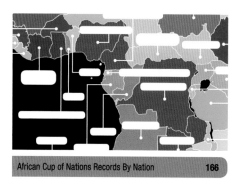

African Cup of Nations Records By Nation | 166

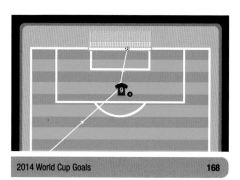

2014 World Cup Goals | 168

Acknowledgements

The publishers would like to thank the following sources for their kind permission to reproduce the pictures in this book.

Colorsport: 133

Getty Images: /AFP: 70; /Allsport: 56; /Matthew Ashton: 66; /Bentley Archive/ Popperfoto: 8; /Marco Bertorello/AFP: 100; /Khaled Desouki/AFP: 166; /Denis Doyle: 31, 58; /Laurence Griffiths: 96; /Jose Jordan/AFP: 118; /Pierre-Philippe Marcou/AFP: 39; /Clive Mason: 152; /Jamie McDonald: 138; /Damien Meyer/ AFP: 126; /Ryan Pierse/FIFA: 168; /Popperfoto: 24, 28; /Andreas Rentz/ Bongarts: 87; /Mike Stone/LatinContent: 97; /Bob Thomas: 61, 88, 98; / VI-Images: 112; /Hector Vivas/LatinContent: 48

Offside Sports Photography: /L'Equipe: 44

PA Images: /Bruno Press: 34

Shutterstock: /Pix4Pix: 121

Every effort has been made to acknowledge correctly and contact the source and/or copyright holder of each picture and Carlton Books Limited apologizes for any unintentional errors or omissions that will be corrected in future editions of this book.